A

SERIES OF PLAYS:

IN WHICH

IT IS ATTEMPTED TO DELINEATE

THE

STRONGER PASSIONS OF THE MIND.

BY

JOANNA BAILLIE.

A NEW EDITION.

VOL. III.

LONDON:

PRINTED FOR

LONGMAN, HURST, REES, ORME, AND BROWN,

PATERNOSTER-ROW.

1821.

TO THE READER.

AFTER an interval of nine years, I offer to the Public a third volume of the "Series of Plays;" hoping that it will be received, as the preceding volumes have been, with some degree of favour and indulgence. This, I confess, is making very slow progress in my promised undertaking; and I could offer some reasonable excuse for an apparent relaxation of industry, were I not afraid it might seem to infer a greater degree of expectation or desire, on the part of my Readers, to receive the remainder of the work, than I am at all entitled to suppose.

With the exception of a small piece, in two acts, at the end of the book, this volume is entirely occupied with different representations of one passion; and a passion, too, which has been supposed to be less adapted to dramatic purposes than any other — Fear. It has been thought that, in Tragedy at least, the principal character could not possibly be actuated by this passion, without becoming so far degraded as to be incapable of engaging the sympathy and interest of the spectator or reader. I am, however, inclined to think, that even Fear, as it is, under certain circumstances and to a certain degree, a universal passion, (for our very admiration of Courage rests upon this idea,) is capable of being made in the tragic drama, as it often is in real life, very interesting, and consequently not abject.

The first of these plays is a Tragedy of five acts, the principal character of which is a woman, under the dominion of Superstitious Fear; and that particular species of it, (the fear of ghosts, or the returning dead,) which is so universal and inherent in our nature, that it cann ever be eradicated from the mind, let the progress of reason or philosophy be what it may. A brave and wise man of the 19th century, were he lodged for the night in a lone apartment where murder has been committed, would not so easily believe, as a brave and wise man of the 14th century, that the restless spirit from its grave might stalk round his bed and open his curtains in the stillness of midnight: but should circumstances arise to impress him with such a belief, he would feel the emotions of Fear as intensely, though firmly persuaded that such beings have no power to injure him. Nay, I am persuaded that, could we suppose any person with a mind so constituted as to hold intercourse with such beings entirely devoid of Fear, we should turn from him with repugnance as something unnatural — as an instance of mental monstrosity. If I am right, then, in believing this impression of the mind to be so universal, I shall not be afraid of having so far infringed on the dignity of my heroine, as to make her an improper object to excite dramatic interest. Those, I believe, who possess strong imagination, quick fancy, and keen feeling, are most easily affected by this species of Fear: I have, therefore, made Orra a lively, cheerful, buoyant character, when not immediately under its influence; and even extracting from her superstitious propensity a kind of wild enjoyment, which tempts her to nourish and cultivate the enemy that destroys her. The catastrophe is such as Fear, I understand, does more commonly produce than any other passion. I have endeavoured to trace the inferior characters of the piece with some degree of variety, so as to stand relieved from the principal figure; but as I am not aware that any particular objection is likely to be made to any of them, they shall be left entirely to the mercy of my Reader.

But if it has been at all necessary to offer any apology for exhibiting Fear as the actuating principle of the heroine of the first play, what must I say in defence of a much bolder step in the one that follows it, in which I have made Fear, and the fear of Death too, the actuating principle of a hero of Tragedy. I can only say, that I believed it might be done without submitting him to any degradation that would affect the sympathy and interest I intended to excite. I must confess, however, that, being unwilling to appropriate this passion in a serious form to my own sex entirely, when the subjects of all the other passions hitherto delineated in this series are men, I have attempted what did indeed appear at first sight almost impracticable. This *esprit de corps* must also plead my excuse for loading the passion in question with an additional play. The fear of Death is here exhibited in a brave character, placed under such new and appalling circumstances as might, I supposed, overcome the most courageous; and as soon as he finds himself in a situation like those in which he has been accustomed to be bold, viz. with arms in his hand and an enemy to encounter, he is made immediately to resume all his wonted spirit. Even after he believes himself to be safe, he returns again to attack, in behalf of his companion, who beseeches him to fly, and who is not exposed to any personal danger, a force so greatly superior to his own as to leave himself scarcely a chance for redemption.

That great active courage in opposing danger, and great repugnance from passive endurance and unknown change which are independent of our exertions, are perfectly consistent, is a point, I believe, very well ascertained. Soldiers, who have distinguished themselves honourably in the field, have died pusillanimously on the scaffold; while men brought up in peaceful habits, who, without some very strong excitement, would have marched with trepidation to battle, have died under the hands of the executioner with magnanimous composure. And, I believe, it has been found by experience, that women have always behaved with as much resolution and calmness in that tremendous situation as men; although I do not believe that women, in regard to uncertain danger, even making allowance for their inferior strength and unfavourable habits of life, are so brave as men. I have therefore supposed that, though active and passive courage are often united, they frequently exist separately, and independently of each other. Nor ought we to be greatly surprised at this, when we consider that a man actively brave, when so circumstanced that no exertion of strength or boldness is of any avail, finds himself in a new situation, contrary to all former experience; and is therefore taken at greater disadvantage than men of a different character. He, who has less of that spirit which naturally opposes an enemy, and still hopes to overcome while the slightest probability remains of success, has often before, in imagination at least, been in a similar predicament, and is consequently better prepared for it. But it is not want of fortitude to bear bodily sufferings, or even deliberately inflicted death under the circumstances commonly attending it, that the character of Osterloo exhibits: it is the horror he conceives on being suddenly awakened to the imagination of the awful retributions of another world, from having the firm belief of them forced at once upon his mind by extraordinary circumstances, which so miserably quells an otherwise undaunted spirit. I only contend for the consistency of brave men shrinking from passive sufferings and unknown change, to shew that, so far from transgressing, I have, in this character, kept much within the bounds which our experience of human nature would have allowed me. If I am tediously anxious to vindicate myself on this subject, let my Reader consider that I am urged to it from the experience I have had of the great reluctance with which people generally receive characters which are not drawn agreeably to the received rules of dramatic dignity and common-place heroism.

It may be objected, that the fear of Death is in him so closely connected with Superstitious Fear, that the picture traced in this play bears too near a resemblance to that which is shewn in the foregoing. But the fears of Orra have nothing to do with apprehension of personal danger, and spring solely from a natural horror of supernatural intercourse: while those of Osterloo arise, as I have already noticed, from a strong sense of guilt, suddenly roused within him by extraordinary circumstances, and the prospect of being plunged almost immediately by death into an unknown state of punishment and horror. Not knowing by what natural means his guilt could be brought to light in a manner so extraordinary, a mind the least superstitious, in those days, perhaps I may even say in these, would have considered it to be supernatural; and the dreadful consequences, so immediately linked to it, are surely sufficiently strong to unhinge the firmest mind, having no time allowed to prepare itself for the tremendous change. If there is any person, who, under such circumstances, could have remained unappalled, he does not belong to that class of men, who, commanding the fleets and armies of their grateful and admiring country, dare every thing by flood and by field that is dangerous and terrific for her sake; but to one far different, whom hard drinking, opium, or impiety, have sunk into a state of unmanly and brutish stupidity. It will probably be supposed that I have carried the consequences of his passion too far in the catastrophe to be considered as natural; but the only circumstance in the piece that is not entirely invention, is the catastrophe. The idea of it I received from a story told to me by my mother, many years ago, of a man condemned to the block, who died in the same manner; and since the play has been written, I have had the satisfaction of finding it confirmed by a circumstance very similar, related in Miss Plumtre's interesting account of the atrocities committed in Lions by the revolutionary tribunals.*

The story of the piece is imaginary, though one of its principal circumstances, by a coincidence somewhat whimsical, I found after it was

* Plumtre's Residence in France, vol. i. p. 339.

written to agree with real history. In looking over Planta's History of Switzerland, I found that a violent pestilence, about the time when I have supposed it to happen, did actually carry off great multitudes of people in that country.* Had it been a real story, handed down by tradition, the circumstances of which were believed to be miraculous, I should have allowed it to remain so; but not thinking myself entitled to assume so much, I have attempted to trace a natural connection from association of ideas, by which one thing produces another, or is insinuated to have done so from beginning to end. The only circumstance that cannot be accounted for on this principle, is the falling of the lot to the guilty hand; and this must be conceded to me as a providential direction, or happy coincidence.

* A plague raged in Switzerland in 1349. It was preceded by terrible earthquakes: about a third part of the inhabitants were destroyed.

The monastery of St. Maurice, where the story of the play is supposed to have happened, is situated in a narrow pass between lofty precipices, where the Rhone gushes from the Valais. The founder was Segismond, King of Burgundy. It was richly endowed; the monks at one period leading very luxurious lives, hunting, and keeping hounds, &c. It was dedicated to St. Maurice and his companions, the holy martyrs of the Theban Legion.

Many of the abbots and priors in Switzerland were, in those days, feudal lords of the empire, and maintained troops of their own. Even some of the abbesses, presiding over convents of nuns, were possessed of the same power and privilege.

Contrary to our established laws of Tragedy, this Play consists only of three acts, and is written in prose. I have made it short, because I was unwilling to mix any lighter matter with a subject so solemn; and in extending it to the usual length without doing so, it would have been in danger of becoming monotonous and harassing. I have written it in prose, that the expressions of the agitated person might be plain, though strong, and kept as closely as possible to the simplicity of nature. Such a subject would, I believe, have been weakened, not enriched, by poetical embellishment. Whether I am right or wrong in this opinion, I assure my Reader it has not been indolence that has tempted me to depart from common rules.

A Comedy on Fear, the chief character being a man, is not liable to the objections I have supposed might be made to a Tragedy under the same circumstances. But a very great degree of constitutional cowardice would have been a picture too humiliating to afford any amusement, or even to engage the attention for any considerable time. The hero of my third Play, therefore, is represented as timid indeed, and endeavouring to conceal it by a boastful affectation of gallantry and courage; but at the same time worked upon by artful contrivances to believe himself in such a situation as would have miserably overcome many a one, who, on ordinary occasions of danger, would have behaved with decorum. Cowardice in him has been cultivated by indulgence of every kind: and self-conceit and selfishness are the leading traits of his character, which might have been originally trained to useful and honourable activity. Fear, in a mixed character of this kind, is, I apprehend, a very good subject for Comedy, and in abler hands would certainly have proved itself to be so.

The last Play in the volume is a drama of two acts, the subject of which is Hope. This passion, when it acts permanently, loses the character of a passion; and when it acts violently, is, like Anger, Joy, or Grief, too transient to become the subject of a piece of any length. It seemed to me, in fact, neither fit for Tragedy nor Comedy; and like Anger, Joy, or Grief, I once thought to have left it out of my Series altogether. However,. what it wanted in strength, it seemed to have in grace; and being of a noble, kindly, and engaging nature, it drew me to itself; and I resolved to do every thing for it that I could, in spite of the objections which had at first deterred me. The piece is very short, and can neither be called Tragedy nor Comedy. It may indeed appear, for a passion so much allied to all our cheerful and exhilarating thoughts, to approach too nearly to the former; but Hope, when its object is of great importance, must so often contend with despondency, that it rides like a vessel on the stormy ocean, rising on the billow's ridge but for a moment. Cheerfulness, the character of common Hope, is, in strong Hope, like glimpses of sunshine in a cloudy sky.

As this passion, though more pleasing, is not so powerfully interesting as those that are more turbulent, and was therefore in danger of becoming languid and tiresome, if long dwelt upon without interruption; and at the same time of being sunk into shade or entirely overpowered, if relieved from it by variety of strong marked characters in the inferior persons of the drama, I have introduced into the scenes several songs. So many, indeed, that I have ventured to call it a Musical Drama. I have, however, avoided one fault so common, I might say universal, in such pieces, viz. making people sing in situations in which it is not natural for them to do so; and creating a necessity for either having the first characters performed by those who can both act and sing, (persons very difficult to find,) or permitting them to be made entirely insipid and absurd. For this purpose, the songs are all sung by those who have little or nothing to act, and introduced when nothing very interesting is going on. They are also supposed not to be spontaneous expressions of sentiment in the singer, but (as songs in ordinary life usually are) compositions of other people, which have been often sung before, and are only generally applicable to the present occasion.

The story is imaginary, but I have endeavoured to make it, as far as my information enabled me to correspond with the circumstances of the time and place in which it is supposed to have happened.

Having said all that appears to me necessary in regard to the contents of the volume, I should now leave my reader to peruse it without further hinderance; but as this will probably be the last volume of Plays I shall ever publish, I must beg to detain him a few moments longer. For I am inclined to think, he may have some curiosity to know what is the extent of my plan in a task I have so far fulfilled; and I shall satisfy it most cheerfully. It is my intention, if I live long enough, to add to this work the passions of Remorse, Jealousy, and Revenge. Joy, Grief, and Anger, as I have already said, are generally of too transient a nature, and are too frequently the attendants of all our other passions to be made the subjects of an entire play. And though this objection cannot be urged in regard to Pride and Envy, two powerful passions which I have not yet named, Pride would make, I should think, a dull subject, unless it were merely taken as the ground-work of more turbulent passions; and Envy, being that state of mind, which, of all others, meets with least sympathy, could only be endured in Comedy or Farce, and would become altogether disgusting in Tragedy. I have besides, in some degree, introduced this latter passion into the work already, by making it a companion or rather a component part of Hatred. Of all our passions, Remorse and Jealousy appear to me to be the best fitted for representation. If this be the case, it is fortunate for me that I have reserved them for the end of my task; and that they have not been already published, read, and very naturally laid aside as unfit for the stage, because they have not been produced upon it.

My Reader may likewise wish to know why, having so many years ago promised to go on publishing this work, I should now intend to leave it off, though I still mean to continue writing till it shall be compleated; and this supposed wish I think myself bound to gratify. — The Series of Plays was originally published in the hope that some of the pieces it contains, although first given to the Public from the press, might in time make their way to the stage, and there be received and supported with some degree of public favour. But the present situation of dramatic affairs is greatly against every hope of this kind; and should they ever become more favourable, I have now good reason to believe, that the circumstance of these plays having been already published would operate strongly against their being received upon the stage. I am therefore strongly of opinion that I ought to reserve the remainder of the work in manuscript, if I would not run the risk of entirely frustrating my original design. Did I believe that their having been already published would not afterwards obstruct their way to the stage, the untowardness of present circumstances should not prevent me from continuing to publish.

Having thus given an account of my views and intentions regarding this work, I hope that, should no more of it be published in my life-time, it will not be supposed I have abandoned or become weary of my occupation, which is in truth as interesting and pleasing to me now as it was at the beginning.

But when I say, present circumstances are unfavourable for the reception of these Plays upon the stage, let it not be supposed that I mean to throw any reflection upon the prevailing taste for dramatic amusements. The Public have now to chuse between what we shall suppose are well-written and well-acted Plays, the words of which are not heard, or heard but imperfectly by two thirds of the audience, while the finer and more pleasing traits of the acting are by a still greater proportion lost altogether; and splendid pantomime, or pieces whose chief object is to produce striking scenic effect, which can be seen and comprehended by the whole. So situated, it would argue, methinks, a very pedantic love indeed for what is called legitimate Drama, were we to prefer the former. A love for active, varied movement, in the objects before us; for striking contrasts of light and shadow; for splendid decorations and magnificent scenery, is as inherent in us as the interest we take in the representation of the natural passions and characters of men: and the most cultivated minds may relish such exhibitions, if they do not, when both are fairly offered to their choice, prefer them. Did our ears and our eyes permit us to hear and see distinctly in a Theatre so large as to admit of chariots and horsemen, and all the "pomp and circumstance of war," I see no reason why we should reject them. They would give variety, and an appearance of truth to the scenes of heroic Tragedy, that would very much heighten its effect. We ought not then to find fault with the taste of the Public for preferring an inferior species of entertainment, good of its kind, to a superior one, faintly and imperfectly given.

It has been urged, as a proof of this supposed bad taste in the Public, by one whose judgment on these subjects is and ought to be high authority, that a play, possessing considerable merit, was produced some years ago on Drury-Lane stage, and notwithstanding the great support it received from excellent acting and magnificent decoration, entirely failed. It is very true that, in spite of all this, it failed, during the eight nights it continued to be acted, to produce houses sufficiently good to induce the Managers to revive it afterwards. But it ought to be acknowledged, that that piece had defects in it as an acting play, which served to counterbalance those advantages; and likewise that, if any supposed merit in the writing ought to have redeemed those defects, in a Theatre, so large and so ill calculated to convey sound as the one in which it was performed, it was impossible this could be felt or comprehended by even a third part of the audience.

The size of our theatres then is what I chiefly allude to when I say, present circumstances are unfavourable for the production of these Plays. While they continue to be of this size, it is a vain thing to complain either of want of taste in the Public, or want of inclination in Managers to bring forward new pieces of merit, taking it for granted that there are such to produce. Nothing can be truly relished by the most cultivated audience that is not distinctly heard and seen, and Managers must produce what will be relished. Shakespeare's Plays, and some of our other old Plays, indeed, attract full houses, though they are often repeated, because, being familiar to the audience, they can still understand and follow them pretty closely, though but imperfectly heard; and surely this is no bad sign of our public taste. And besides this advantage, when a piece is familiar to the audience, the expression of the actors' faces is much better understood, though seen imperfectly; for the stronger marked traits of feeling which even in a large theatre may reach the eyes of a great part of the audience, from the recollection of finer and more delicate indications, formerly seen so delightfully mingled with them in the same countenances during the same passages of the Play, will, by association, still convey them to the mind's eye, though it is the mind's eye only which they have reached.

And this thought leads me to another defect in large theatres, that ought to be considered.

Our great tragic actress, Mrs. Siddons, whose matchless powers of expression have so long been the pride of our stage, and the most admired actors of the present time, have been brought up in their youth in small theatres, where they were encouraged to enter thoroughly into the characters they represented, and to express in their faces that variety of fine fleeting emotion which nature in moments of agitation assumes, and the imitation of which we are taught by nature to delight in. But succeeding actors will only consider expression of countenance as addressed to an audience removed from them to a greater distance, and will only attempt such strong expression as can be perceived and have effect at a distance. It may easily be imagined what exaggerated expression will then get into use; and I should think, even this strong expression will not only be exaggerated but false: for, as we are enabled to assume the outward signs of passion, not by mimicking what we have beheld in others, but by internally assuming, in some degree, the passion itself; a mere outline of it cannot, I apprehend, be given as an outline of figure frequently is, where all that is delineated is true, though the whole is not filled up. Nay, besides having it exaggerated and false, it will perpetually be thrust in where it ought not to be. For real occasions of strong expression not occurring often enough, and weaker being of no avail, to avoid an apparent barrenness of countenance, they will be tempted to introduce it where it is not wanted, and thereby destroy its effect where it is. — I say nothing of expression of voice, to which the above observations obviously apply. This will become equally, if not in a greater degree, false and exaggerated, in actors trained from their youth in a large theatre.

But the department of acting that will suffer most under these circumstances, is that which particularly regards the gradually unfolding of the passions, and has, perhaps, hitherto been less understood than any other part of the art— I mean Soliloquy. What actor in his senses will then think of giving to the solitary musing of a perturbed mind, that muttered, imperfect articulation, which grows by degrees into words; that heavy, suppressed voice, as of one speaking through sleep; that rapid burst of sounds which often succeeds the slow languid tones of distress; those sudden, untuned exclamations, which, as if frightened at their own discord, are struck again into silence as sudden and abrupt, with all the corresponding variety of countenance that belongs to it; — what actor, so situated, will attempt to exhibit all this? No; he will be satisfied, after taking a turn or two across the front of the stage, to place himself directly in the middle of it; and there, spreading out his hands, as if he were addressing some person whom it behoved him to treat with great ceremony, to tell to himself, in an audible, uniform voice, all the secret thoughts of his own heart. When he has done this, he will think, and he will think rightly, that he has done enough.

The only valuable part of acting that will then remain to us, will be expression of gesture, grace, and dignity, supposing that these also shall not become affected by being too much attended to and studied.

It may be urged against such apprehensions, that, though the theatres of the metropolis should be large, they will be supplied with actors who have been trained to the stage in small country theatres. An actor of ambition (and all actors of genius are such) will practise with little heart in the country what he knows will be of no use to him on a London stage; not to mention that the style of acting in London will naturally be the fashionable and prevailing style elsewhere. Acting will become a less respectable profession than it has continued to be from the days of Garrick; and the few actors who add to the natural advantages requisite to it, the accomplishments of a scholar and a gentleman, will soon be wed away by the hand of time, leaving nothing of the same species behind them to spring from a neglected and sapless root.

All I have said on this subject may still in a greater degree be applied to actresses; for the features and voice of a woman being naturally more delicate than those of a man, she must suffer in proportion from the defects of a large theatre.

The great disadvantage of such over-sized buildings to natural and genuine acting, is, I believe, very obvious; but they have other defects which are not so readily noticed, because they in some degree run counter to the common opinion of their great superiority in every thing that regards general effect. The diminutive appearance of individual figures, and the straggling poverty of grouping, which unavoidably takes place when a very wide and lofty stage is not filled by a great number of people, is very injurious to general effect. This is particularly felt in Comedy, and all plays on domestic subjects; and in those scenes also of the grand drama, where two or three persons only are produced at a time. To give figures who move upon it proper effect, there must be depth as well as width of stage; and the one must bear some proportion to the other, if we would not make every closer or more confined scene appear like a section of a long passage, in which the actors move before us, apparently in one line, like the figures of a magic lanthorn.

It appears to me, that when a stage is of such a size that as many persons as generally come

16

into action at one time in our grandest and best-peopled plays, can be produced on the front of it in groups, without crowding together more than they would naturally do any where else for the convenience of speaking to one another, all is gained in point of general effect that can well be gained. When modern gentlemen and ladies talk to one another in a spacious saloon, or when ancient warriors and dames conversed together in an old baronial hall, they do not, and did not stand further apart than when conversing in a room of common dimensions; neither ought they to do so on the stage. All width of stage, beyond what is convenient for such natural grouping, is lost; and worse than lost, for it is injurious. It is continually presenting us with something similar to that which always offends us in a picture, where the canvass is too large for the subject; or in a face, where the features are too small for the bald margin of cheeks and forehead that surrounds them.

Even in the scenes of professed show and spectacle, where nothing else is considered, it appears to me that a very large stage is in some degree injurious to general effect. Even when a battle is represented in our theatres, the great width of the stage is a disadvantage; for as it never can nor ought to be represented but partially, and the part which is seen should be crowded and confused, opening a large front betrays your want of numbers; or should you be rich enough in this respect to fill it sufficiently, imposes upon you a difficulty seldom surmounted, viz. putting the whole mass sufficiently in action to sustain the deception.* When a moderate number of combatants, so as to make one connected groupe, are fighting on the front of a moderately wide stage, which they sufficiently occupy, it is an easy thing, through the confusion of their brandished weapons and waving banners, to give the appearance of a deep active battle beyond them, seen, as it were, through a narrow pass; and beholding all the tumult of battle in the small view opened before us, our imagination supplies what is hid. If we open a wider view, we give the imagination less to do, and supply what it would have done less perfectly. In narrowing our battle, likewise, we could more easily throw smoke or an appearance

* The objections above do not apply to scenes where sieges are represented; for then the more diminished the actors appear, the greater is the importance and magnitude given to the walls or castle which they attack, while the towers and buttresses, &c. sufficiently occupy the width and heighth of the stage, and conceal the want of numbers and general activity in the combatants. And the managers of our present large theatre have, in my opinion, shewn great judgment in introducing into their mixed pieces of late so many good scenes of this kind, that have, to my fancy at least, afforded a grand and animating show. Nor do they fairly apply to those combats or battles into which horses are introduced; for a moderate number of those noble animals may be made to occupy and animate, in one connected groupe, the front of the widest stage that we are in danger of having, and to conceal the want of a numerous host and tumultuous battle behind them.

of dust over the back ground, and procure for our fancy an unlimited space.

In processions, also, the most pleasing effect to our imaginations is, when the marshalled figures are seen in long perspective, which requires only depth of stage; and the only advantage a wide stage has on such occasions is containing the assembled mass of figures, when the moving line stops and gathers itself together on the front. The rich confusion of such a crowd is indeed very brilliant and pleasing for a short time, but it is dearly purchased at the price of many sacrifices.

On those occasions too, when many people are assembled on the front of the stage to give splendour and importance to some particular scene, or to the conclusion of a piece, the general effect is often injured by great width of stage: for the crowd is supposed to be attracted to the spot by something which engages their attention; and, as they must not surround this object of attention, (which would be their natural arrangement,) lest they should conceal it from the audience, they are obliged to spread themselves out in a long straight line on each side of it: now the shorter those lines or wings are spreading out from the centre figures, the less do they offend against natural arrangement, and the less artificial and formal does the whole scene appear.

In short, I scarcely know of any advantage which a large stage possesses over one of a moderate size, without great abatements, even in regard to general effect, unless it be when it is empty, and scenery alone engages our attention, or when figures appear at a distance on the back ground only. Something in confirmation of what I have been saying has perhaps been felt by most people on entering a grand cathedral, where figures moving in the long aisles at a distance add grandeur to the building by their diminished appearance; but in approaching near enough to become themselves distinct objects of attention, look stunted and mean, without serving to enlarge by comparison its general dimensions.

There is also, I apprehend, greater difficulty, in a very wide and lofty stage, to produce variety of light and shadow; and this often occasions the more solemn scenes of Tragedy to be represented in a full, staring, uniform light that ought to be dimly seen in twilight uncertainty; or to have the objects on them shewn by partial gleams only, while the deepened shade around gives a sombre indistinctness to the other parts of the stage, particularly favourable to solemn or terrific impressions. And it would be more difficult, I imagine, to throw down light upon the objects on such a stage, which I have never indeed seen attempted in any theatre, though it might surely be done in one of moderate dimensions with admirable effect. In short, a great variety of pleasing effects from light and shadow might be more easily produced on a smaller stage, that would give change and even interest to pieces otherwise monotonous and heavy; and would often be very useful in relieving the exhausted strength of the chief actors, while want of skill in the inferior could be craftily concealed.* On this part of the subject, however, I speak with great diffidence, not knowing to what perfection machinery for the management of light may be brought in a large theatre. But at the same time, I am certain that, by a judicious use of light and scenery, an artificial magnitude may be given to a stage of a moderate size, that would, to the eye, as far as distance in perspective is concerned, have an effect almost equal to any thing that can be produced on a larger stage: for that apparent magnitude, arising from succession of objects, depends upon the depth of the stage, much more than its width and loftiness, which are often detrimental to it; and a small or moderate sized theatre may have, without injury to proportion, a very deep stage.

It would be, I believe, impertinent to pursue this subject any farther; and I beg pardon for having obtruded it so far, where it may not appear naturally to be called for. I plead in my excuse an almost irresistible desire to express my thoughts, in some degree, upon what has occupied them considerably; and a strong persuasion that I ought not, how unimportant soever they may be, entirely to conceal them.

* See Note at the end.

I must now beg leave to return my thanks to the public for that indulgent favour which for so many years has honoured and cheered my labour; and whether more or less liberally dealt to me, has at all times been sufficient to prevent me from laying down my pen in despair. Favour, which has gratified me the more sensibly, because I have shared it with cotemporary writers of the highest poetic genius, whose claims to such distinction are so powerful.

NOTE.

THAT strong light cast up from lamps on the front of the stage which has long been in use in all our theatres, is certainly very unfavourable to the appearance and expression of individual actors, and also to the general effect of their grouped figures. When a painter wishes to give intelligence and expression to a face, he does not make his lights hit upon the under part of his chin, the nostrils, and the under curve of the eye-brows, turning of course all the shadows upwards. He does the very reverse of all this; that the eye may look hollow and dark under the shade of its brow; that the shadow of the nose may shorten the upper lip, and give a greater character of sense to the mouth; and that any fulness of the under chin may be the better concealed. From this disposition of the light in our theatres, whenever an actor, whose features are not particularly sharp and pointed, comes near the front of the stage, and turns his face fully to the audience, every feature immediately becomes shortened and snub, and less capable of any expression, unless it be of the ludicrous kind. This at least will be the effect produced to those who are seated under or on the same level with the stage, making now a considerable proportion of an audience; while to those who sit above it, the lights and shadows, at variance with the natural bent of the features, will make the whole face appear confused, and (compared to what it would have been with light thrown upon it from another direction) unintelligible. — As to the general effect of grouped figures: close groupes or crowds, ranged on the front of the stage, when the light is thrown up upon them, have a harsh glaring appearance; for the foremost figures catch the light, and are too much distinguished from those behind, from whom it is intercepted. But when the light is thrown down upon the objects, this cannot be the case: for then it will glance along the heads of the whole crowd, even to the very bottom of the stage, presenting a varied harmonious mass of figures to the eye, deep, mellow, and brilliant.

It may, perhaps, be objected to these last observations, that the most popular of our night-scenes in nature, and those which have been most frequently imitated by the painter, are groupes of figures with strong light thrown up upon them, such as gypsies or banditti round a fire, or villagers in a smith's forge, &c. But the striking and pleasing effect of such scenes is owing to the deep darkness which surrounds them; while the ascending smoke, tinged with flame-colour in the one case, and the rafters or higher parts of the wall catching a partial gleam in the other, connect the brilliant colouring of the figures with the deep darkness behind them, which would else appear hard and abrupt, and thus at the same time produce strong contrast with harmonious gradation. I need scarcely mention, for it is almost too obvious, that the effect of the light so thrown on the faces of those figures abundantly confirm my first observations, regarding the features and expression of individuals' faces. Yet I do not mean to say that light thrown up from the front of a stage, where light is also admitted from many other quarters, can have so strong an effect upon the countenances as in such situations.

Groupes of gypsies, &c. are commonly composed but of one circle of figures; for did they amount to any thing like a deepened groupe or crowd, the figures behind would be almost entirely lost. But those grand night-scenes containing many figures which we admire in nature or in painting, — processions by torch-light or in an illuminated street, — crowds gathered to behold a conflagration, &c. always have the light thrown down upon them.—It may be urged, indeed, that the greater part of our stage-scenes are meant to represent day and not night, so that the observations above are but partially applicable. It is very true that stage-scenes generally are supposed to be seen by day-light; but day-light comes from heaven, not from the earth; even within-doors our whitened ceilings are made to throw down reflected light upon us, while our pavements and carpets are of a darker colour.

In what way this great defect of all our theatres could be rectified, I am not at all competent to say. Yet, I should suppose, that by bringing forward the roof of the stage as far as its boards or floor, and placing a row of lamps with reflectors along the inside of the wooden front-piece, such a light as is wanted might be procured. The green curtain in this case behoved not to be let down, as it now is, from the front-piece, but some feet within it; and great care taken that nothing should be placed near the lamps capable of catching fire. If this were done, no boxes, I suppose, could be made upon the stage; but the removal of stage-boxes would in itself be a great advantage. The front-piece at the top; the boundary of the stage from the orchestra at the bottom; and the pilasters on each side, would then represent the frame of a great moving picture, entirely separated and distinct from the rest of the theatre: whereas, at present, an unnatural mixture of audience and actors, of house and stage takes place near the front of the stage, which destroys the general effect in a very great degree.

O R R A:

A TRAGEDY,

IN FIVE ACTS.

PERSONS OF THE DRAMA.

MEN.

HUGHOBERT, *Count of* Aldenberg.

GLOTTENBAL, *his Son.*

THEOBALD OF FALKENSTEIN, *a Nobleman of reduced Fortune, and Co-burgher of Basle.*

RUDIGERE, *a Knight, and Commander of one of the Free Companies returned from the Wars, and Bastard of a Branch of the Family of* Aldenberg.

HARTMAN, *friend of* Theobald, *and Banneret of Basle.*

URSTON, *a Confessor.*

FRANKO, *Chief of a Band of Outlaws.*

MAURICE, *an Agent of* Rudigere's.

Soldiers, Vassals, Outlaws, &c.

WOMEN.

ORRA, *Heiress of another Branch of the Family of* Aldenberg, *and Ward to* Hughobert.

ELEANORA, *Wife to* Hughobert.

CATHRINA, } *Ladies attending on* Orra.
ALICE, }

Scene, *Switzerland, in the Canton of Basle, and afterwards in the Borders of the Black Forest in Suabia.*

Time, *towards the end of the* 14*th Century.*

ORRA.

ACT I.

SCENE I. — *An open Space before the Walls of a Castle, with wild Mountains beyond it; enter* GLOTTENBAL, *armed as from the Lists, but bare-headed and in Disorder, and his Arms soiled with Earth or Sand, which an Attendant is now and then brushing off, whilst another follows bearing his Helmet; with him enters* MAURICE, *followed by* RUDIGERE, *who is also armed, and keeps by himself, pacing to and fro at the bottom of the Stage, whilst the others come forward.*

GLOTTENBAL (*speaking as he enters, loud and boastingly.*)

AYE, let him triumph in his paltry honours,
Won by mere trick and accident. Good faith!
It were a shame to call it strength or skill.
Were it not, Rudigere?
(*Calling to* Rudigere, *who answers not.*)
Maur. His brow is dark, his tongue is lock'd, my Lord;
There come no words from him; he bears it not
So manfully as thou dost, noble Glottenbal.
Glot. Fy on't! I mind it not.

Maur. And wherefore should'st thou? This same Theobald,
Count and co-burgher — mixture most unseemly
Of base and noble, — know we not right well
What powers assist him? Mark'd you not, my Lord,
How he did turn him to the witchy north,
When first he mounted; making his fierce steed,
That paw'd and rear'd and shook its harness'd neck
In generous pride, bend meekly to the earth
Its mained crest, like one who made obeisance?

Glot. Ha! did'st thou really see it?

Maur. Yes, brave Glottenbal,
I did right truly; and besides myself,
Many observ'd it.

Glot. Then 'tis manifest
How all this foil hath been. Who e'er before
Saw one with such advantage of the field,
Lose it so shamefully? By my good fay!
Barring foul play and other dev'lish turns,
I'd keep my courser's back with any Lord,
Or Knight, or Squire that e'er bestrode a steed.
Think'st thou not, honest Maurice, that I could?

Maur. Who doubts it, good my Lord? This Falkenstein
Is but a clown to you.

Glot. Well let him boast:
Boasting I scorn; but I will shortly shew him
What these good arms, with no foul play against them,
Can honestly atchieve.

Maur. Yes, good my Lord; but chuse you well your day:
A moonless Friday luck did never bring
To honest combatant.

Glot. Ha! blessing on thee! I ne'er thought of this:
Now it is clear how our mischance befell.
Be sure thou tell to every one thou meet'st,
Friday and a dark moon suit Theobald.
Ho there! Sir Rudigere! hear'st thou not this?

Rud. (*as he goes off, aside to* Maurice)
Flatter the fool a while and let me go,
I cannot join thee now. [Exit.

Glot. (*looking after* Rudigere)
Is he so crest-fallen?

Maur. He lacks your noble spirit.

Glot. Fy upon't!
I heed it not. Yet, by my sword and spurs!
'Twas a foul turn, that for my rival earn'd
A branch of victory from Orra's hand.

Maur. Aye, foul indeed! My blood boil'd high to see it.
Look where he proudly comes.

Enter Theobald *arm'd, with Attendants, having a green sprig stuck in his helmet.*

Glot. (*going up to* Theobald)
Comest thou to face me so? Audacious Burgher!
The Lady Orra's favour suits thee not,
Tho' for a time thou hast upon me gain'd
A seeming 'vantage.

Theo. A seeming 'vantage!—Then it is not true,
That thou, unhors'd, layd'st rolling in the dust,

Asking for quarter? —Let me crave thy pardon;
Some strange delusion hung upon our sight
That we believed it so.

Glot. Off with thy taunts!
And pull that sprig from its audacious perch:
The favour of a Dame too high for thee.

Theo. Too high indeed; and had'st thou also added,
Too good, too fair, I had assented to it.
Yet, be it known unto your courteous worth,
That were this sprig a Queen's gift, or received
From the brown hand of some poor mountain maid;
Yea, or bestow'd upon my rambling head,
As in the hairy sides of brouzing kid
The wild rose sticks a spray, unprized, unbidden,
I would not give it thee.

Glot. Dost thou so face me out? Then I will have it. (*Snatching at it with rage.*)

Enter HARTMAN.

Hart. (*separating them*)
What! Malice! after fighting in the lists
As noble courteous knights!

Glot. (*to* Hartman) Go, paltry Banneret! Such friends as thou
Become such Lords as he, whose ruined state
Seeks the base fellowship of restless burghers;
Thinking to humble still, with envious spite,
The great and noble houses of the land.
I know ye well, and I defy you both,
With all your damned witchery to-boot,

[EXIT *grumbling, followed by* Maurice, &c.

Manent Theobald *and* Hartman.

Theo. How fierce the creature is, and full of folly!
Like a shent cur to his own door retired,
That bristles up his furious back, and there
Each passenger annoys. — And this is he,
Whom sordid and ambitious Hughobert,
The guardian in the selfish father sunk,
Destines for Orra's husband. — O foul shame!
The carrion-crow and royal eagle join'd,
Make not so cross a match. — But think'st thou, Hartman,
She will submit to it?

Hart. That may be as thou pleasest, Falkenstein.

Theo. Away with mockery!

Hart. I mock thee not.

Theo. Nay, Banneret, thou dost. Saving this favour,
Which every victor in these listed combats
From Ladies' hands receive, nor then regard
As more than due and stated courtesy,
She ne'er hath honour'd me with word or look
Such hope to warrant.

Hart. Wait not thou for looks.

Theo. Thou would'st not have me to a Dame like this,
With rich domains and titled rights encompass'd,
These simple limbs, girt in their soldier's gear,
My barren hills and ruin'd tower present,
And say, "Accept — these will I nobly give
In fair exchange for thee and all thy wealth."

No, Rudolph, Hartman, woo the maid thyse lf,
If thou hast courage for it.

Hart. Yes, Theobald of Falkenstein, I will,
And win her too; but all for thy behoof.
And when I do present, as thou hast said,
Those simple limbs, girt in their soldier's geer,
Adding thy barren hills and ruin'd tower,
With some few items more of gen'rous worth
And native sense and manly fortitude,
I'll give her in return for all that she
Or any maid can in such barter yield,
Its fair and ample worth.

Theo. So dost thou reckon.

Hart. And so will Orra. Do not shake thy head.
I know the maid: for still she has received me
As one who knew her noble father well,
And in the bloody field in which he died
Fought by his side with kind familiarity:
And her stern guardian, viewing these grey hairs
And this rough visage with no jealous eye,
Hath still admitted it.——— I'll woo her for thee.

Theo. I do in truth believe thou mean'st me well.

Hart. And this is all thou say'st? Cold frozen words!
What has bewitch'd thee, man? Is she not fair?

Theo. O fair indeed as woman need be form'd
To please and be belov'd! Tho', to speak honestly,
I've fairer seen; yet such a form as Orra's

For ever in my busy fancy dwells,
Whene'er I think of wiving my lone state.
It is not this; she has too many lures;
Why wilt thou urge me on to meet her scorn?
I am not worthy of her.

Hart. (*pushing him away with gentle anger*)
Go to! I praised thy modesty short-while,
And now with dull and senseless perseverance,
Thou would'st o'erlay me with it. Go thy ways!
If thro' thy fault, thus shrinking from the onset,
She should with this untoward cub be matched,
'Twill haunt thy conscience like a damning sin,
And may it gnaw thee shrewdly!

[EXEUNT.

SCENE II.

A small Apartment in the Castle; enter RUDIGERE *musing gloomily, and muttering to himself some time before he speaks aloud.*

Rud. No, no; it is to formless air dissolved,
This cherish'd hope, this vision of my brain!
(*Pacing to and fro, and then stopping and musing as before.*)
I daily stood contrasted in her sight
With an ungainly fool; and when she smiled,
Methought ——— But wherefore still upon this thought,
Which was perhaps but a delusion then,
Brood I with ceaseless torment? Never, never!
O never more on me, from Orra's eye,
Approving glance shall light, or gentle look!

This day's disgrace mars all my goodly dreams.
My path to greatness is at once shut up.
Still in the dust my grov'ling fortune lies.
(*Striking his breast in despair*)
Tame thine aspiring spirit, luckless wretch!
There is no hope for thee!
And shall I tame it? No, by saints and devils!
The laws have cast me off from every claim
Of house and kindred, and within my veins
Turn'd noble blood to baseness and reproach:
I'll cast them off: why should they be to me
A bar, and no protection?
(*Pacing again to and fro, and muttering low for some time before he speaks aloud*)
Aye; this may still within my toils enthral her:
This is the secret weakness of her mind
On which I'll clutch my hold.

Enter CATHRINA *behind him, laying her hand upon him.*

Cath. Ha! speak'st thou to thyself?
Rud. (*starting*) I did not speak.
Cath. Thou did'st; thy busy mind gave sound to thoughts
Which thou didst utter with a thick harsh voice,
Like one who speaks in sleep. Tell me their meaning.
Rud. And dost thou so presume? Be wise; be humble.
(*After a pause*)
Has Orra oft of late requested thee

To tell her stories of the restless dead?
Of spectres rising at the midnight watch
By the lone trav'ller's bed?

Cath. Wherefore of late dost thou so oft enquire
Of what she says and does?

Rud. Be wise, and answer what I ask of thee;
This is thy duty now.

Cath. Alas, alas! I know that one false step
Has o'er me set a stern and ruthless master.

Rud. No, madam; 'tis thy grave and virtuous seeming;
Thy saint-like carriage, rigid and demure,
On which thy high repute so long has stood,
Endowing thee with right of censorship
O'er every simple maid, whose cheerful youth
Wears not so thick a mask, that o'er thee sets
This ruthless master. Hereon rests my power:
I might expose, and therefore I command thee.

Cath. Hush, hush! approaching steps!
They'll find me here!
I'll do whate'er thou wilt.

Rud. It is but Maurice: hie thee to thy closet,
Where I will shortly come to thee. Be thou
My faithful agent in a weighty matter,
On which I now am bent, and I will prove
Thy stay and shelter from the world's contempt.

Cath. Maurice to find me here! Where shall I hide me?

Rud. No where, but boldly pass him as he enters.

I'll find some good excuse; he will be silent:
He is my agent also.

Cath. Dost thou trust him?

Rud. Avarice his master is, as shame is thine
Therefore I trust to deal with both. — Away!

Enter MAURICE, *passing* CATHRINA *as she goes out.*

Maur. What, doth the grave and virtuous Cathrina,
Vouchsafe to give thee of her company?

Rud. Yes, rigid saint! she has bestowed upon me
Some grave advice to bear with pious meekness
My late discomfiture.

Maur. Aye, and she call'd it,
I could be sworn! heaven's judgment on thy pride.

Rud. E'en so: thou'st guessed it. — Shall we to the ramparts
And meet the western breeze?

[EXEUNT.

SCENE III.

A spacious Apartment; enter HUGHOBERT *and* URSTON.

Hugh. (*speaking with angry gesticulation as he enters*)
I feed and clothe these drones, and in return
They cheat, deceive, abuse me; nay, belike,
Laugh in their sleeve the while. By their advice,
This cursed tourney I proclaim'd; for still

They puffed me up with praises of my son —
His grace, his skill in arms, his horsemanship —
Count Falkenstein to him was but a clown —
And so, in Orra's eyes to give him honour,
Full surely did I think — I'll hang them all!
I'll starve them in a dungeon shut from light:
I'll heap my boards no more with dainty fare
To feed false flatterers.

Urst. That indeed were wise:
But art thou sure, when men shall speak the truth,
That thou wilt feed them for it? I but hinted
In gentle words to thee, that Glottenbal
Was praised with partial or affected zeal,
And thou receiv'dst it angrily.

Hugh. Aye, true indeed: but thou did'st speak of him
As one bereft of all capacity.
Now tho', God wot! I look on his defects
With no blind love, and even in my ire
Will sometimes call him fool; yet, ne'ertheless,
He still has parts and talents, tho' obscured
By some untoward failings. — Heaven be praised!
He wants not strength at least and well turn'd limbs,
Had they but taught him how to use them. Knaves!
They have neglected him.

(*Enter* Glottenbal, *who draws back on seeing his Father.*)

Advance, young Sir: art thou afraid of me?

That thus thou shrinkest like a sculking thief
To make disgrace the more apparent on thee?

Glot. Yes, call it then disgrace, or what you please;
Had not my lance's point somewhat awry
Glanced on his shield ——

Hugh. E'en so; I doubt it not;
Thy lance's point, and every thing about thee
Hath glanced awry. Go, rid my house, I say,
Of all those feasting flatterers that deceive thee;
They harbour here no more: dismiss them quickly.

Glot. Do it yourself, my Lord; you are, I trow,
Angry enough to do it sharply.

Hugh. (*turning to* Urston) Faith!
He gibes me fairly here; there's reason in't;
Fools speak not thus. (*to* Glottenbal) Go to! if I am angry,
Thou art a graceless son to tell me so.

Glot. Have you not bid me still to speak the truth?

Hugh. (*to* Urston) Again thou hear'st he makes an apt reply.

Urst. He wants not words.

Hugh. Nor meaning neither, Father.

(*Enter* Eleonora.)

Well Dame; where hast thou been?

El. I came from Orra.

Hugh. Hast thou been pleading in our son's excuse?

And how did she receive it?

El. I tried to do it, but her present humour
Is jest and merriment. She is behind me,
Stopping to stroke a hound, that in the corridor
Came to her fawningly to be carest.

Glot. (*listening*) Aye, she is coming; light and quick her steps;
So sound they, when her spirits are unruly;
But I am bold; she shall not mock me now.

(*Enter* ORRA, *tripping gaily, and playing with the folds of her scarf.*)

Methinks you trip it briskly, gentle Dame.

Or. Does it offend you, noble Knight.

Glot. Go to!
I know your meaning. Wherefore smile you so?

Or. Because, good sooth! with tired and aching sides
I have not power to laugh.

Glot. Full well I know why thou so merry art.
Thou think'st of him to whom thou gav'st that sprig
Of hopeful green, his rusty casque to grace,
Whilst at thy feet his honour'd glave he laid.

Or. Nay, rather say, of him, who at my feet,
From his proud courser's back, more gallantly
Laid his most precious self; then stole away,
Thro' modesty, unthank'd, nor left behind
Of all his geer that flutter'd in the dust,
Or glove or band, or fragment of torn hose,
For dear remembrance-sake, that in my sleeve

I might have stuck it. O! thou wrong'st me much
To think my merriment a ref'rence hath
To any one but him. (*Laughing.*)

El. Nay, Orra; these wild fits of uncurb'd laughter,
Athwart the gloomy tenor of your mind,
As it has low'r'd of late, so keenly cast,
Unsuited seem and strange.

Or. O nothing strange, my gentle Eleonora!
Did'st thou ne'er see the swallow's veering breast,
Winging the air beneath some murky cloud
In the sunn'd glimpses of a stormy day,
Shiver in silv'ry brightness?
Or boatman's oar, as vivid lightning flash
In the faint gleam, that like a spirit's path
Tracks the still waters of some sullen lake?
Or lonely Tower, from its brown mass of woods,
Give to the parting of a wintry sun
One hasty glance in mockery of the night
Closing in darkness round it? — Gentle Friend!
Chide not her mirth, who was sad yesterday,
And may be so to-morrow.

Glot. And wherefore art thou sad, unless it is
From thine own wayward humour? Other Dames,
Were they so courted, would be gay and happy.

Or. Wayward it needs must be, since I am sad
When such perfection woos me.
Pray good Glottenbal,

How dids't thou learn with such a wond'rous grace
So high in air to toss thine armed heels,
And clutch with outspread hands the slipp'ry sand?
I was the more amaz'd at thy dexterity,
As this, of all thy many gallant feats
Before-hand promised, most modestly
Thou did'st forbear to mention.

Glot. Gibe away!
I care not for thy gibing. With fair lists,
And no black arts against me —

Hugh. (*advancing angrily from the bottom of the stage to* Glottenbal.) Hold thy peace!
(*To* Orra.) And, Madam, be at least somewhat restrained
In your unruly humour.

Or. Pardon, my Lord: I knew not you were near me.
My humour is unruly: with your leave,
I will retire till I have curb'd it better.
(*To* Eleanora.) I would not lose your company, sweet Countess.

El. We'll go together, then.

[EXEUNT Orra *and* Eleanora.

(*Manet* Hughobert; *who paces angrily about the stage, while* Glottenbal *stands on the front, thumping his legs with his sheathed rapier.*)

There is no striving with a forward girl,
Nor pushing on a fool. My harassed life
Day after day more irksome grows. Curs'd bane!
I'll toil no more for this untoward match.

(*Enter* RUDIGERE, *stealing behind, and listening.*)

Rud. You are disturb'd, my Lord.

Hugh. What, is it thou? I am disturb'd in sooth.

Rud. Aye, Orra has been here; and some light words
Of girlish levity have mov'd you. How!
Toil for this match no more! What else remains,
If this should be abandoned, noble Aldenberg,
That can be worth your toil?

Hugh. I'll match the cub elsewhere.

Rud. What call ye matching?

Hugh. Surely for him some other virtuous maid
Of high descent, tho' not so richly dowried,
May be obtain'd.

Rud. Within your walls, perhaps,
Some waiting gentlewoman, who perchance
May be some fifty generations back
Descended from a king, he will himself
Ere long obtain, without your aid, my Lord.

Hugh. Thou mak'st me mad! the dolt! the senseless dolt!
What can I do for him? I cannot force
A noble maid entrusted to my care:
I, the sole guardian of her helpless youth!

Rud. That were indeed unfit; but there are means
To make her yield consent.

Hugh. Then by my faith, good friend, I'll call thee wizard,
If thou can'st find them out. What means already,

Short of compulsion, have we left untried?
And now the term of my authority
Wears to its close.

Rud. I know it well; and therefore powerful means,
And of quick operation, must be sought.

Hugh. Speak plainly to me.

Rud. I have watch'd her long.
I've seen her cheek, flush'd with the rosy glow
Of jocund spirits, deadly pale become
At tale of nightly sprite or apparition,
Such as all hear, 'tis true, with greedy ears,
Saying, "Saints, save us!" but forget as quickly.
I've mark'd her long: she has, with all her shrewdness
And playful merriment, a gloomy fancy,
That broods within itself on fearful things.

Hugh. And what doth this avail us?

Rud. Hear me out.
Your ancient castle in the Suabian forest
Hath, as too well you know, belonging to it,
Or false or true, frightful reports. There hold her
Strictly confin'd in sombre banishment;
And doubt not but she will, ere long, full gladly
Her freedom purchase at the price you name.

Hugh. On what pretence can I confine her there?
It were most odious.

Rud. Can pretence be wanting?
Has she not favour shewn to Theobald,

Who in your neighbourhood, with his sworn friend
The Banneret of Basle, suspiciously
Prolongs his stay? A poor and paltry Count,
Unmeet to match with her. And want ye then
A reason for removing her with speed
To some remoter quarter? Out upon it!
You are too scrupulous.

Hugh. Thy scheme is good, but cruel.

(Glottenbal—*who has been drawing nearer to them, and attending to the last part of their discourse.*)

Glot. O much I like it, dearly wicked Rudigere!
She then will turn her mind to other thoughts
Than scornful gibes at me.

Hugh. I to her father swore I would protect her:
I must fulfil his will.

Rud. And, in that will, her father did desire
She might be match'd with this your only son;
Therefore you're firmly bound all means to use
That may the end attain.

Hugh. Walk forth with me, we'll talk of this at large. [Exeunt Hugh. *and* Rud.

(*Manet* Glottenbal, *who comes forward from the bottom of the stage, with the action of a knight advancing to the charge.*)

Glot. Yes, thus it is: I have the slight o't now:
And were the combat yet to come, I'd shew them
I'm not a whit behind the bravest knight,
Cross luck excepted.

Enter MAURICE.

Maur. My Lord, indulge us of your courtesy.

Glot. In what, I pray?

Maur. Did not Fernando tell you?
We are all met within our social bower;
And I have wager'd on your head, that none
But you alone, within the Count's domains,
Can to the bottom drain the chased horn.
Come, do not linger here when glory calls you.

Glot. Think'st thou that Theobald could drink so stoutly?

Maur. He, paltry chief! he herds with sober burghers;
A goblet, half its size, would conquer him.

[EXEUNT.

ACT II.

SCENE I. — *A Garden with Trees and Shrubs, &c.* ORRA, THEOBALD, *and* HARTMAN, *are discovered in a shaded Walk at the bottom of the Stage, speaking in dumb Show, which they cross, disappearing behind the Trees; and are presently followed by* CATHRINA *and* ALICE, *who continue walking there.* OR. THEO. *and* HART. *then appear again, entering near the front of the Stage.*

OR. (*talking to* Hart. *as she enters.*) And so, since fate has made me, woe the day!
That poor and good-for-nothing, helpless being,
Woman yclept, I must consign myself
With all my lands and rights into the hands
Of some proud man, and say, "Take all, I pray,
And do me in return the grace and favour
To be my master."

Hart. Nay, gentle lady, you constrain my words,
And load them with a meaning harsh and foreign
To what they truly bear. — A master! No;
A valiant, gentle mate, who in the field
Or in the council will maintain your right:
A noble, equal partner.

Or. (*shaking her head.*) Well I know,
In such a partnership, the share of power

Allotted to the wife. See, noble Falkenstein
Hath silent been the while, nor spoke one word
In aid of all your specious arguments.
What's your advice, my Lord? (*to* Theo.)

Theo. Ah, noble Orra,
'Twere like self-murder to give honest counsel;
Then urge me not. I frankly do confess
I should be more heroic than I am.

Or. Right well I see thy head approves my plan,
And by and by so will thy gen'rous heart.
In short, I would, without another's leave,
Improve the low condition of my peasants,
And cherish them in peace. Ev'n now methinks
Each little cottage of my native vale
Swells out its earthen sides, up-heaves its roof,
Like to a hillock mov'd by lab'ring mole,
And with green trail-weeds clamb'ring up its walls,
Roses and ev'ry gay and fragrant plant
Before my fancy stands, a fairy bower:
Aye, and within it too do fairies dwell.

(*Looking playfully through her fingers like a shew-glass.*)

Peep thro' its wreathed window, if indeed
The flowers grow not too close, and there within
Thou'lt see some half a dozen rosy brats
Eating from wooden bowls their dainty milk;—
Those are my mountain elves. See'st thou not
Their very forms distinctly?

Theo. Distinctly; and most beautiful the sight!
A sight which sweetly stirreth in the heart
Feelings that gladden and ennoble it,
Dancing like sun-beams on the rippled sea;
A blessed picture! Foul befall the man
Whose narrow, selfish soul would shade or mar it!

Hart. To this right heartily I say Amen!
But if there be a man whose gen'rous soul
(*turning to* Orra.)
Like ardour fills; who would with thee pursue
Thy gen'rous plan; who would his harness don—

Or. (*putting her hand on him in gentle interruption.*)
Nay, valiant Banneret, who would, an't please you,
His harness doff: all feuds, all strife forbear,
All military rivalship, all lust
Of added power, and live in steady quietness,
A mild and fost'ring Lord. Know you of one
That would so share my task?—You answer not;
And your brave friend, methinks, casts on the ground
A thoughtful look: wots he of such a Lord?
(*to* Theo.)

Theo. Wot I of such a Lord? No, noble Orra,
I do not; nor does Hartman, tho' perhaps
His friendship may betray his judgment. No;
None such exist: we are all fierce, contentious,
Restless and proud, and prone to vengeful feuds;
The very distant sound of war excites us,

Like the curb'd courser list'ing to the chase,
Who paws, and frets, and bites the rein. Trust none
To cross thy gentle, but most princely purpose,
Who hath on head a circling helmet wore,
Or ever grasp'd a glave. — But ne'ertheless
There is — I know a man. — Might I be bold?

Or. Being so honest, boldness is your right.

Theo. Permitted then, I'll say, I know a man,
Tho' most unworthy Orra's Lord to be,
Who, as her champion, friend, devoted soldier,
Might yet commend himself; and, so received,
Who would at her command, for her defence
His sword right proudly draw. An honour'd sword,
Like that which at the gate of Paradise
From steps prophane the blessed region guarded.

Or. Thanks to the gen'rous knight! I also know
The man thou would'st commend; and when my state
Such service needeth, to no sword but his
Will I that service owe.

Theo. Most noble Orra! greatly is he honour'd;
And will not murmur that a higher wish,
Too high, and too presumptuous, is represt.
(*Kissing her hand with great respect.*)

Or. Nay, Rodolph Hartman, clear that cloudy brow,
And look on Falkenstein and on myself,
As two co-burghers of thy native city,
(For such I mean ere long to be,) and claiming

From thee, as cadets from an elder born,
Thy chearing equal kindness.

Enter a Servant.

Serv. The Count is now at leisure to receive
The Lord of Falkenstein, and Rodolph Hartman.

Hart. We shall attend him shortly.

(*Exit* Servant.)

(*Aside to* Theo.) Must we now
Our purpos'd suit to some pretended matter
Of slighter import change?

Theo. (*to* Hart. *aside.*) Assuredly.—
Madam, I take my leave with all devotion.

Hart. I with all friendly wishes.

[Exeunt Theo. *and* Hart.

(Cathrina *and* Alice *now advance through the shrubs, &c. at the bottom of the stage, while* Orra *remains, wrapped in thought, on the front.*)

Cath. Madam, you're thoughtful; something occupies
Your busy mind.

Or. What was't we talk'd of, when the worthy Banneret
With Falkenstein upon our converse broke?

Cath. How we should spend our time, when in your castle
You shall your state maintain in ancient splendour,
With all your vassals round you.

Or. Aye, so it was.

Al. And you did say, my Lady,

It should not be a cold unsocial grandeur:
That you would keep, the while, a merry house.

Or. O doubt it not! I'll gather round my board
All that heav'n sends to me of way-worn folks,
And noble travellers, and neighb'ring friends,
Both young and old. Within my ample hall,
The worn-out man of arms, (of whom too many,
Nobly descended, rove like reckless vagrants
From one proud chieftain's castle to another,
Half chid, half honour'd,) shall o'tip-toe tread,
Tossing his grey locks from his wrinkled brow
With cheerful freedom, as he boasts his feats
Of days gone by. — Music we'll have; and oft
The bick'ring dance upon our oaken floors
Shall, thund'ring loud, strike on the distant ear
Of 'nighted trav'llers, who shall gladly bend
Their doubtful footsteps tow'rds the cheering din.
Solemn, and grave, and cloister'd, and demure
We shall not be. Will this content ye, damsels?

Al. O passing well! 'twill be a pleasant life;
Free from all stern subjection; blithe and fanciful;
We'll do whate'er we list.

Cath. That right and prudent is, I hope thou meanest.

Al. Why ever so suspicious and so strict?
How could'st thou think I had another meaning?
(*To* Orra.) And shall we ramble in the woods full oft
With hound and horn?—that is my dearest joy.

Or. Thou runn'st me fast, good Alice. Do not doubt
This shall be wanting to us. Ev'ry season
Shall have its suited pastime: even Winter
In its deep noon, when mountains piled with snow,
And chok'd up valleys from our mansion bar
All entrance, and nor guest nor traveller
Sounds at our gate; the empty hall forsaking,
In some warm chamber, by the crackling fire
We'll hold our little, snug, domestic court,
Plying our work with song and tale between.

Cath. And stories too, I ween, of ghosts and spirits,
And things unearthly, that on Michael's eve
Rise from the yawning tombs.

Or. Thou thinkest then one night o'th' year is truly
More horrid than the rest.

Cath. Perhaps 'tis only silly superstition:
But yet it is well known the Count's brave father
Would rather on a glacier's point have lain,
By angry tempests rock'd, than on that night
Sunk in a downy couch in Brunier's castle.

Or. How, pray? What fearful thing did scare him so?

Cath. Hast thou ne'er heard the story of Count Hugo,
His ancestor, who slew the hunter-knight?

Or. (*eagerly.*) Tell it, I pray thee.

Al. Cathrina, tell it not: it is not right:

Such stories ever change her cheerful spirits
To gloomy pensiveness; her rosy bloom
To the wan colour of a shrouded corse.
(*To* Orra.) What pleasure is there, Lady, when thy hand,
Cold as the valley's ice, with hasty grasp
Seizes on her who speaks, while thy shrunk form
Cow'ring and shiv'ring stands with keen turn'd ear
To catch what follows of the pausing tale?

Or. And let me cow'ring stand, and be my touch
The valley's ice: there is a pleasure in it.

Al. Say'st thou indeed there is a pleasure in it?

Or. Yea, when the cold blood shoots through every vein:
When every hair's-pit on my shrunken skin
A knotted knoll becomes, and to mine ears
Strange inward sounds awake, and to mine eyes
Rush stranger tears, there is a joy in fear.
(*Catching hold of* Cathrina.)
Tell it, Cathrina, for the life within me
Beats thick, and stirs to hear it.
He slew the hunter-knight?

Cath. Since I must tell it, then, the story goes
That grim Count Aldenbergh, the ancestor
Of Hughobert, and also of yourself,
From hatred or from envy, to his castle
A noble knight, who hunted in the forest,
Well the Black Forest named, basely decoyed,
And there, within his chamber, murder'd him —

Or. Merciful Heaven! and in my veins there runs
A murderer's blood. Said'st thou not, *murder'd him?*

Cath. Aye; as he lay asleep, at dead of night.

Or. A deed most horrible!

Cath. It was on Michael's eve; and since that time,
The neighb'ring hinds oft hear the midnight yell
Of spectre-hounds, and see the spectre shapes
Of huntsmen on their sable steeds, with still
A nobler hunter riding in their van
To cheer the chase, shewn by the moon's pale beams,
When wanes its horn in long October nights.

Or. This hath been often seen?

Cath. Aye, so they say.
But, as the story goes, on Michael's eve,
And on that night alone of all the year,
The hunter-knight himself, having a horn
Thrice sounded at the gate, the castle enters;
And, in the very chamber where he died,
Calls on his murd'rer, or in his default
Some true descendant of his house, to loose
His spirit from its torment; for his body
Is laid i'the earth unbless'd, and none can tell
The spot of its interment.

Or. Call on some true descendant of his race!
It were to such a fearful interview.
But in that chamber, on that night alone—

Hath he elsewhere to any of the race
Appear'd? or hath he power —

Al. Nay, nay, forbear:
See how she looks. (*To* Orra.) I fear thou art not well.

Or. There is a sickly faintness come upon me.

Al. And did'st thou say there is a joy in fear?

Or. My mind of late has strange impressions ta'en.
I know not how it is.

Al. A few nights since,
Stealing o'tiptoe, softly thro' your chamber,
Towards my own —

Or. O heaven defend us! did'st thou see aught there?

Al. Only your sleeping self. But you appear'd
Distress'd and troubled in your dreams; and once
I thought to wake you ere I left the chamber,
But I forbore.

Or. And glad I am thou did'st.
It is not dreams I fear; for still with me
There is an indistinctness o'er them cast,
Like the dull gloom of misty twilight, where
Before mine eyes pass all incongruous things,
Huge, horrible and strange, on which I stare
As idiots do upon this changeful world,
With nor surprise nor speculation. No;
Dreams I fear not: it is the dreadful waking,
When, in deep midnight stillness, the roused fancy
Takes up th' imperfect shadows of its sleep,

Like a marr'd speech snatch'd from a bungler's mouth,
Shaping their forms distinctively and vivid
To visions horrible: — this is my bane; —
It is the dreadful waking that I fear.

Al. Well, speak of other things. There in good time
Your ghostly father comes with quicken'd steps,
Like one who bears some tidings good or ill.
Heaven grant they may be good!

Enter URSTON.

Or. Father, you seem disturb'd.

Ur. Daughter, I am in truth disturb'd. The Count
All o'the sudden, being much enrag'd
That Falkenstein still lingers near these walls,
Resolves to send thee hence, to be a while
In banishment detain'd, till on his son
Thou look'st with better favour.

Or. Aye, indeed!
That is to say perpetual banishment:
A sentence light or heavy, as the place
Is sweet or irksome he would send me to.

Ur. He will contrive to make it, doubt him not,
Irksome enough. Therefore I would advise thee
To feign at least, but for a little time,
A disposition to obey his wishes.
He's stern, but not relentless; and his dame,
The gentle Eleanor, will still befriend you,
When fit occasion serves.

Or. What said'st thou, Father?
To feign a disposition to obey!
I did mistake thy words.

Urst. No, gentle daughter;
So press'd, thou mayest feign and yet be blameless.
A trusty guardian's faith with thee he holds not,
And therefore thou art free to meet his wrongs
With what defence thou hast.

Or. (*proudly.*) Nay pardon me; I, with an unshorn crown,
Must hold the truth in plain simplicity,
And am in nice distinctions most unskilful.

Urst. Lady, have I deserv'd this sharpness? oft
Thine infant hand has strok'd this shaven crown:
Thou'st ne'er till now reproach'd it.

Or. (*bursting into tears.*)
Pardon, O pardon me, my gentle Urston!
Pardon a wayward child, whose eager temper
Doth sometimes mar the kindness of her heart.
Father, am I forgiven? (*Hanging on him.*)

Urst. Thou art, thou art:
Thou art forgiven; more than forgiven, my child.

Or. Then lead me to the Count, I will myself
Learn his stern purpose.

Urst. In the hall he is,
Seated in state, and waiting to receive you.

[Exeunt.

SCENE III.

A spacious Apartment, or Baron's Hall, with a Chair of State, HUGHOBERT, ELEANORA, *and* GLOTTENBAL *enter near the Front, speaking as they enter; and afterwards enter Vassals and Attendants, who range themselves at the bottom of the Stage.*

Hugh. Cease, Dame! I will not hear; thou striv'st in vain
With thy weak pleadings. Orra hence must go
Within the hour, unless she will engage
Her plighted word to marry Glottenbal.

Glot. Aye, and a mighty hardship, by the mass!

Hugh. I've summon'd her in solemn form before me,
That these my vassals should my act approve,
Knowing my right of guardianship; and also
That her late father, in his dying moments,
Did will she should be married to my son;
Which will, she now must promise to obey,
Or take the consequence.

El. But why so hasty?

Hugh. Why, say'st thou? Falkenstein still in these parts
Lingers with sly intent. Even now he left me,
After an interview of small importance,
Which he and Hartman, as a blind pretence
For seeing Orra, formally requested.
I say again she must forthwith obey me,
Or take the consequence of wayward will.

El. Nay, not for Orra do I now intreat
So much as for thyself. Bethink thee well
What honour thou shalt have, when it is known
Thy ward from thy protecting roof was sent;
Thou who should'st be to her a friend, a father.
Hugh. But do I send her unprotected? No!
Brave Rudigere conducts her with a band
Of trusty spearmen. In her new abode
She will be safe as here.
El. Ha! Rudigere!
Put'st thou such trust in him? Alas, my Lord!
His heart is full of cunning and deceit.
Wilt thou to him the flower of all thy race
Rashly intrust? O be advised, my Lord!
Hugh. Thy ghostly father tells thee so, I doubt not.
Another priest confesses Rudigere,
And Urston likes him not. But can'st thou think,
With aught but honest purpose, he would chuse
From all her women the severe Cathrina,
So strictly virtuous, for her companion?
This puts all doubt to silence. Say no more,
Else I shall think thou plead'st against my son,
More with a stĕp-dame's than a mother's feelings.
Glot. Aye, marry does she, father! And forsooth!
Regards me as a fool. No marvel then
That Orra scorns me; being taught by her, —
How should she else? — So to consider me.
Hugh. (*to* Glottenbal.) Tut! hold thy tongue.
El. He wrongs me much, my Lord.

Hugh. No more, for here she comes.

Enter ORRA, *attended by* URSTON, ALICE *and* CATHRINA, *and* HUGHOBERT *seats himself in his chair of state, the vassals, &c. ranging themselves on each side.*

Hugh. (*to* Orra.) Madam and ward, placed under mine authority,
And to my charge committed by my kinsman,
Ulric of Aldenberg, thy noble father;
Having all gentle means essay'd to win thee
To the fulfilment of his dying will,
That did decree his heiress should be married
With Glottenbal my heir; I solemnly
Now call upon thee, ere that rougher means
Be used for this good end, to promise truly,
Thou wilt, within a short and stated time,
Before the altar give thy plighted faith
To this my only son. I wait thine answer.
Orra of Aldenberg, wilt thou do this?

Or. Count of the same, my lord and guardian,
I will not.

Hugh. Have a care, thou froward maid!
'Tis thy last opportunity: ere long
Thou shalt, within a dreary dwelling pent,
Count thy dull hours, told by the dead man's watch,
And wish thou had'st not been so proudly wilful.

Or. And let my dull hours by the dead man's watch
Be told; yea, make me too the dead man's mate,

My dwelling place the nailed coffin; still
I would prefer it to the living Lord
Your goodness offers me.

Hugh. Art thou bewitch'd?
Is he not young, well featured and well form'd?
And dost thou put him in thy estimation
With bones and sheeted clay?
Beyond endurance is thy stubborn spirit.
Right well thy father knew that all thy sex
Stubborn and headstrong are; therefore, in wisdom,
He vested me with power that might compel thee
To what he will'd should be.

Or. O not in wisdom!
Say rather in that weak, but gen'rous faith,
Which said to him, the cope of heaven would fall
And smother in its cradle his swath'd babe,
Rather than thou, his mate in arms, his kinsman,
Who by his side in many a field had fought,
Should'st take advantage of his confidence
For sordid ends. —
My brave and noble father!
A voice comes from thy grave and cries against it,
And bids me to be bold. Thine awful form
Rises before me, — and that look of anguish
On thy dark brow! — O no! I blame thee not.

Hugh. Thou seem'st beside thyself with such wild gestures

And strangely-flashing eyes. Repress these fancies,
And to plain reason listen. Thou hast said,
For sordid ends I have advantage ta'en.
Since thy brave father's death, by war and compact,
Thou of thy lands hast lost a third; whilst I,
By happy fortune, in my heir's behalf,
Have doubled my domains to what they were
When Ulric chose him as a match for thee.

Or. O, and what speaketh this, but that my father
Domains regarded not; and thought a man
Such as the son should be of such a man
As thou to him appear'dst, a match more honourable
Than one of ampler state. Take thou from Glottenbal
The largely added lands of which thou boastest,
And put, in lieu thereof, into his stores
Some weight of manly sense and gen'rous worth,
And I will say thou keep'st faith with thy friend:
But as it is, altho' a king's domains
Encreas'd thy wealth, thou poorly would'st deceive him.

Hugh. (*rising from his chair in anger.*)
Now, Madam, be all counsel on this matter
Between us closed. Prepare thee for thy journey.

El. Nay, good my Lord! consider.

Hugh. (*to* Eleanora.) What, again!

Have I not said thou hast an alien's heart
From me and mine. Learn to respect my will:
— Be silent, as becomes a youthful Dame.

Urst. For a few days may she not still remain?

Hugh. No, priest; not for an hour. It is my pleasure
That she for Brunier's castle do set forth
Without delay.

Or. (*with a faint starting movement.*) In Brunier's castle!

Hug. Aye;
And doth this change the colour of thy cheek,
And give thy alter'd voice a feebler sound?
(*Aside to* Glottenbal.)
She shrinks, now to her, boy; this is thy time.

Glot. (*to* Orra.) Unless thou wilt, thou need'st not go at all.
There is full many a maiden would right gladly
Accept the terms we offer, and remain.
(*A pause.*) Wilt thou not answer me?

Or. I heard thee not. —
I heard thy voice but not thy words. What said'st thou?

Glot. I say, there's many a maiden would right gladly
Accept the terms we offer, and remain.
The daughter of a King hath match'd ere now
With mine inferior. We are link'd together
As 'twere by right and natural property.
And as I've said before I say again,
I love thee too: What more couldst thou desire?

Or. I thank thee for thy courtship, tho' uncouth;
For it confirms my purpose: and my strength
Grows as thou speak'st, firm like the deep-bas'd rock.
(*To* Hughobert.) Now for my journey when you will, my Lord;
I'm ready.

Hugh. Be it so! on thine own head
Rest all the blame.

(*Going from her.*)

Perverse past all belief!

(*Turning round to her sternly.*)

Orra of Aldenberg, wilt thou obey me?

Or. Count of that noble house, with all respect,
Again I say I will not.

(EXIT Hughobert *in anger, followed by* Glottenbal, Urston, *&c. Manent only* Eleanora, Cathrina, Alice *and* Orra, *who keeps up with stately pride till* Hughobert *and all Attendants are gone out, and then throwing herself into the arms of* Eleanora, *gives vent to her feelings.*)

El. Sweet Orra! be not so depress'd; thou goest
For a short term, soon to return again;
The banishment is mine who stays behind.
But I will beg of heaven with ceaseless prayers
To have thee soon restored: and, when I dare,
Will plead with Hughobert in thy behalf;
He is not always stern.

Or. Thanks, gentle friend! Thy voice to me doth sound
Like the last sounds of kindly nature; dearly
In my remembrance shall they rest. — What sounds,
What sights, what horrid intercourse I may,
Ere we shall meet again, be doom'd to prove,
High heaven alone doth know. — If that indeed
We e'er shall meet again!

(*Falls on her neck and weeps.*)

El. Nay, nay! come to my chamber. There awhile
Compose your spirits. Be not so deprest.

[EXEUNT.

(Rudigere, *who has appear'd, during the last part of the above scene, at the bottom of the stage, half concealed, as if upon the watch, now comes forward.*)

(*Speaking as he advances.*)

Hold firm her pride till fairly from these walls
Our journey is begun; then fortune hail!
Thy favours are secured.

(*Looking off the stage.*)

Ho, Maurice there!

Enter MAURICE.

My faithful Maurice, I would speak with thee
I leave thee here behind me; to thy care,
My int'rests I commit; be it thy charge
To counteract thy Lady's influence,
Who will entreat her Lord the term to shorten

Of Orra's absence, maiming thus my plan,
Which must, belike, have time to be effected.
Be vigilant, be artful; and be sure
Thy services I amply will repay.

Maur. Aye, thou hast said so, and I have believed thee.

Rud. And dost thou doubt?

Maur. No; yet meantime, good sooth!
If somewhat of thy bounty I might finger,
'Twere well: I like to have some actual proof.
Did'st thou not promise it?

Rud. 'Tis true I did,
But other pressing calls have drain'd my means.

Maur. And other pressing calls my ebbing faith
May also drain, and change my promis'd purpose.

Rud. Go to! I know thou art a greedy leech,
Tho' ne'ertheless thou lov'st me.

(*Taking a small case from his pocket, which he opens.*)

See'st thou here?
I have no coin; but look upon these jewels:
I took them from a knight I slew in battle.
When I am Orra's lord, thou shalt receive,
Were it ten thousand crowns, whate'er their worth
Shall by a skilful lapidary be
In honesty esteem'd.

(*Gives him the jewels.*)

Maur. I thank thee, but methinks their lustre's dim.
I've seen the stones before upon thy breast

In gala days, but never heard thee boast
They were of so much value.

Rud. I was too prudent : I had lost them else.
To no one but thyself would I entrust
The secret of their value.

Enter Servant.

Serv. Sir Rudigere, the spearmen are without,
Waiting your further orders, for the journey.

Rud. (*to* Servant.) I'll come to them anon.

[Exit Servant.

Before I go, I'll speak to thee again.

[Exeunt *severally*.

ACT III.

SCENE I. — *A Forest with a half-ruined Castle in the Back-Ground, seen through the Trees by Moon-light.* FRANKO *and several* Outlaws *are discovered sitting on the Ground, round a Fire, with Flaggons, &c. by them, as if they had been drinking.*

Song of several voices.

The chough and crow to roost are gone,
The owl sits on the tree,
The hush'd wind wails with feeble moan,
Like infant charity.
The wild-fire dances on the fen,
The red star sheds its ray,
Up-rouse ye, then, my merry men!
It is our op'ning day.

Both child and nurse are fast asleep,
And clos'd is every flower,
And winking tapers faintly peep
High from my Lady's bower;
Bewilder'd hinds with shorten'd ken
Shrink on their murky way,
Up-rouse ye, then, my merry men!
It is our op'ning day.

Nor board nor garner own we now,
Nor roof nor latched door,
Nor kind mate, bound by holy vow
To bless a good man's store;

Noon lulls us in a gloomy den,
And night is grown our day,
Up-rouse ye, then, my merry men!
And use it as ye may.

Frank. (*to* 1*st.* Out.) How lik'st thou this, Fernando?

1*st Out.* Well sung i'faith! but serving ill our turn,
Who would all trav'llers and benighted folks
Scare from our precincts. Such sweet harmony
Will rather tempt invasion.

Frank. Fear not, for mingled voices, heard afar,
Thro' glade and glen and thicket, stealing on
To distant list'ners, seem wild-goblin-sounds;
At which the lonely trav'ller checks his steed,
Pausing with long-drawn breath and keen-turn'd ear;
And twilight pilferers cast down in haste
Their ill-got burthens, while the homeward hind
Turns from his path, full many a mile about,
Thro' bog and mire to grope his blund'ring way.
Such, to the startled ear of superstition,
Were seraph's song, could we like seraphs sing.

Enter 1*st* Outlaw *hastily.*

2*d Out.* Disperse ye diff'rent ways: we are undone.

Frank. How say'st thou, shrinking poltron? we undone!
Outlaw'd and ruin'd men, who live by daring!

2d Out. A train of armed men, some noble Dame
Escorting, (so their scatter'd words discover'd
As unperceived I hung upon their rear,)
Are close at hand, and mean to pass the night
Within the castle.

Frank. Some benighted travellers,
Bold from their numbers, or who ne'er have heard
The ghostly legend of this dreaded place.

1st Out. Let us keep close within our vaulted haunts;
The way to which is tangled and perplex'd,
And cannot be discover'd: with the morn
They will depart.

Frank. Nay, by the holy mass! within those walls
Not for a night must trav'llers quietly rest,
Or few or many. Would we live securely,
We must uphold the terrors of the place:
Therefore, let us prepare our midnight rouse.
See, from the windows of the castle gleam
(*lights seen from the castle.*)
Quick passing lights, as tho' they moved within
In hurried preparation; and that bell,
(*bell heard.*)
Which from yon turret its shill 'larum sends,
Betokens some unwonted stir. Come hearts!
Be all prepared, before the midnight watch,
The fiend-like din of our infernal chace
Around the walls to raise. — Come; night advances. [EXEUNT.

SCENE II.

A Gothic Room in the Castle, with the Stage darkened; enter Cathrina, *bearing a Light, followed by* Orra.

Or. (*Catching her by the robe and pulling her back.*)
Advance no further: turn, I pray! This room
More dismal and more ghastly seems than that
Which we have left behind. Thy taper's light,
As thus aloft thou wav'st it to and fro,
The fretted ceiling gilds with feeble brightness;
Whilst over-head its carved ribs glid past
Like edgy waves of a dark sea, returning
To an eclipsed moon its sullen sheen.

Cath. To me it seems less dismal than the other.
See, here are chairs around the table set,
As if its last inhabitants had left it
Scarcely an hour ago.
(*Setting the light upon the table.*)

Or. Alas! how many hours and years have past
Since human forms have round this table sat,
Or lamp or taper on its surface gleam'd!
Methinks I hear the sound of time long past
Still murm'ring o'er us in the lofty void
Of those dark arches, like the ling'ring voices
Of those who long within their graves have slept.
It was their gloomy home; now it is mine.
(*Sits down, resting her arm upon the table, and covering her eyes with her hand.*)

(*Enter* RUDIGERE, *beckoning* CATHRINA *to come to him; and speaks to her in a low voice at the corner of the stage.*)

Go and prepare thy Lady's chamber; why
Dost thou for ever closely near her keep?

Cath. She charged me so to do:

Rud. I charge thee also,
With paramount authority, to leave her:
I for a while will take thy station here.
Thou art not mad? Thou dost not hesitate?

(*Fixing his eyes on her with a fierce threatening look, from which she shrinks.*)

[EXIT Cath.

Or. This was the home of bloody lawless power.
The very air rests thick and heavily
Where murder hath been done.
(*Sighing heavily.*) There is a strange oppression in my breast:
Dost thou not feel a close unwholesome vapour?

Rud. No; ev'ry air to me is light and healthful,
That with thy sweet and heavenly breath is mix'd.

Or. (*starting up.*) Thou here!
(*Looking round.*) Cathrina gone?

Rud. Does Orra fear to be alone with one,
Whose weal, whose being on her favour hangs?

Or. Retire, Sir Knight. I chuse to be alone.

Rud. And dost thou chuse it, here, in such a place,
Wearing so near the midnight hour? — Alas!
How loath'd and irksome must my presence be!

Or. Dost thou deride my weakness?
Rud. I deride it!
No, noble Maid! say rather that from thee
I have a kindred weakness caught. In battle
My courage never shrunk, as my arm'd heel
And crested helm do fairly testify:
But now when midnight comes, I feel by sympathy,
With thinking upon thee, fears rise within me
I never knew before.
Or. (*in a softened kindlier voice.*)
Ha! dost thou too
Such human weakness own?
Rud. I plainly feel
We are all creatures, in the wakeful hour
Of ghastly midnight, form'd to cower together,
Forgetting all distinctions of the day,
Beneath its awful and mysterious power.
(*Stealing closer to her as he speaks, and putting his arms round her.*)
Or. (*breaking from him.*)
I pray thee hold thy parley further off:
Why dost thou press so near me?
Rud. And art thou so offended, lovely Orra?
Ah! wherefore am I thus presumptuous deem'd?
The blood that fills thy veins enriches mine;
From the same stock we spring; tho' by that glance
Of thy disdainful eye, too well I see
My birth erroneously thou countest base.
Or. Erroneously!
Rud. Yes, I will prove it so.

Longer I'll not endure a galling wrong
Which makes each word of tenderness that bursts
From a full heart, bold and presumptuous seem,
And severs us so far.

Or. No, subtile snake!
It is the baseness of thy selfish mind,
Full of all guile, and cunning, and deceit,
That severs us so far, and shall do ever.

Rud. Thou prov'st how far my passion will endure
Unjust reproaches from a mouth so dear.

Or. Out on hypocrisy! who but thyself
Did Hughobert advise to send me hither?
And who the jailor's hateful office holds
To make my thraldom sure?

Rud. Upbraid me not for this: had I refused,
One less thy friend had ta'en th' ungracious task.
And, gentle Orra! dost thou know a man,
Who might in ward all that his soul holds dear
From danger keep, yet would the charge refuse,
For that strict right such wardship doth condemn?
O! still to be with thee; to look upon thee;
To hear thy voice, makes ev'n this place of horrours, —
Where, as 'tis said, the spectre of a chief,
Slain by our common grandsire, haunts the night,
A paradise — a place where I could live
In penury and gloom, and be most bless'd.
Ah! Orra! if there's misery in thraldom,
Pity a wretch who breathes but in thy favour:

Who till he look'd upon that beauteous face,
Was free and happy. — Pity me or kill me!
(*Kneeling and catching hold of her hand.*)

Or. Off, fiend! let snakes and vipers cling to me
So thou dost keep aloof.

Rud. (*rising indignantly.*)
And is my love with so much hatred met?
Madam, beware lest scorn like this should change me
Ev'n to the baleful thing your fears have fancied.

Or. Dar'st thou to threaten me?

Rud. He, who is mad with love and gall'd with scorn,
Dares any thing. — But O! forgive such words
From one who rather, humbled at your feet,
Would of that gentleness, that gen'rous pity,
The native inmate of each female breast,
Receive the grace on which his life depends.
There was a time when thou did'st look on me
With other eyes.

Or. Thou dost amaze me much.
Whilst I believ'd thou wert an honest man,
Being no fool, and an adventurous soldier,
I look'd upon thee with good-will; if more
Thou did'st discover in my looks than this,
Thy wisdom with thine honesty, in truth
Was fairly match'd.

Rud. Madam, the proud derision of that smile
Deceives me not. It is the Lord of Falkenstein,
Who better skill'd than I in tournay-war,
Tho' not i' th' actual field more valiant found,

Engrosses now your partial thoughts. And yet
What may he boast which, in a lover's suit,
I may not urge? He's brave, and so am I.
In birth I am his equal; for my mother,
As I shall prove, was married to Count Albert,
My noble father, tho' for reasons tedious
Here to be stated, still their secret nuptials
Were unacknowledged, and on me hath fallen
A cruel stigma which degrades my fortunes.
But were I—O forgive th' aspiring thought!—
But were I Orra's Lord, I should break forth
Like the unclouded sun, by all acknowledg'd
As ranking with the highest in the land.

Or. Do what thou wilt when thou art Orra's Lord;
But being as thou art, retire and leave me:
I chuse to be alone. (*Very proudly.*)

Rud. Then be it so.
Thy pleasure, mighty Dame, I will not balk.
This night, to-morrow's night, and every night,
Shalt thou in solitude be left; if absence
Of human beings can secure it for thee.
(*Pauses and looks on her, while she seems struck and disturb'd.*)
It wears already on the midnight hour;
Good night!
(*Pauses again, she still more disturb'd.*)
Perhaps I understood too hastily
Commands you may retract.

Or. (*recovering her state.*)
Leave me, I say; that part of my commands
I never can retract.

Rud. You are obey'd.
[EXIT.

(*Or. paces up and down hastily for some time, then stops short, and after remaining a little while in a thoughtful posture*)

Can spirit from the tomb, or fiend from hell,
More hateful, more malignant be than man —
Than villanous man? Altho' to look on such,
Yea, even the very thought of looking on them,
Makes natural blood to curdle in the veins,
And loosen'd limbs to shake.
There are who have endur'd the visitation
Of supernatural Beings. — O forfend it!
I would close couch me to my deadliest foe
Rather than for a moment bear alone
The horrours of the sight.
Who's there? Who's there?

(*looking round.*)

Heard I not voices near? That door ajar
Sends forth a cheerful light. Perhaps my women,
Who now prepare my chamber. Grant it be!

[EXIT, *running hastily to a door from which a light is seen.*

SCENE III.

A Chamber, with a small Bed or Couch in it; enter RUDIGERE *and* CATHRINA, *wrangling together.*

Rud. I say begone, and occupy the chamber
I have appointed for thee: here I'm fix'd,
And here I pass the night.

Cath. Thou said'st my chamber
Should be adjoining that which Orra holds?
I know thy wicked thoughts: they meditate
Some dev'lish scheme; but think not I'll abet it.

Rud. Thou wilt not!—angry, restive, simple fool!
Dost thou stop short and say, "I'll go no further?"
Thou, whom concealed shame hath bound so fast,—
My tool,—my instrument?—Fulfil thy charge
To the full bent of thy commission, else
Thee, and thy bantling too, I'll from me cast
To want and infamy.

Cath. O shameless man!
Thou art the son of a degraded mother
As low as I am, yet thou hast no pity.

Rud. Aye, and dost thou reproach my bastardy
To make more base the man who conquer'd thee,
With all thy virtue, rigid and demure?
Who would have thought less than a sov'reign Prince
Could e'er have compass'd such achievement? Mean
As he may be, thou'st given thyself a master,
And must obey him.—Dost thou yet resist?
Thou know'st my meaning.

(*Tearing open his vest in vehemence of action.*)

Cath. Under thy vest a dagger!—Ah! too well,
I know thy meaning, cruel, ruthless man!

Rud. Have I discover'd it?—I thought not of it:
The vehemence of gesture hath betray'd me.
I keep it not for thee, but for myself;
A refuge from disgrace. Here is another:
He who with high, but dangerous fortune grapples,
Should he be foil'd, looks but to friends like these.

(*Pulling out two daggers from his vest.*)

This steel is strong to give a vig'rous thrust;
The other on its venom'd point hath that
Which, in the feeblest hand, gives death as certain,
As tho' a giant smote the destin'd prey.

Cath. Thou desp'rate man! so arm'd against thyself!

Rud. Aye; and against myself with such resolves,
Consider well how I shall deal with those
Who may withstand my will or mar my purpose.
Think'st thou I'll feebly ——

Cath. O be pacified.
I will be gone: I am a humbled wretch
On whom thou tramplest with a tyrant's cruelty.

[Exit.

(*Rud. looks after her with a malignant laugh, and then goes to the door of an adjoining chamber, to the lock of which he applies his ear.*)

All still within.—I'm tired and heavy grown:
I'll lay me down to rest. She is secure:
No one can pass me here to gain her chamber.

If she hold parley now with any thing,
It must in truth be ghost or sprite.—Heigh ho!
I'm tir'd, and will to bed.

(*Lays himself on the couch and falls asleep. The cry of hounds is then heard without at a distance, with the sound of a horn; and presently* ORRA *enters, bursting from the door of the adjoining chamber, in great alarm.*)

Or. Cathrina! sleepest thou? Awake! Awake!

(*Running up to the couch and starting back on seeing* Rudigere.)

That hateful viper here!
Is this my nightly guard? Detested wretch!
I will steal back again.

(*Walks softly on tiptoe to the door of her chamber, when the cry of hounds, &c. is again heard without, nearer than before.*)

O no! I dare not.
Tho' sleeping, and most hateful when awake,
Still he is natural life and may be 'waked.

(*listening again.*)

'Tis nearer now: that dismal thrilling blast!
I must awake him.

(*Approaching the couch and shrinking back again.*)

O no! no, no!
Upon his face he wears a horrid smile
That speaks bad thoughts.

(Rud. *speaks in his sleep.*)

He mutters too my name.—

I dare not do it. (*Listening again.*)
The dreadful sound is now upon the wind,
Sullen and low, as if it wound its way
Into the cavern'd earth that swallow'd it.
I will abide in patient silence here;
Tho' hateful and asleep, I feel me still
Near something of my kind.

(*Crosses her arms, and leans in a cowering posture over the back of a chair at a distance from the couch; when presently the horn is heard without, louder than before, and she starts up.*)

O it returns! as tho' the yawning earth
Had given it up again, near to the walls.
The horribly mingled din! 'tis nearer still:
'Tis close at hand: 'tis at the very gate!
(*running up to the couch.*)
Were he a murd'rer, clenching in his hands
The bloody knife, I must awake him. — No!
That face of dark and subtile wickedness!
I dare not do it. (*listing again.*) Aye; 'tis at the gate —
Within the gate. —
What rushing blast is that
Shaking the doors? Some awful visitation
Dread entrance makes! O mighty God of Heaven!
A sound ascends the stairs.
Ho, Rudigere!
Awake, awake! Ho! Wake thee, Rudigere!

Rud. (*waking.*) What cry is that so terribly strong? — Ha! Orra!
What is the matter?

Or. It is within the walls. Did'st thou not hear it?
Rud. What? The loud voice that call'd me?
Or. No, it was mine.
Rud. It sounded in my ears
With more than human strength.
Or. Did it so sound?
There is around us, in this midnight air,
A power surpassing nature. List, I pray:
Altho' more distant now, dost thou not hear
The yell of hounds; the spectre-huntsman's horn?
Rud. I hear, indeed, a strangely mingled sound:
The wind is howling round the battlements.
But rest secure where safety is, sweet Orra!
Within these arms, nor man nor fiend shall harm thee.

(*Approaching her with a softened winning voice, while she pushes him off with abhorrence.*)

Or. Vile reptile! touch me not.
Rud. Ah! Orra! thou art warp'd by prejudice,
And taught to think me base; but in my veins
Lives noble blood, which I will justify.
Or. But in thy heart, false traitor! what lives there?
Rud. Alas! thy angel-faultlessness conceives not
The strong temptations of a soul impassion'd
Beyond controul of reason. —— At thy feet —
(*kneeling.*)
O spurn me not.

(*Enter several* Servants, *alarmed.*)

Rud. What all these fools upon us! Staring knaves,
What brings ye here at this untimely hour?

1st Serv. We have all heard it—'twas the yell of hounds
And clatt'ring steeds, and the shrill horn between.

Rud. Out on such folly!

2d Serv. In very truth it pass'd close to the walls;
Did not your honour hear it?

Rud. Ha! say'st thou so? thou art not wont to join
In idle tales.—I'll to the battlements
And watch it there: it may return again.

[EXEUNT *severally,* Rudigere *followed by* Servants, *and* Orra *into her own chamber.*

SCENE IV.

The Outlaws' *Cave; enter* THEOBALD.

Theo. (*looking round.*) Here is a place in which some traces are
Of late inhabitants. In yonder nook
The embers faintly gleam, and on the walls
Hang spears and ancient arms: I must be right.
A figure thro' the gloom moves towards me.
Ho! there! Whoe'er you are: Holla! good friend!

Enter an Outlaw.

Out. A stranger! Who art thou, who art thus bold,
To hail us here unbidden?

Theo. That thou shalt shortly know. Thou art, I guess,
One of the Outlaws, who this forest haunt.

Out. Be thy conjecture right or wrong, no more
Shalt thou return to tell where thou hast found us.
Now for thy life!

(*drawing his sword.*)

Theo. Hear me, I do entreat thee.

Out. Nay, nay! no foolish pleadings; for thy life
Is forfeit now; have at thee!

(*Falls fiercely upon* Theobald, *who also draws and defends himself bravely, when another* Outlaw *enters and falls likewise upon him.* Theo. *then recedes, fighting, till he gets his back to the wall of the cavern, and there defends himself stoutly.*)

Enter Franko.

Frank. Desist, I charge you! Fighting with a stranger,
Two swords to one — a solitary stranger!

1st Out. We are discover'd: had he master'd me,
He had return'd to tell his mates above

What neighbours in these nether caves they have.
Let us dispatch him.

Frank. No, thou hateful butcher!
Dispatch a man alone and in our power!
Who art thou, stranger, who dost use thy sword
With no mean skill; and in this perilous case
So bold an air and countenance maintainest?
What brought thee hither?

Theo. My name is Theobald of Falkenstein;
To find the valiant Captain of these bands,
And crave assistance of his gen'rous arm:
This is my business here.

Frank. (*struck and agitated, to his men.*)
Go, join your comrades in the further cave.
[EXEUNT Outlaws.
And thou art Falkenstein? In truth thou art.
And who think'st thou am I?

Theo. Franco, the gen'rous leader of those Outlaws.

Frank. So am I call'd, and by that name alone
They know me. Sporting on the mountain's side,
Where Garva's wood waves green, in other days,
Some fifteen years ago, they call'd me Albert.

Theo. (*rushing into his arms.*)
Albert; my play-mate Albert! Woe the day!
What cruel fortune drove thee to this state?

Frank. I'll tell thee all; but tell thou first to me
What is the aid thou camest here to ask.

Theo. Aye, thou wert ever thus: still forward bent

To serve, not to be serv'd.
But wave we this.
Last night a Lady to the castle came,
In thraldom by a villain kept, whom I
Ev'n with my life would rescue. Of arm'd force
At present destitute, I come to thee
Craving thy aid in counsel and in arms.

Frank. When did'st thou learn that Outlaws harbour here,
For 'tis but lately we have held these haunts?

Theo. Not till within the precincts of the forest,
Following the traces of that villain's course,
One of your band I met, and recogniz'd
As an old soldier, who, some few years back,
Had under my command right bravely serv'd.
Seeing himself discover'd, and encouraged
By what I told him of my story, freely
He offer'd to conduct me to his captain.
But in a tangled path some space before me,
Alarm'd at sight of spearmen thro' the brake,
He started from his way, and so I miss'd him,
Making, to gain your cave, my way alone.

Frank. Thou'rt welcome here: and gladly I'll assist thee,
Tho' not by arms, the force within the castle
So far out-numbering mine.
But other means may serve thy purpose better.

Theo. What other means, I pray?

Frank. From these low caves, a passage under ground
Leads to the castle—to the very tower

Where, as I guess, the Lady is confin'd.
When sleep has still'd the house, we'll make our
way.

Theo. Aye, by my faith it is a noble plan!
Guarded or not we well may overcome
The few that may compose her midnight guard.

Frank. We shall not shrink from that.——
But by my fay!
To-morrow is St. Michael's Eve: 'twere well
To be the spectre-huntsman for a night,
And bear her off, without pursuit or hindrance.

Theo. I comprehend thee not.

Frank. Thou shalt ere long.
But stand not here; an inner room I have,
Where thou shalt rest and some refreshment
take,
And then we will more fully talk of this,
Which, slightly mention'd, seems chimerical.
Follow me.
(*Turning to him as they go out.*)
Hast thou still upon thine arm
That mark which from mine arrow thou re-
ceiv'dst
When sportively we shot? The wound was
deep,
And gall'd thee much, but thou mad'st light of
it.

Theo. Yes, here it is. (*Pulling up his sleeve as they go out, and* EXEUNT.)

ACT IV.

SCENE I.—*The Ramparts of the Castle. Enter* ORRA *and* CATHRINA.

Cath. (*after a pause in which* Orra *walks once or twice across the stage, thoughtfully.*)
GO in, I pray; thou wand'rest here too long.
(*A pause again.*)
The air is cold; behind those further mountains
The sun is set. I pray thee now go in.

Or. Ha! sets the sun already? Is the day
Indeed drawn to its close?

Cath. Yes, night approaches.
See, many a gather'd flock of cawing rooks
Are to their nests returning.

Or. (*solemnly.*) Night approaches!—
This awful night which living beings shrink from;
All now of every kind scour to their haunts,
While darkness, peopled with its hosts unknown,
Awful dominion holds. Mysterious night!
What things unutterable thy dark hours
May lap!—What from thy teeming darkness burst
Of horrid visitations, ere that sun
Again shall rise on the enlighten'd earth!
(*A pause.*)

Cath. Why dost thou gaze intently on the sky?
See'st thou aught wonderful?

Or. Look there; behold that strange gigantic form
Which yon grim cloud assumes; rearing aloft
The semblance of a warrior's plumed head,
While from its half-shaped arm a streamy dart
Shoots angrily? Behind him, too, far stretch'd,
Seems there not, verily, a seried line
Of fainter misty forms?

Cath. I see, indeed,
A vasty cloud, of many clouds composed,
Towering above the rest; and that behind
In misty faintness seen, which hath some likeness
To a long line of rocks with pine-wood crown'd:
Or, if indeed the fancy so incline,
A file of spearmen, seen thro' drifted smoke.

Or. Nay, look how perfect now the form becomes:
Dost thou not see?—Aye, and more perfect still.
O thou gigantic Lord, whose robed limbs
Beneath their stride span half the heavens! art thou
Of lifeless vapour form'd? Art thou not rather
Some air-clad spirit—some portentous thing—
Some mission'd Being?—Such a sky as this
Ne'er usher'd in a night of nature's rest.

Cath. Nay, many such I've seen; regard it not.
That form, already changing, will ere long
Dissolve to nothing. Tarry here no longer.
Go in, I pray.

Or. No; while one gleam remains
Of the sun's blessed light, I will not go.

Cath. Then let me fetch a cloak to keep thee warm,
For chilly blows the breeze.
Or. Do as thou wilt.
[EXIT Cath.

Enter an Outlaw, *stealing softly behind her.*

Out. (*in a low voice.*) Lady!—the Lady Orra!
Or. (*starting.*) Heaven protect me!
Sounds it beneath my feet, in earth or air?
(*He comes forward.*)
Welcome is aught that wears a human face.
Did'st thou not hear a sound?
Out. What sound, an't please you?
Or. A voice which call'd me now: it spoke, methought,
In a low, hollow tone, suppress'd and low,
Unlike a human voice.
Out. It was my own.
Or. What would'st thou have?
Out. Here is a letter, Lady.
Or. Who sent thee hither?
Out. It will tell thee all. (*Gives a letter.*)
I must be gone, your chieftain is at hand.
[EXIT.
Or. Comes it from Falkenstein? It is his seal.
I may not read it here. I'll to my chamber.

[EXIT *hastily, not perceiving* Rudigere, *who enters by the opposite side, before she has time to get off.*

Rud. A letter in her hand, and in such haste!
Some secret agent here from Falkenstein?
It must be so. (*Hastening after her*, EXIT.)

SCENE II.

The Outlaws' *Cave; enter* THEOBALD *and* FRANKO *by opposite sides.*

Theo. How now, good Captain; draws it near the time?
Are those the keys?
Frank. They are: this doth unlock
The entrance to the staircase, known alone
To Gomez, ancient keeper of the castle,
Who is my friend in secret, and deters
The neighb'ring peasantry with dreadful tales
From visiting by night our wide domains.
The other doth unlock a secret door,
That leads us to the chamber where she sleeps.
Theo. Thanks, gen'rous friend! thou art my better genius.
Did'st thou not say, until the midnight horn
Hath sounded thrice, we must remain conceal'd?
Frank. Even so. And now I hear my men without
Telling the second watch.
Theo. How looks the night?
Frank. As we could wish: the stars do faintly twinkle
Thro' sever'd clouds, and shed but light sufficient
To shew each nearer object closing on you

In dim unshapely blackness. Aught that moves
Across your path, or sheep or straggling goat,
Is now a pawing steed or grizzly bull,
Large and terrific; every air-mov'd bush
Or jutting crag, some strange gigantic thing.

Theo. Is all still in the castle?

Frank. There is an owl sits hooting on the tower,
That answer from a distant mate receives,
Like the faint echo of his dismal cry;
While a poor houseless dog, by dreary fits,
Sits howling at the gate. All else is still.

Theo. Each petty circumstance is in our favour,
That makes the night more dismal.

Frank. Aye, all goes well: as I approach'd the walls,
I heard two centinels—for now I ween,
The boldest spearman will not watch alone—
Together talk in the deep hollow voice
Of those who speak at midnight, under awe
Of the dead stillness round them.

Theo. Then let us put ourselves in readiness,
And heaven's good favour guide us!

[EXEUNT.

SCENE III.

A gloomy Apartment; enter ORRA *and* RUDIGERE.

Or. (*aside.*) The room is darken'd: yesternight a lamp
Did shed its light around on roof and walls,
And made the dreary space appear less dismal.

Rud. (*overhearing her, and calling to a* Servant *without.*)

Ho! more lights here!

(Servant *enters with a light, and* EXIT.)

Thou art obey'd: in aught
But in the company of human kind,
Thou shalt be gratified. Thy lofty mind
For higher super-human fellowship,
If such there be, may now prepare it's strength.

Or. Thou ruthless tyrant! They who have in battle
Fought valiantly, shrink like a helpless child
From any intercourse with things unearthly.
Art thou a man? And bear'st thou in thy breast
The feelings of a man? It cannot be!

Rud. Yes, madam; in my breast I bear too keenly
The feelings of a man — a man most wretched:
A scorn'd, rejected man. — Make me less miserable;
Nay rather should I say, make me most blest;
And then — (*attempting to take her hand, while she steps back from him, drawing herself up with an air stately and determined, and looking stedfastly in his face.*)
I too am firm. Thou know'st my fix'd resolve:
Give me thy solemn promise to be mine.
This is the price, thou haughty, scornful maid,
That will redeem thee from the hour of terrour!
This is the price —

Or. Which never shall be paid.

(*Walks from him to the further end of the apartment.*)

Rud. (*after a pause.*) Thou art determin'd then. Be not so rash:
Bethink thee well what flesh and blood can bear:
The hour is near at hand.

(*She, turning round, waves him with her hand to leave her.*)

Thou deign'st no answer.
Well; reap the fruits of thine unconquer'd pride. [Exit.

Manet Orra.

Or. I am alone: that closing door divides me
From ev'ry being owning nature's life.—
And shall I be constrain'd to hold communion
With that which owns it not?

(*After pacing to and fro for a little while.*)

O that my mind
Could raise its thoughts in strong and steady fervour
To Him, the Lord of all existing things,
Who lives, and is where'er existence is;
Grasping its hold upon His skirted robe,
Beneath whose mighty rule Angels and Spirits,
Demons and nether powers, all living things,
Hosts of the earth, with the departed dead
In their dark state of mystery, alike
Subjected are!—And I will strongly do it.—
Ah! would I could! Some hidden powerful hindrance

Doth hold me back, and mars all thought.—

(After a pause, in which she stands fixed with her arms crossed on her breast.)

Dread intercourse!
O! if it look on me with its dead eyes!
If it should move its lock'd and earthy lips,
And utt'rance give to the grave's hollow sounds!
If it stretch forth its cold and bony grasp —
O horror, horror!

(Sinking lower at every successive idea, as she repeats these four last lines, till she is quite upon her knees on the ground.)

Would that beneath these planks of senseless matter
I could, until the dreadful hour is past,
As senseless be! *(striking the floor with her hands.)*
O open and receive me,
Ye happy things of still and lifeless being,
That to the awful steps which tread upon ye
Unconscious are!

Enter Cathrina *behind her.*

Who's there? Is't any thing?

Cath. 'Tis I, my dearest Lady; 'tis Cathrina.

Or. *(embracing her.)* How kind! such blessed kindness! keep thee by me;
I'll hold thee fast; an angel brought thee hither.
I needs must weep to think thou art so kind
In mine extremity.—Where wert thou hid?

Cath. In that small closet, since the supper hour,
I've been conceal'd. For searching round the chamber,

I found its door, and enter'd. Fear not now,
I will not leave thee till the break of day.

Or. Heaven bless thee for it! Till the break of day!
The very thought of day-break gives me life.
If but this night were past, I have good hope
That noble Theobald will soon be here
For my deliv'rance.

Cath. Wherefore think'st thou so?

Or. A stranger, when thou left'st me on the ramparts,
Gave me a letter, which I quickly open'd,
As soon as I, methought, had gain'd my room
In privacy; but close behind me came
That dæmon, Rudigere, and, snatching at it,
Forced me to cast it to the flames, from which,
I struggling with him still, he could not save it.

Cath. You have not read it then.

Or. No; but the seal
Was Theobald's, and I could swear ere long
He will be here to free me from this thraldom.

Cath. God grant he may!

Or. If but this night were past! How goes the time?
Has it not enter'd on the midnight watch?

Cath. (*pointing to a small slab at the corner of the stage on which is placed a sand-glass.*)
That glass I've set to measure it. As soon
As all the sand is run, you are secure;
The midnight watch is past.

Or. (*running to the glass, and looking at it eagerly.*)

There is not much to run: O an't were finish'd!
But it so slowly runs!

Cath. Yes; watching it,
It seemeth slow. But heed it not; the while,
I'll tell thee some old tale, and ere I've finish'd,
The midnight watch is gone. Sit down, I pray.

(*They sit,* Orra *drawing her chair close to* Cathrina.)

What story shall I tell thee?

Or. Something, my friend, which thou thyself hast known,
Touching the awful intercourse which spirits
With mortal men have held at this dread hour.
Did'st thou thyself e'er meet with one whose eyes
Had look'd upon the spectred dead—had seen
Forms from another world?

Cath. Never but once.

Or. (*eagerly.*) Once then thou did'st. O tell it! tell it me!

Cath. Well, since I needs must tell it, once I knew
A melancholy man, who did aver,
That journeying on a time o'er a wild waste,
By a fell storm o'erta'en, he was compell'd
To pass the night in a deserted tower,
Where a poor hind, the sole inhabitant
Of the sad place, prepared for him a bed:
And, as he told his tale, at dead of night,
By the pale lamp that in his chamber burn'd,
As it might be an arm's-length from his bed—

Or. So close upon him?

Cath. Yes.

Or. Go on; what saw he?

Cath. An upright form, wound in a clotted shroud —
Clotted and stiff, like one swaith'd up in haste
After a bloody death.

Or. O horrible!

Cath: He started from his bed, and gaz'd upon it.

Or. And did he speak to it?

Cath. He could not speak.
Its visage was uncover'd, and at first
Seem'd fix'd and shrunk, like one in coffin'd sleep;
But, as he gaz'd, there came, he wist not how,
Into its beamless eyes a horrid glare,
And turning towards him, for it did move —
Why dost thou grasp me thus?

Or. Go on, go on!

Cath. Nay, heaven forfend! Thy shrunk and sharpen'd features
Are of the corse's colour, and thine eyes
Are full of tears. How's this?

Or. I know not how.
A horrid sympathy jarr'd on my heart,
And forc'd into mine eyes these icy tears.
A fearful kindredship there is between
The living and the dead — an awful bond!
Wo's me! that we do shudder at ourselves —
At that which we must be! —— A dismal thought!
Where dost thou run? thy story is not told.

(*Seeing* Cath. *go towards the sand-glass.*)

Cath. (*shewing the glass.*) A better story I will tell thee now;
The midnight watch is past.

Or. Ha! let me see.

Cath. There's not one sand to run.

Or. But it is barely past.

Cath. 'Tis more than past.
For I did set it later than the hour,
To be assur'dly sure.

Or. Then it is gone indeed. O heaven be praised!
The fearful gloom gone by!

(*Holding up her hands in gratitude to heaven, and then looking round her with cheerful animation.*)

In truth, already
I feel as if I breath'd the morning air:
I'm marvellously lighten'd.

Cath. Ne'ertheless,
Thou art forspent: I'll run to my apartment,
And fetch some cordial drops that will revive thee.

Or. Thou need'st not go; I've ta'en thy drops already:
I'm bold and buoyant grown.

(*Bounding lightly from the floor.*)

Cath. I'll soon return:
Thou art not fearful now?

Or. No; I breathe lightly;
Valour within me grows most powerfully,
Would'st thou but stay to see it, gentle Cathrine.

Cath. I will return to see it, ere thou canst
Three times repeat the letters of thy name.
[EXIT *hastily by the concealed door.*

Or. (*alone.*) This burst of courage shrinks most shamefully.
I'll follow her. — (*Striving to open the door.*)
'Tis fast: it will not open.
I'll count my footsteps as I pace the floor
Till she return again.

(*Paces up and down, muttering to herself, when a horn is heard without, pausing and sounding three times, each time louder than before.*)

(Orra *runs again to the door.*)

Despair will give me strength: where is the door?
Mine eyes are dark, I cannot find it now.
O God! protect me in this awful pass!

(*After a pause, in which she stands with her body bent in a cowering posture, with her hands locked together, and trembling violently, she starts up and looks wildly round her.*)

There's nothing, yet I felt a chilly hand
Upon my shoulder press'd. With open'd eyes
And ears intent I'll stand. Better it is
Thus to abide the awful visitation,
Than cower in blinded horror, strain'd intensely
With ev'ry beating of my goaded heart.

(*Looking round her with a steady sternness, but shrinking again almost immediately.*)

I cannot do it: on this spot I'll hold me
In awful stillness.

(*Bending her body as before; then, after a momentary pause, pressing both her hands upon her head.*)

The icy scalp of fear is on my head;
The life stirs in my hair; it is a sense
That tells the nearing of unearthly steps,
Albeit my ringing ears no sounds distinguish.

(*Looking round, as if by irresistible impulse, to a great door at the bottom of the stage, which bursts open, and the form of a huntsman, cloathed in black, with a horn in his hand, enters and advances towards her. She utters a loud shriek, and falls senseless on the ground.*)

Theo. (*running up to her, and raising her from the ground.*)
No semblance, but real agony of fear.
Orra, oh, Orra! know'st thou not my voice?
Thy knight, thy champion, the devoted Theobald?
Open thine eyes and look upon my face:
(*Unmasking.*)
I am no fearful waker from the grave.
Dost thou not feel? 'Tis the warm touch of life.
Look up, and fear will vanish.—Words are vain!
What a pale countenance of ghastly strength
By horrour chang'd! O ideot that I was,
To hazard this!—The villain hath deceiv'd me:
My letter she has ne'er received. O fool!
That I should trust to this!
(*Beating his head distractedly.*)

Enter FRANKO, *by the same door.*

Frank. What is the matter? what strange turn is this?

Theo. O cursed sanguine fool! could I not think —
She moves, she moves! — rouse thee, my gentle Orra!
'Tis no strange voice that calls thee; 'tis thy friend.

Frank. She opens now her eyes.

Theo. But, oh, that look!

Frank. She knows thee not, but gives a stifled groan,
And sinks again in stupor.
Make no more fruitless lamentation here,
But bear her hence: the cool and open air
May soon restore her. Let us, while we may,
Occasion seize, lest we should be surprised.

[EXEUNT, Orra *borne off in a state of insensibility.*

ACT V.

SCENE I. — *The great Hall of the Castle. Enter* RUDIGERE, CATHRINA, *and* Attendants, *by different Doors.*

Rud. (*to* Attend.) Return'd again! Is any thing discover'd?
Or door or passage, garment dropt in haste,
Or footstep's track, or any mark of flight?

1st Att. No, by my faith! tho' from its highest turrets
To its deep vaults, the castle we have search'd.

Cath. 'Tis vain to trace the marks of trackless feet.
If that in truth it hath convey'd her hence,
The yawning earth has yielded them a passage,
Or else, thro' rifted roofs, the buoyant air.

Rud. Fools! search again. I'll raze the very walls
From their foundations, but I will discover
If door or pass there be to us unknown.
Ho! Gomez, there! (*Calling off the stage.*)
He keeps himself aloof.
Nor aids the search with true and hearty will.
I am betray'd. — Ho! Gomez, there, I say!
He shrinks away: go, drag the villain hither,
And let the torture wring confession from him.
(*A loud knocking heard at the gate.*)

Ha! who seeks entrance at this early hour
In such a desert place?

Cath. Some hind, perhaps,
Who brings intelligence. Heaven grant it be!

Enter an armed Vassal.

Rud. Ha! one from Aldenberg! What brings thee hither?

Vass. (*seizing* Rud.) Thou art my prisoner.
(*To* Attendants.) Upon your peril,
Assist me to secure him.

Rud. Audacious hind! by what authority
Speak'st thou such bold commands? Produce thy warrant.

Vass. 'Tis at the gate, and such as thou must yield to:
Count Hughobert himself, with armed men,
A goodly band, his pleasure to enforce.

(*Secures him.*)

Rud. What sudden freak is this? am I suspected
Of aught but true and honourable faith?

Vass. Aye, by our holy Saints! more than suspected.
Thy creature Maurice, whom thou thought'st to bribe
With things of seeming value, hath discover'd
The cunning fraud; on which his tender conscience,
Good soul! did o'the sudden so upbraid him,
That to his Lord forthwith he made confession

Of all the plots against the Lady Orra,
In which thy wicked arts had tempted him
To take a wicked part. All is discover'd.

Cath. (*aside.*) All is discover'd! Where then shall I hide me?
(*Aloud to* Vass.) What is discover'd?

Vass. Ha! most virtuous Lady!
Art thou alarm'd? Fear not: the world well knows
How good thou art; and to the Countess shortly,
Who with her Lord is near, thou wilt no doubt
Give good account of all that thou hast done.

Cath. (*aside, as she retires in agitation.*)
O heaven forbid! What hole o' th' earth will hide me! [EXIT.

(*Enter by the opposite side,* HUGHOBERT, ELEANORA, ALICE, GLOTTENBAL, URSTON, MAURICE, *and* Attendants.)

Hug. (*speaking as he enters.*) Is he secured?

Vass. He is, my Lord; behold!
(*pointing to* Rud.)

Hugh. (*to* Rud.) Black artful traitor! Of a sacred trust,
Blindly reposed in thee, the base betrayer
For wicked ends; full well upon the ground
May'st thou decline those darkly frowning eyes,
And gnaw thy lip in shame.

Rud. And rests no shame with him, whose easy faith

Entrusts a man unproved; or, having proved him,
Lets a poor hireling's unsupported testimony
Shake the firm confidence of many years?

Hugh. Here the accuser stands; confront him boldly,
And spare him not.

(*Bringing forward* Maurice.

Maur. (*to* Rud.) Deny it if thou canst. Thy brazen front,
All brazen as it is, denies it not.

Rud. (*to* Mau.) Fool! that of prying curiosity
And av'rice art compounded! I in truth
Did give to thee a counterfeited treasure
To bribe thee to a counterfeited trust;
Meet recompence! Ha, ha! Maintain thy tale,
For I deny it not. (*With careless derision.*)

Maur. O subtile traitor!
Dost thou so varnish it with seeming mirth?

Hugh. Sir Rudigere, thou dost, I must confess,
Out-face him well. But call the Lady Orra;
If towards her thou hast thyself comported
In honesty, she will declare it freely.
Bring Orra hither. (*To* Attendant.)

1st Attend. Would that we could; last night i' the midnight watch
She disappear'd; but whether man or devil
Hath borne her hence, in truth we cannot tell.

Hugh. O both! Both man and devil together join'd.

(*To* Rud. *furiously.*) Fiend, villain, murderer!
Produce her instantly.
Dead or alive, produce thy hapless charge.

Rud. Restrain your rage, my Lord; I would right gladly
Obey you, were it possible: the place,
And the mysterious means of her retreat,
Are both to me unknown.

Hugh. Thou liest! thou liest!

Glot. (*coming forward.*) Thou liest, beast, villain, traitor! think'st thou still
To fool us thus? Thou shalt be forced to speak.
(*To* Hugh.) Why lose we time in words when other means
Will quickly work? Straight to those pillars bind him,
And let each sturdy varlet of your train
Inflict correction on him.

Maur. Aye, this alone will move him.

Hugh. Thou say'st well:
By heaven it shall be done!

Rud. And will Count Hughobert degrade in me
The blood of Aldenberg to shame himself?

Hugh. That plea avails thee not; thy spurious birth
Gives us full warrant, as thy conduct varies,
To reckon thee or noble or debased.
(*To* Att.) Straight bind the traitor to the place of shame.

(*As they are struggling to bind* Rud. *he gets one of his hands free, and, pulling out a dagger from under his clothes, stabs himself.*)

Rud. Now, take your will of me, and drag my corse
Thro' mire and dust; your shameless fury now
Can do me no disgrace.

Urston. (*advancing.*)
Rash, daring, thoughtless wretch! dost thou so close
A wicked life in hardy desperation?

Rud. Priest, spare thy words: I add not to my sins
That of presumption, in pretending now
To offer up to Heaven the forced repentance
Of some short moments for a life of crimes.

Urst. My son, thou dost mistake me: let thy heart
Confession make ——

Glot. (*interrupting* Urst.) Yes, dog! Confession make
Of what thou'st done with Orra; else I'll spurn thee,
And cast thy hateful carcase to the kites.

Hugh. (*pulling back* Glot. *as he is going to spurn* Rud. *with his foot, who is now fallen upon the ground.*)
Nay, nay, forbear; such outrage is unmanly.

(Eleanora, *who with* Alice *had retired from the shocking sight of* Rudigere, *now comes forward to him.*)

El. Oh, Rudigere! thou art a dying man,
And we will speak to thee without upbraiding.
Confess, I do entreat thee, ere thou goest

To thy most awful change, and leave us not
In this our horrible uncertainty.
Is Orra here conceal'd?

Al. Thou hast not slain her?
Confession make, and heaven have mercy on thee!

Rud. Yes, Ladies; with these words of gentle meekness
My heart is changed; and that you may perceive
How greatly changed, let Glottenbal approach me;
Spent am I now, and can but faintly speak —
Ev'n unto him in token of forgiveness,
I'll tell what ye desire.

El. Thank heaven, thou art so changed!

Hugh. (*to* Glot.) Go to him, boy.

(Glottenbal *goes to* Rudigere, *and stooping over him to hear what he has to say,* Rudigere, *taking a small dagger from his bosom, strikes* Glottenbal *on the neck.*)

Glot. Oh, he has wounded me! — Detested traitor!
Take that and that; would thou had'st still a life
For every thrust. (*Killing him.*)

Hugh. (*alarmed.*) Ha! has he wounded thee, my son?

Glot. A scratch;
'Tis nothing more. He aim'd it at my throat,
But had not strength to thrust.

Hugh. Thank God, he had not!
(*A trumpet sounds without.*)
Hark! martial notice of some high approach!
(*To* Attendants.) Go to the gate.
[EXEUNT Attendants.
El. Who may it be? This castle is remote
From every route which armed leaders take.

Enter a Servant.

Ser. The banneret of Basle is at the gate.
Hugh. Is he in force?
Ser. Yes, thro' the trees his distant bands are seen
Some hundreds strong, I guess; tho' with himself
Two followers only come.

Enter HARTMAN *attended.*

Hugh. Forgive me, banneret, if I receive thee
With more surprise than courtesy. How is it?
Com'st thou in peace.
Hart. To you, my Lord, I frankly will declare
The purpose of my coming: having heard it,
It is for you to say if I am come,
As much I wish, in peace.
(*To* El.) Countess, your presence much emboldens me
To think it so shall be.
Hugh. (*impatiently.*) Proceed, I beg.
When burghers gentle courtesy affect,
'It chafes me more than all their sturdy boasting.

Hart. Then with a burgher's plainness, Hughobert,
I'll try my tale to tell, — nice task I fear!
So that it may not gall a baron's pride.
Brave Theobald, the Lord of Falkenstein,
Co-burgher also of our ancient city,
Whose cause of course is ours, declares himself
The suitor of thy ward, the Lady Orra;
And learning that within these walls she is,
By thine authority, in durance kept,
In his behalf I come to set her free;
As an oppressed Dame, such service claiming
From every gen'rous knight. What is thy answer?
Say, am I come in peace? Wilt thou release her?

Hugh. Ah, would I could! In faith thou gall'st me shrewdly.

Hart. I've been inform'd of all that now disturbs you,
By one who held me waiting at the gate.
Until the maid be found, if 'tis your pleasure,
Cease enmity.

Hugh. Then let it cease. A traitor has deceived me,
And there he lies.

(*Pointing to the body of* Rud.)

Hart. (*looking at the body.*)
A ghastly smile of fell malignity
On his distorted face death has arrested.
(*Turning again to* Hugh.)
And has he died, and no confession made?

All means that may discover Orra's fate
Shut from us?

Hugh. Ah! the fiend hath utter'd nothing
That could betray his secret. If she lives——

El. Alas, alas! think you he murder'd her?

Al. Merciful heaven forefend!

Enter a Soldier *in haste.*

Sold. O, I have heard a voice, a dismal voice!

Omnes. What hast thou heard?

El. What voice?

Sold. The Lady Orra's.

El. Where? Lead us to the place.

Hugh. Where did'st thou hear it, Soldier?

Sold. In a deep-tangled thicket of the wood,
Close to a ruin'd wall, o'ergrown with ivy,
That marks the ancient out-works of the castle.

Hugh. Haste; lead the way.

[EXEUNT *all eagerly, without order, following the* Soldier; Glottenbal *and one* Attendant *excepted.*

Att. You do not go, my Lord?

Glot. I'm sick, and strangely dizzy grows my head,
And pains shoot from my wound. It is a scratch,
But from a devil's fang.—There's mischief in it.
Give me thine arm, and lead me to a couch:
I'm very faint.

Att. This way, my Lord, there is a chamber near.

[EXEUNT Glottenbal, *supported by the* Attendant.

SCENE II.

The Forest near the Castle; in front a rocky Bank crowned with a ruined Wall o'ergrown with Ivy, and the Mouth of a Cavern shaded with Bushes: Enter FRANCO, *conducting* HUGHOBERT, HARTMAN, ELEONORA, ALICE, *and* URSTON, *the* Soldier *following them.*

Frank. (*to* Hugh.) This is the entry to our secret haunts.
And now, my Lord, having inform'd you truly
Of the device, well meant, but most unhappy,
By which the Lady Orra from her prison
By Falkenstein was ta'en, myself, my outlaws,
Unhappy men—who better days have seen,
Drove to this lawless life by hard necessity,
Are on your mercy cast.

Hugh. Which shall not fail you, valiant Franko. Much
Am I indebted to thee: had'st thou not
Of thine own free good will become our guide,
As wand'ring here thou found'st us, we had ne'er
The spot discover'd; for this honest soldier,
A stranger to the forest, sought in vain
To thread the tangled path.

El. (*to* Frank.) She is not well thou say'st, and from her swoon
Imperfectly recover'd.

Frank. When I left her,
She so appear'd.—But enter not, I pray,

Till I give notice.—Holla, you within!
Come forth and fear no ill.

(*A shriek heard from the cave.*)

Omnes. What dismal shriek is that?

Al. 'Tis Orra's voice.

El. No, no! it cannot be! It is some wretch,
In maniac's fetters bound.

Hart. The horrid thought that bursts into my mind!
Forbid it, righteous Heaven!

(*Running into the cave, he is prevented by* Theobald, *who rushes out upon him.*)

Theo. Hold, hold! no entry here but o'er my corse,
When ye have master'd me.

Hart. My Theobald
Dost thou not know thy friends?

Theo. Ha! thou, my Hartman! Art thou come to me?

Hart. Yes, I am come. What means that look of anguish?
She is not dead!

Theo. Oh, no! it is not death!

Hart. What mean'st thou? Is she well?

Theo. Her body is.

Hart. And not her mind?——Oh! direst wreck of all!
That noble mind!——But 'tis some passing seizure,
Some powerful movement of a transient nature;
It is not madness?

Theo. (*shrinking from him, and bursting into tears.*)
'Tis heaven's infliction; let us call it so;
Give it no other name. (*Covering his face.*)

El. (*to* Theo.) Nay, do not thus despair: when she beholds us,
She'll know her friends, and, by our kindly soothing,
Be gradually restored.

Al. Let me go to her.

Theo. Nay, forbear, I pray thee;
I will myself with thee, my worthy Hartman,
Go in and lead her forth.

(Theobald *and* Hartman *go into the cavern, while those without wait in deep silence, which is only broken once or twice by a scream from the cavern and the sound of* Theobald's *voice speaking soothingly, till they return, leading forth* Orra, *with her hair and dress disordered, and the appearance of wild distraction in her gait and countenance.*)

Or. (*shrinking back as she comes from under the shade of the trees, &c. and dragging* Theobald *and* Hartman *back with her.*)
Come back, come back! The fierce and fiery light!

Theo. Shrink not, dear love! it is the light of day.

Or. Have cocks crow'd yet?

Theo. Yes; twice I've heard already
Their mattin sound. Look up to the blue sky;

Is it not day-light there? And these green boughs
Are fresh and fragrant round thee: every sense
Tells thee it is the cheerful early day.

Or. Aye, so it is; day takes his daily turn,
Rising between the gulphy dells of night
Like whiten'd billows on a gloomy sea;
Till glow-worms gleam, and stars peep thro' the dark,
And will-o'-the-wisp his dancing taper light,
They will not come again.

(*Bending her ear to the ground*)

Hark, hark! Aye, hark:
They are all there: I hear their hollow sound
Full many a fathom down.

Theo. Be still, poor troubled soul! they'll ne'er return:
They are for ever gone. Be well assured
Thou shalt from henceforth have a cheerful home
With crackling faggots on thy midnight fire,
Blazing like day around thee; and thy friends —
Thy living, loving friends still by thy side,
To speak to thee and cheer thee.—See, my Orra!
They are beside thee now; dost thou not know them? (*Pointing to* Eleanora *and* Alice.)

Or. (*gazing at them with her hand held up to shade her eyes.*)
No, no! athwart the wav'ring garish light,
Things move and seem to be, and yet are nothing.

El. (*going near her.*) My gentle Orra! hast thou then forgot me?
Dost thou not know my voice?

Or. 'Tis like an old tune to my ear return'd.
For there be those, who sit in cheerful halls,
And breathe sweet air, and speak with pleasant sounds;
And once I liv'd with such; some years gone by;
I wot not now how long.

Hugh. Keen words that rend my heart! — Thou had'st a home,
And one whose faith was pledged for thy protection.

Urst. Be more composed, my Lord, some faint remembrance
Returns upon her with the well-known sound
Of voices once familiar to her ear.
Let Alice sing to her some fav'rite tune,
That may lost thoughts recall.

(Alice *sings an old tune, and* Orra, *who listens eagerly and gazes on her while she sings, afterwards bursts into a wild laugh.*)

Or. Ha, ha! the witched air sings for thee bravely.
Hoot owls thro' mantling fog for mattin birds?
It lures not me. — I know thee well enough:
The bones of murder'd men thy measure beat,
And fleshless heads nod to thee. — Off, I say!
Why are ye here? — That is the blessed sun.

El. Ah, Orra! do not look upon us thus!
These are the voices of thy loving friends.

That speak to thee: this is a friendly hand
That presses thine so kindly.

(*Putting her hand upon* Orra's, *who gives a loud shriek, and shrinks from her with horror.*)

Hart. O grievous state. (*Going up to her.*)
What terror seizes thee?

Or. Take it away! It was the swathed dead!
I know its clammy, chill, and bony touch.

(*Fixing her eyes fiercely on* Eleanora.)

Come not again; I'm strong and terrible now:
Mine eyes have look'd upon all dreadful things;
And when the earth yawns, and the hell-blast sounds,
I'll 'bide the trooping of unearthly steps
With stiff-clench'd, terrible strength.

(*Holding her clenched hands over her head with an air of grandeur and defiance.*)

Hugh. (*beating his breast.*)
A murd'rer is a guiltless wretch to me.

Hart. Be patient; 'tis a momentary pitch;
Let me encounter it.

(*Goes up to* Orra, *and fixes his eyes upon her, which she, after a moment, shrinks from and seeks to avoid, yet still, as if involuntarily, looks at him again.*)

Or. Take off from me thy strangely-fasten'd eye:
I may not look upon thee, yet I must.

(*Still turning from him, and still snatching a hasty look at him as before.*)

Unfix thy baleful glance: Art thou a snake?

Something of horrid power within thee dwells.
Still, still that powerful eye doth suck me in
Like a dark eddy to its wheeling core.
Spare me! O spare me, Being of strange power,
And at thy feet my subject head I'll lay.
(*Kneeling to* Hartman, *and bending her head submissively.*)

El. Alas, the piteous sight! to see her thus;
The noble, generous, playful, stately Orra!

Theo. (*running to* Hartman, *and pushing him away with indignation.*)
Out on thy hateful and ungenerous guile!
Think'st thou I'll suffer o'er her wretched state
The slightest shadow of a base controul?
(*Raising* Orra *from the ground.*)
No, rise thou stately flower with rude blasts rent;
As honour'd art thou with thy broken stem
And leafets strew'd, as in thy summer's pride.
I've seen thee worshipp'd like a regal dame
With ev'ry studied form of mark'd devotion,
Whilst I, in distant silence, scarcely proffer'd
Ev'n a plain soldier's courtesy; but now,
No liege-man to his crowned mistress sworn,
Bound and devoted is as I to thee;
And he who offers to thy alter'd state
The slightest seeming of diminish'd rev'rence,
Must in my blood——(*To* Hartman.) O pardon me, my friend!
Thou'st wrung my heart.

Hart. Nay, do thou pardon me: I am to blame:

Thy nobler heart shall not again be wrung.
But what can now be done? O'er such wild ravings,
There must be some controul.

Theo. O none! none, none! but gentle sympathy
And watchfulness of love.
My noble Orra!
Wander where'er thou wilt; thy vagrant steps
Shall follow'd be by one, who shall not weary,
Nor e'er detach him from his hopeless task;
Bound to thee now as fairest, gentlest beauty
Could ne'er have bound him.

Al. See how she gazes on him with a look,
Subsiding gradually to softer sadness,
Half saying that she knows him.

El. There is a kindness in her changing eye.
Yes, Orra, 'tis the valiant Theobald,
Thy knight and champion, whom thou gazest on,

Or. The brave are like the brave; so should it be.
He was a goodly man — a noble knight.
(*To* Theobald.) What is thy name, young soldier? — Woe is me!
For prayers of grace are said o'er dying men,
Yet they have laid thy clay in unblest earth —
Shame! shame! not with the still'd and holy dead.
This shall be rectified; I'll find it out;
And masses shall be said for thy repose;
Thou shalt not troop with these.

El. 'Tis not the dead, 'tis Theobald himself,
Alive and well, who standeth by thy side.

Or. (*looking wildly round.*)
Where, where? All dreadful things are near me, round me,
Beneath my feet and in the loaded air.
Let him begone! The place is horrible!
Baneful to flesh and blood. —— The dreadful blast!
Their hounds now yell below i'the centre gulph;
They may not rise again till solemn bells
Have given the stroke that severs night from morn.

El. O rave not thus! Dost thou not know us, Orra?

Or. (*hastily.*) Aye, well enough I know ye.

Urst. Ha! think ye that she does?

El. It is a terrible smile of recognition,
If such it be.

Hart. Nay, do not thus your restless eye-balls move,
But look upon us steadily, sweet Orra.

Or. Away! your faces waver to and fro;
I'll know you better in your winding-sheets,
When the moon shines upon ye.

Theo. Give o'er, my friends; you see it is in vain;
Her mind within itself holds a dark world
Of dismal phantasies and horrid forms!
Contend with her no more.

Enter an Attendant *in an abrupt disturbed manner.*

Att. (*to* Eleanor, *aside.*)
Lady, I bring to you most dismal news:
Too grievous for my Lord, so suddenly
And unprepar'd, to hear.

El. (*aside*) What is it? Speak.

Att. (*aside to* El.) His son is dead, all swell'd and rack'd with pain;
And on the dagger's point, which the sly traitor
Still in his stiffen'd grasp retains, foul stains,
Like those of limed poison, shew full well
The wicked cause of his untimely death.

Hugh. (*overhearing them.*)
Who speaks of death? What did'st thou whisper there?
How is my son? —— What look is that thou wear'st?
He is not dead? —— Thou dost not speak! O God!
I have no son.
(*After a pause*)
I am bereft! —— But this!
But only him! — Heaven's vengeance deals the stroke.

Urst. Heaven oft in mercy smites ev'n when the blow
Severest is.

Hugh. I had no other hope.
Fell is the stroke, if mercy in it be!
Could this — could this alone atone my crime?

Urst. Submit thy soul to Heaven's all-wise decree.
Perhaps his life had blasted more thy hopes
Than ev'n his grievous end.

Hugh. He was not all a father's heart could wish;
But, oh! he was my son! — my only son:
My child — the thing that from his cradle grew,
And was before me still. — Oh, oh! Oh, oh!

(*Beating his breast, and groaning deeply.*)

Or. (*running up to him.*)
Ha! dost thou groan, old man? Art thou in trouble?
Out on it! tho' they lay him in the mould,
He's near thee still. — I'll tell thee how it is:
A hideous burst hath been: the damn'd and holy,
The living and the dead, together are
In horrid neighbourship — 'Tis but thin vapour,
Floating around thee, makes the wav'ring bound.
Poh! blow it off, and see th' uncurtain'd reach.
See! from all points they come; earth casts them up!
In grave-clothes swath'd are those but new in death;
And there be some half bone, half cased in shreds
Of that which flesh hath been; and there be some
With wicker'd ribs, thro' which the darkness scowls.
Back, back! — They close upon us. — Oh! the void

Of hollow unball'd sockets staring grimly,
And lipless jaws that move and clatter round
us
In mockery of speech! — Back, back, I say!
Back, back!

(*Catching hold of* Hughobert *and* Theobald, *and dragging them back with her in all the wild strength of frantic horror, whilst the curtain drops.*)

THE END OF ORRA.

THE DREAM:

A TRAGEDY, IN PROSE,

IN THREE ACTS.

PERSONS OF THE DRAMA.

MEN.

OSTERLOO, *an Imperial General.*
Prior *of the Monastery.*
BENEDICT, JEROME, PAUL, } *Monks,*
MORAND, WOVELREID, } *Officers in the Service of the* Prior.
The Imperial Ambassador.
Officers *serving under* Osterloo.
Sexton, Monks, Soldiers, Peasants, &c.

WOMEN.

LEONORA.
AGNES.

Scene, *the Monastery of St. Maurice in Switzerland; a Castle near it.*

Time, *the middle of the 14th Century.*

THE DREAM.

ACT I.

SCENE I. — *A Court within the Monastery, with a grated iron Gate opening into an outer Court, through which are seen several Peasants waiting;* JEROME *is discovered on the front of the stage, walking backwards and forwards in a disturbed manner, then stopping and speaking to himself.*

Jer. TWICE in one night the same awful vision repeated! And Paul also terrified with a similar visitation! This is no common accidental mimicry of sleep: the shreds and remnants of our day-thoughts, put together at night in some fantastic incongruous form, as the drifting clouds of a broken-up storm piece themselves again into uncertain shapes of rocks and animals. No, no! there must be some great and momentous meaning in this.

Enter BENEDICT *behind him.*

Ben. Some great and momentous meaning in this! What art thou musing upon?

Jer. Be satisfied! be satisfied! It is not always fitting that the mind should lay open the things it is busy withal, though an articulate sound may sometimes escape it to set curiosity on the rack. Where is brother Paul? Is he still at his devotions?

Ben. I believe so. But look where the poor Peasants are waiting without: it is the hour when they expect our benefactions. Go, and speak to them: thou hast always been their favourite confessor, and they want consolation.

(*Beckoning the* Peasants, *who thereupon advance through the gate, while* Jerome *stretches out his hand to prevent them.*)

Jer. Stop there! come not within the gates! I charge you advance no farther. (*To* Benedict *angrily.*) There is death and contagion in every one of them, and yet thou would'st admit them so near us. Dost thou indeed expect a miracle to be wrought in our behalf? Are we not flesh and blood? and does not the grave yawn for us as well as other men?

(*To the* Peasants *still more vehemently.*)

Turn, I charge you, and retire without the gate.

1*st Peas.* Oh! be not so stern with us, good Father! There are ten new corpses in the village since yesterday, and scarcely ten men left in it with strength enough to bury them. The best half of the village are now under ground, who, but three weeks gone by, were all alive and well. O, do not chide us away!

2d Peas. God knows if any of us shall ever enter these gates again; and it revives us to come once a day to receive your blessings, good Fathers.

Jer. Well, and you shall have our blessing, my children; but come not so near us; we are mortal men like yourselves, and there is contagion about you.

1st Peas. Ah! no, no! Saint Maurice will take care of his own; there is no fear of you, Fathers.

Jer. I hope he will; but it is presumptuous to tempt danger. Retire, I beseech you, and you shall have relief given to you without the gates. If you have any love for us, retire.

(*The* Peasants *retire.*)

Ben. Well, I feel a strong faith within me, that our Saint, or some other good spirit, will take care of us. How is it that thou art so alarmed and so vehement with those good people? It is not thy usual temper.

Jer. Be satisfied, I pray thee: I cannot tell thee now. Leave me to myself a little while.— Would to God brother Paul were come to me! Ha! here he is.

Enter PAUL; *and* JEROME, *after waiting impatiently till* BENEDICT *retires, advances to him eagerly.*

Was it to a spot near the black monument in the stranger's burying vault, that it pointed?

Paul. Yes, to the very spot described by thee yesterday morning, when thou first told'st me thy dream: and, indeed, every circumstance of my last night's vision strongly resembled thine; or rather, I should say, was the same. The fixed frown of it's ghastly face ——

Jer. Aye, and the majestic motion of its limbs. Did it not wear a mantle over its right shoulder, as if for concealment rather than grace?

Paul. I know not; I did not mark that; but it strode before me as distinctly as ever mortal man did before my waking sight; and yet as no mortal man ever did before the waking sight.

Jer. But it appeared to thee only once.

Paul. Only once; for I waked under such a deep horror, that I durst not go to sleep again.

Jer. When it first appeared to me, as I told thee, the night before last, the form, though distinctly, was but faintly imaged forth; and methought it rose more powerfully to my imagination as I told it to thee, than in the dream itself. But last night, when it returned, it was far more vivid than before. I waked indeed as thou did'st, impressed with a deep horror, yet irresistible sleep seized upon me again; and O, how it appeared to me the third time, like a palpable, horrid reality! (*After a pause*) What is to be done?

Paul. What can be done? We can stop no division of the Imperial army till one shall really march by this pass.

Jer. And this is not likely; for I received a letter from a friend two days ago, by an express messenger, who says, he had delayed sending it, hoping to have it conveyed to me by one of Count Osterloo's soldiers, who, with his division, should have marched through our pass, but was now, he believed, to conduct them by a different route.

Paul. What noise and commotion is that near the gate?

(*Calling to those without.*)

Ho there! What is the matter?

1st. Peas. (*without.*) Nothing, Father; but we hear a trumpet at a distance, and they say, there is an army marching amongst the mountains.

Jer. By all our holy saints, if it be so—

(*Calling again to the 1st* Peas.)

Are ye sure it is trumpets you hear?

1st. Peas. As sure as we ever heard any sound; and here is a lad too, who saw from the top-most crag, with his own eyes, their banners waving at a distance.

Jer. (*to* Paul.) What think'st thou of it?

Paul. We must go to the Prior, and reveal the whole to him directly. Our own lives and those of the whole brotherhood depend upon it; there can be no hesitation now.

Jer. Come then; lose no time. We have a solemn duty imposed upon us. [EXEUNT.

SCENE II.

An open Space by the Gate of the Monastery, with a View of the Building on one Side, while Rocks and Mountains, wildly grand, appear in every other Direction, and a narrow Pass through the Mountains opening to the bottom of the Stage. Several Peasants, *both Men and Women, are discovered, waiting as if to see some Sight; a Trumpet and warlike Music heard at a little distance.*

1st Peas. Hear how it echoes amongst the rocks: it is your true warlike sound, that makes a man's heart stir within him, and his feet beat the ground to its measure.

2d Peas. Ah! what have our hearts to do with it now, miserable as we are!

1st Peas. What have we to do with it! Speak for thyself. Were I to be laid in the grave this very night, it would rouse me to hear those sounds, which remind me of the battle of Laupen.

2d Peas. Well; look not so proudly at me: though I have not yet fought for my country, I am of a good stock, nevertheless: my father lost is life at Morgarten.

(*Calling up to* Morand, *who now appears scrambling down the sides of the rocks.*)

Are they near us, Lieutenant?

Mor. They'll be here in a trice. I know their ensigns already: they are those brave fellows under the command of Count Osterloo, who did such good service to the Emperor in his last battle.

3d Peas. (*Woman.*) Aye; they be goodly men, no doubt, and bravely accoutred, I warrant ye.

4th Peas. (*Old Woman.*) Aye, there be many a brave man amongst them I trow, returning to his mother again. My Hubert never returned.

2d Peas. (*to* Mor.) Count Osterloo! Who is he?

Mor. Did'st thou never hear of him? He has been in as many battles as thou hast been in harvest fields.

2d Peas. And won them too?

Mor. Nay, some of them he has won, and some he has lost; but whether his own side were fighting or flying, he always kept his ground, or retreated like a man. The enemy never saw his back.

1st Peas. True, Lieutenant; I once knew an old soldier of Osterloo's who boasted much of his General; for his men are proud of him, and would go through flood and flame for his sake.

Mor. Yes, he is affable and indulgent to them, although passionate and unreasonable when provoked; and has been known to punish even his greatest favourites severely for a slight offence. I remember well, the officer I first served under, being a man of this kidney, and ——

1st Peas. Hist, hist! the gates are thrown

open, and yonder come the Monks in procession with the Prior at their head.

(*Enter* Prior *and* Monks *from the Monastery, and range themselves on one side of the stage.*)

Prior. (*to the Peasants*) Retire, my children, and don't come so near us. Don't stand near the soldiers as they pass neither, but go to your houses.

1*st Woman.* O bless St. Maurice and your holy reverence! We see nothing now but coffins and burials, and hear nothing but the ticking of the death-watch, and the tolling of bells: do let us stand here and look at the brave sight. Lord knows if any of us may be above ground to see such another, an' it were to pass this way but a week hence.

Prior. Be it so then, daughter, but keep at a distance on the rocks, where you may see every thing without communicating infection.

(*The* Peasants *retire, climbing amongst the rocks: then enter by the narrow pass at the bottom of the stage,* Soldiers *marching to martial music, with* Officers *and* Osterloo.)

Prior. (*advancing, and lifting up his hands with solemnity.*)

Soldiers and officers, and the noble chief commanding this band! in the name of our patron St. Maurice, once like yourselves a valiant soldier upon earth, now a holy powerful saint in heaven, I conjure you to halt.

1*st Off.* (*in the foremost rank.*)
Say you so, reverend Prior, to men pressing forward as we do, to shelter our heads for the night, and that cold wintry sun going down so fast upon us?

1*st Sold.* By my faith! if we pass the night here amongst the mountains, it will take something besides prayers and benedictions to keep us alive.

2*d Sold.* Spend the night here amongst chamois and eagles! Some miracle no doubt will be wrought for our accommodation.

1*st Off.* Murmur not, my friends: here comes your general, who is always careful of you.

Ost. (*advancing from the rear.*)
What is the matter?

Prior. (*to* Ost.) You are the commander in chief?

Ost. Yes, reverend Father: and, with all respect and deference, let me say, the night advances fast upon us. Martigny is still at a good distance, and we must not be detained. With many thanks, then, for your intended civilities, we beg your prayers, holy Prior, with those of your pious Monks, and crave leave to pass on our way.

Prior. (*lifting his hands as before.*)
If there be any piety in brave men, I conjure you, in the name of St. Maurice, to halt! The lives of our whole community depend upon it;

men who, for your lives, have offered to heaven many prayers.

Ost. How may this be, my Lord? Who will attack your sacred walls, that you should want any defence?

Prior. We want not, general, the service of your arms: my own troops, with the brave captain who commands them, are sufficient to defend us from mortal foes.

Soldiers. (*murmuring*) Must we fight with devils then?

Ost. Be quiet, my good comrades. (*To* Prior.) Well, my Lord, proceed.

Prior. A fatal pestilence rages in this neighbourhood; and by command of a vision, which has appeared three times to the Senior of our order, and also to another of our brotherhood, threatening, in case of disobedience, that the whole community shall fall victims to the dreadful disease, we are compelled to conjure you to halt.

Ost. And for what purpose?

Prior. That we may chuse by lot from the first division of the Imperial army which marches through this pass, (so did the vision precisely direct us,) a man who shall spend one night within the walls of our monastery; there to undergo certain penances for the expiation of long-concealed guilt.

Ost. This is very strange. By lot did you say? It will be tedious. There are a hundred of my men who will volunteer the service.—What say ye, Soldiers?

1st Sold. Willingly, General, if you desire it. Yet I marvel what greater virtue there can be in beleag'ring the war-worn hide of a poor soldier, than the fat sides of a well-fed monk.

Ost. Wilt thou do it, then?

1st Sold. Aye; and more than that, willingly, for my General. It is not the first time a cat-o'-nine-tails has been across my back for other men's misdeeds. Promise me a good flask of brandy when I'm done with it, and I warrant ye I'll never winch. As to the saying of Pater-nosters, if there be any thing of that kind tacked to it, I let you to wit my dexterity is but small.

Ost. Then be it as thou wilt, my good friend; yet I had as lief my own skin should smart for it as thine, thou art such a valiant fellow.

Prior. No, noble General, this must not be; we must have our man chosen by lot. The lives of the whole community depending upon it; we must strictly obey the vision.

Ost. It will detain us long.

Prior. Nay, my Lord; the lots are already prepared. In the first place, six men only shall draw; four representing the soldiers, and two the officers. If the soldiers are taken, they shall draw by companies, and the company that is taken shall draw individually; but if the lot falls to the officers, each of them shall draw for himself.

Ost. Let it be so; you have arranged it well. Produce the lots.

(*The* Prior *giving the sign, a* Monk *advances, bearing a stand, on which are placed three vases, and sets it near the front of the stage.*)

Prior. Now, brave Soldiers, let four from your body advance.

(Ost. *points to four men, who advance from the ranks.*)

Ost. And two from the officers, my Lord?

Prior. Even so, noble Count.

(Ost. *then points to two* Officers, *who, with the four* Soldiers, *draw lots from the smallest vase directed by the* Prior.)

1*st Sold.* (*speaking to his comrades as the others are drawing.*) This is strange mummery i' faith! but it would have been no joke, I suppose, to have offended St. Maurice.

Prior. (*after examining the lots.*) Soldiers, ye are free; it is your Officers who are taken.

1*st Sold.* (*as before*) Ha! the vision is dainty it seems; it is not vulgar blood like ours, that will serve to stain the ends of his holy lash.

(*A* Monk *having removed two of the vases, the* Prior *beckons the* Officers *to draw from the remaining one.*)

Prior. Stand not on order; let him who is nearest put in his hand first.

1*st Sold.* (*aside to the others as the* Officers *are drawing*)

Now by these arms! I would give a month's

pay that the lot should fall on our prim, pompous lieutenant. It would be well worth the money to look in at one of their narrow windows, and see his dignified back-bone winching under the hands of a good brawny friar.

Ost. (*aside, unrolling his lot.*)
Mighty heaven! Is fate or chance in this?

1st Off. (*aside to* Ost.) Have you got it, General? Change it for mine if you have.

Ost. No, no, my noble Albert; let us be honest; but thanks to thy generous friendship!

Prior. Now shew the lots. (*All the Officers shew their lots, excepting* Osterloo, *who continues gloomy and thoughtful.*) Has no one drawn the sable scroll of election? (*To* Osterloo.) You are silent, my Lord; of what colour is your lot?

Ost. (*holding out his scroll.*)
Black as midnight.

(Soldiers *quit their ranks and crowd round* Osterloo, *tumultuously.*

1st Sold. Has it fallen upon our General? 'tis a damned lot — an unfair lot.

2d Sold. We will not leave him behind us, though a hundred St. Maurices commanded it.

3d Sold. Get within your walls again, ye cunning Friars.

1st Sold. An' we should lie i' the open air all night, we will not leave brave Osterloo behind us.

Prior. (*to* Ost.) Count, you seem gloomy and irresolute: have the goodness to silence these clamours. I am in truth as sorry as any of your soldiers can be, that the lot has fallen upon you.

1*st Off.* (*aside to* Ost.) Nay, my noble friend, let me fulfil this penance in your stead. It is not now a time for scruples: the soldiers will be mutinous.

Ost. Mutinous! Soldiers, return to your ranks. (*Looking at them sternly as they seem unwillingly to obey.*) Will you brave me so far that I must repeat my command? (*They retire.*) I thank thee, dear Albert. (*To* 1*st* Off.) Thou shalt do something in my stead; but it shall not be the service thou thinkest of. (*To* Prior.) Reverend Father, I am indeed somewhat struck at being marked out by fate from so many men; but, as to how I shall act thereupon, no wise irresolute. (*To the* Sold.) Continue your march. The brave Albert shall conduct you to Martigny; and there you will remain under his command, till I join you again.

1*st Sold.* God preserve you then, my noble General! and if you do not join us again by to-morrow evening, safe and sound, we will not leave one stone of that building standing on another.

Many Soldiers at once. So swear we all! So swear, &c.

Ost. (*assuming a cheerful look.*)
Go to, foolish fellows? Were you to leave me in a den of lions, you could not be more apprehensive. Will watching all night by some holy shrine, or walking bare-foot through their mid-

night aisles, be such a hardship to one, who has passed so many nights with you all on the cold field of battle? Continue your march without delay; else these good Fathers will count you no better than a band of new-raised city troops, with some jolly tankard-chief for your leader. A good march to you, my friends, with kind hostesses and warm fire-sides where you are going.

1st Sold. Ah! What good will our fire-sides do us, when we think how our General is lodged?

Ost. Farewell! March on as quickly as you may: you shall all drink my health to-morrow evening in a good hogshead of Rhenish.

1st Sold. (*with others.*) God grant we may! (*1st to* Prior.) Look to it, reverend Prior: if our General be not with us by to-morrow's sunset, St. Maurice shall neither have monastery nor monks on this mountain.

Ost. No more! (*Embracing first Officer, and shaking hands with others.*) Farewell! Farewell!

(*The* Soldiers, *after giving him a loud cheer, march off with their* Officers *to martial music, and* EXEUNT Osterloo, Prior, *and* Monks *into the monastery, while the* Peasants *disappear amongst the rocks.* MANENT Morand *and* Agnes, *who has for some time appeared, looking over a crag.*)

Agn. Morand, Morand!

Mor. Ha! art thou there? I might have guessed indeed, that so brave a sight would not escape thee. What made thee perch thyself like an eagle upon such a crag as that?

Agn. Chide not, good Morand, but help me down, lest I pay a dearer price for my sight than thou, with all thy grumbling, wouldst wish.

(*He helps her down.*)

Mor. And now thou art going no doubt to tell the Lady Leonora, what a band of gallant fellows thou hast seen.

Agn. Assuredly, if I can find in my heart to speak of any but their noble leader!—What is his name? What meaning had all that drawing of lots in it? What will the monks do with him? Walk with me a little way towards the castle, brave Morand, and tell me what thou knowest.

Mor. I should walk to the castle and miles beyond it too, ere I could answer so many questions, and I have duty in the monastery, besides.

Agn. Come with me a little way, at least.

Mor. Ah, Witch! thou knowest too well that I must always do what thou biddest me.

[Exeunt.

SCENE III.

The Refectory of the Monastery, with a small Table, on which are placed Refreshments, discovered in one Corner. Enter OSTERLOO, Prior, BENEDICT, JEROME, *and* PAUL, *&c.*

Prior. Noble Osterloo, let me welcome you here, as one appointed by heaven to purchase our deliverance from this dreadful malady; and I hope the price to be paid for it will not be a heavy one. Yet ere we proceed further in this matter, be entreated, I pray, to take some refreshment after your long march.

(*The table is placed near the front of the stage.*)

Ost. I thank you, my Lord; this is a gentle beginning to my penance: I will, then, by your leave. (*Sitting down at the table.*) I have fasted long, and am indeed somewhat exhausted. (*After taking some refreshment.*) Ah! My poor Soldiers! You must still endure two hours' weary march, before you find such indulgence. Your wine is good, reverend Father.

Prior. I am glad you find it so; it is old.

Ost. (*cheerfully.*) And your viands are good too; and your bread is delicious.

(*Drinking another cup.*)

I shall have vigour now for any thing.——— Pray tell me something more of this wonderful vision: was it a Saint or an Angel that appeared to the Senior Brother?

Prior. (*pointing to* Jerome.)
He will answer for himself, and (*pointing to* Paul) this man saw it also.

Jer. It was neither Angel nor Saint, noble Count, but a mortal form wonderfully noble.

Ost. And it appeared to you in the usual manner of a dream?

Jer. It did; at least I know no sensible distinction. A wavy envelopement of darkness preceded it, from which appearances seemed dimly to wake into form, till all was presented before me in the full strength of reality.

Paul. Nay, Brother, it broke upon me at once; a vivid distinct apparition.

Ost. Well, be that as it may; what did appear to you? A mortal man, and very noble?

Jer. Yes, General. Methought I was returning from mass, through the cloisters that lead from the chapel, when a figure, as I have said, appeared to me, and beckoned me to follow it. I did follow it; for at first I was neither afraid, nor even surprised; but so wonderfully it rose in stature and dignity as it strode before me, that, ere it reached the door of the stranger's burying vault, I was struck with unaccountable awe.

Ost. The stranger's burying vault!

Prior. Does any sudden thought strike you, Count?

Ost. No, no! here's your health, Fathers; (*drinking;*) your wine is excellent.

Prior. But that is water you have just now swallowed: this is the wine.

Ost. Ha! is it? No matter, no matter! it is very good too. (*A long pause;* Osterloo *with his eyes fixed thoughtfully on the ground.*)

Prior. Shall not our brother proceed with his story, General?

Ost. Most certainly: I have been listening for it.

Jer. Well, then, as I have said, at the door of the stranger's burying vault it stopped, and beckoned me again. It entered, and I followed it. There, through the damp mouldering tombs, it strode still before me, till it came to the farther extremity, as nearly as I could guess, two yards westward from the black marble monument; and then, stopping and turning on me its fixed and ghastly eyes, it stretched out its hands ——

Ost. Its hands! Did you say, its hands?

Jer. It stretched out one of them; the other was covered with its mantle; and in a voice that sounded—I know not how it sounded——

Paul. Aye, Brother; it was something like a voice, at least it conveyed words to the mind, though it was not like a voice neither.

Jer. Be that as you please: these words it solemnly uttered,—"Command the Brothers of this monastery, on pain of falling victims to the pestilence now devastating the country, to stop on its way the first division of the Imperial army that shall march through your mountain pass; and chuse from it, by lot, a man who shall abide one night within these walls, to make expiation for long concealed guilt. Let the suffering be such as the nature of the crime and the connection of the expiator therewith shall dictate. This spot of earth shall reveal —" It said no more, but bent its eyes steadfastly upon me with a stern threatening frown, which became, as it looked, keener than the looks of any mortal being, and vanished from my sight.

Paul. Aye, that look; that last terrible look! it awoke me with terror, and I know not how it vanished.

Jer. This has been repeated to me three times; last night twice in the course of the night, while brother Paul here was at the same time terrified with a similar apparition.

Prior. This, you will acknowledge, Count, was no common visitation, and could not but trouble us.

Ost. You say well. ——— Yet it was but a dream.

Prior. True; it was but a dream, and as such these pious men strove to consider it; when the march of your troops across our mountains, a thing so unlikely to happen, compelled them to reveal to me, without loss of time, what had appeared to them.

Ost. A tall figure, you say, and of a noble aspect?

Jer. Like that of a King, though habited more in the garb of a foreign soldier of fortune than of a state so dignified.

(Osterloo *rises from table agitated.*)

Prior. What is the matter, General? Will you not finish your repast?

Ost. I thank you; I have had enough. The night grows cold; I would rather walk than sit.

(*Going hastily to the bottom of the stage, and pacing to and fro.*)

Jer. (*aside to* Paul *and the* Prior.) What think ye of this?

Prior. (*aside to* Jerome.) His countenance changed several times as he listened to you; there is something here different from common surprise on hearing a wonderful thing.

(*Enter a* Peasant *by the bottom of the stage, bearing a torch.*)

Peas. (*eagerly, as he enters.*) We have found it.

Ost. (*stopping short in his walk.*) What hast thou found?

Peas. What the Prior desired us to dig for.

Ost. What is that?

Peas. A grave.

(Osterloo *turns from him suddenly, and paces up and down very rapidly.*)

Prior. (*to* Peas.) Thou hast found it?

Peas. Aye, please you, and in the very spot, near the black monument, where your reverence desired us to dig. And it is well you sent for my kinsman and I to do it, for there is not a lay-brother in the monastery strong enough to raise up the great stones that covered it.

Prior. In the very spot, sayest thou?

Peas. In the very spot.

Prior. Bear thy torch before us, and we'll follow thee.

Omnes. (*eagerly*, Osterloo *excepted.*)
Let us go immediately.

Prior. (*to* Osterloo, *who stands fixed to the spot.*)
Will not Count Osterloo go also? It is fitting that he should.

Ost. (*rousing himself.*) O, most assuredly: I am perfectly ready to follow you.

[EXEUNT.

ACT II.

SCENE I.—*A burying Vault, almost totally dark; the Monuments and Grave-stones being seen very dimly by the Light of a single Torch, stuck by the side of a deep open Grave, in which a* Sexton *is discovered, standing leaning on his Mattock, and* Morand, *above Ground, turning up, with his sheathed Sword, the loose Earth about the Mouth of the Grave.*

Mor. There is neither scull nor bone amongst this earth: the ground must have been newly broken up, when that coffin was let down into it.

Sex. So one should think; but the earth here has the quality of consuming whatever is put into it in a marvellous short time.

Mor. Aye; the flesh and more consumable parts of a body; but hath it grinders in its jaws like your carnivorous animal, to cransh up bones and all? I have seen bones on an old field of battle, some hundred years after the action, lying whitened and hard in the sun.

Sex. Well, an't be new ground, I'll warrant ye somebody has paid money enough for such a good tenement as this: I could not wish my own father a better.

Mor. (*looking down.*) The coffin is of an uncommon size: there must be a leaden one within it, I should think.

Sex. I doubt that: it is only a clumsy shell that has been put together in haste; and I'll be hanged if he who made it ever made another before it. Now it would pine me with vexation to think I should be laid in such a bungled piece of workmanship as this.

Mor. Aye; it is well for those who shall bury thee, Sexton, that thou wilt not be a looker-on at thine own funeral. —— Put together in haste, sayest thou! How long may it be since this coffin was laid in the ground?

Sex. By my fay, now, I cannot tell; though many a grave I have dug in this vault, instead of the lay-brothers, who are mighty apt to take a cholic or shortness of breath, or the like, when any thing of hard labour falls to their share. (*After pausing.*) Ha! now I have it. When I went over the mountain some ten years ago to visit my father-in-law, Baldwick, the stranger, who died the other day, after living so long as a hermit amongst the rocks, came here; and it was shrewdly suspected he had leave from our late Prior, for a good sum of money, to bury a body privately in this vault. I was a fool not to think of it before. This, I'll be sworn for it, is the place.

Enter the Prior, OSTERLOO, JEROME, PAUL, BENEDICT, *and other* Monks, *with the* Peasant *carrying light before them. They enter by an arched door at the bottom of the stage, and walk on to the front, when every one, but* Osterloo, *crowds eagerly to the grave, looking down into it.*

Prior. (*to* Sexton.) What hast thou found, friend?

Sex. A coffin an't please you, and of a size, too, that might almost contain a giant.

Omnes. (Osterloo *excepted.*) The inscription — is there an inscription on it?

Sex. No, no! They who put these planks together had no time for inscriptions.

Omnes. (*as before.*) Break it open: — break it open.

(*They crowd more eagerly about the grave, when, after a pause, the* Sexton *is heard wrenching open the lid of the coffin.*)

Omnes. (*as before.*) What is there in it? What hast thou found, Sexton?

Sex. An entire skeleton, and of no common size.

Ost. (*in a quick hollow voice.*) Is it entire?

Sex. (*after a pause.*) No, the right hand is wanting, and there is not a loose bone in the coffin. (Ost. *shudders and steps back.*)

Jer. (*to* Prior, *after a pause.*) Will you not speak to him, Father? His countenance is changed, and his whole frame seems moved by some sudden convulsion.

(*The* Prior *remains silent.*)

How is this? You are also changed, reverend Father. Shall I speak to him?

Prior. Speak thou to him.

Jer. (*to* Osterloo.) What is the matter with you, General? Has some sudden malady seized you?

Ost. (*to* Jerome.) Let me be alone with you, holy Prior; let me be alone with you instantly.

Jer. (*pointing.*) This is the Prior.—He would be alone with you, Father: he would make his confession to you.

Prior. I dare not hear him alone: there must be witnesses. Let him come with me to my apartment.

Jer. (*to* Osterloo, *as they leave the grave.*) Let me conduct you, Count.

(*After walking from it some paces.*)

Come on, my Lord, why do you stop short?

Ost. Not this way—not this way, I pray you.

Jer. What is it you would avoid?

Ost. Turn aside, I pray you; I cannot cross over this.

Jer. Is it the grave you mean? We have left it behind us.

Ost. Is it not there? It yawns across our path, directly before us.

Jer. Indeed, my Lord, it is some paces behind.

Ost. There is delusion in my sight then; lead me as thou wilt.

[Exeunt.

SCENE II.

The private Apartment of the Prior; *enter* Benedict, *looking round as he enters.*

Ben. Not yet come; aye, penitence is not very swift of foot.

(*Speaking to himself as he walks up and down.*) Miserable man! — brave, goodly creature! — but alas, alas! most subdued; most miserable; and, I fear, most guilty!

Enter Jerome.

Jerome here! — Dost thou know, Brother, that the Prior is coming here immediately to confess the penitent?

Jer. Yes, Brother; but I am no intruder; for he has summoned me to attend the confession as well as thyself.

Ben. Methinks some other person of our order, unconcerned with the dreaming part of this business, would have been a less suspicious witness.

Jer. Suspicious! Am I more concerned in this than any other member of our community? Heaven appoints its own agents as it listeth: the stones of these walls might have declared its awful will as well as the dreams of a poor friar.

Ben. True, brother Jerome; could they listen to confessions as he does, and hold reveries upon them afterwards.

Jer. What dost thou mean with thy reveries and confessions? Did not Paul see the terrible vision as well as I?

Ben. If thou hadst not revealed thy dream to him, he would have slept sound enough, or, at worst, have but flown over the pinnacles with his old mate the horned serpent, as usual: and had the hermit Baldwick never made his death-bed confession to thee, thou wouldst never have had such a dream to reveal.

Jer. Thinkest thou so? Then what brought Osterloo and his troops so unexpectedly by this route? With all thy heretical dislike to miraculous interposition, how wilt thou account for this?

Ben. If thou hadst no secret intelligence of Osterloo's route, to set thy fancy a working on the story the hermit confessed to thee, I never wore cowl on my head.

Jer. Those, indeed, who hear thee speak so lightly of mysterious and holy things, will scarcely believe thou ever didst. — But hush! the Prior comes with his penitent; let us have no altercation now.

Enter Prior *and* Osterloo.

Prior. (*after a pause, in which he seems agitated.*)
Now, Count Osterloo, we are ready to hear your confession. To myself and these pious Monks; men appointed by our holy religion to search into the crimes of the penitent, unburthen

your heart of its terrible secret; and God grant you afterwards, if it be his righteous will, repentance and mercy.

Ost. (*making a sign, as if unable to speak, then uttering rapidly.*) Presently, presently.

Jer. Don't hurry him, reverend Father; he cannot speak.

Ben. Take breath awhile, noble Osterloo, and speak to us when you can.

Ost. I thank you.

Ben. He is much agitated. (*to* Osterloo.) Lean upon me, my Lord.

Prior. (*to* Benedict.) Nay, you exceed in this. (*to* Osterloo.) Recollect yourself, General, and try to be more composed, You seem better now; endeavour to unburden your mind of its fatal secret; to have it labouring within your breast is protracting a state of misery.

Ost. (*feebly.*) I have voice now.

Jer. (*to* Osterloo.) Give to Heaven, then, as you ought —

Ben. Hush, brother Jerome! no exhortations now! let him speak it as he can. (*to* Osterloo.) We attend you most anxiously.

Ost. (*after struggling for utterance.*)
I slew him.

Prior. The man whose bones have now been discovered?

Ost. The same: I slew him.

Jer. In the field, Count?

Ost. No, no! many a man's blood has been on my hands there: — this is on my heart.

Prior. It is then premeditated murder you have committed.

Ost. (*hastily.*) Call it so, call it so.

Jer. (*to* Osterloo, *after a pause.*) And is this all? Will you not proceed to tell us the circumstances attending it?

Ost. Oh! they were terrible! — But they are all in my mind as the indistinct horrors of a frenzied imagination.

(*After a short pause.*)

I did it in a narrow pass on St. Gothard, in the stormy twilight of a winter day.

Prior. You murdered him there?

Ost. I felt him dead under my grasp; but I looked at him no more after the last desperate thrust that I gave him. I hurried to a distance from the spot; when a servant, who was with me, seized with a sudden remorse, begged leave to return and remove the body, that, if possible, he might bury it in consecrated ground, as an atonement for the part he had taken in the terrible deed.——I gave him leave, with means to procure his desire: — I waited for him three days, concealed in the mountains; — but I neither saw him, nor heard of him again.

Ben. But what tempted a brave man like Osterloo to commit such a horrible act?

Ost. The torments of jealousy stung me to it. (*Hiding his face with his hands, and then uncovering it.*) I loved her, and was beloved: —— He came, — a noble stranger ——

Jer. Aye, if he was in his mortal state, as I

in my dream beheld him, he was indeed most noble.

Ost. (*waving his hand impatiently.*)
Well, well! he did come, then, and she loved me no more.—— With arts and enchantments he besotted her.—————— Even from her own lips I received——

(*Tossing up his arms violently, and then covering his face as before.*)

But what is all this to you? Maimed as he was, having lost his right arm in a battle with the Turks, I could not defy him to the field.——
——After passing two nights in all the tossing agony of a damned spirit, I followed him on his journey 'cross the mountains.—On the twilight of the second day, I laid wait for him in a narrow pass; and as soon as his gigantic form darkened the path before me——I have told you all.

Prior. (*eagerly.*) You have not told his name.

Ost. Did I not say Montera? He was a noble Hungarian.

Prior. (*much agitated.*) He was so!—He was so. He was noble and beloved.

Jer. (*aside to* Prior.) What is the matter with you, reverend Father? Was he your Friend?

Prior. (*aside to* Jerome.) Speak not to me now, but question the murderer as ye will.

Ben. (*overhearing the* Prior.)
He is indeed a murderer, reverend Father, but he is our penitent.

Prior. Go to! what are names?—Ask him what questions you will, and finish the confession quickly.

Ben. (*to* Osterloo.) But have you never till now confessed this crime; nor in the course of so many years reflected on its dreadful turpitude?

Ost. The active and adventurous life of a soldier is most adverse to reflection: but often, in the stillness of midnight, the remembrance of this terrible deed has come powerfully upon me; till morning returned, and the noise of the camp began, and the fortunes of the day were before me.

Prior. (*in a severe voice.*)
Thou hast indeed been too long permitted to remain in this hardened state. But Heaven, sooner or later, will visit the man of blood with its terrours. Sooner or later, he shall feel that he stands upon an awful brink; and short is the step which engulphs him in that world, where the murdered and the murderer meet again, in the tremendous presence of HIM who is the Lord and Giver of life.

Ost. You believe then in such severe retribution?

Prior. I believe in it as in my own existence.

Ost. (*turning to* Jerome *and* Benedict.)
And you, good Fathers, you believe in this?

Ben. Nature teaches this, as well as revelation: we must believe it.

Jer. Some presumptuous minds, dazzled with

the sunshine of prosperity, have dared to doubt; but to us in the sober shade of life, visited too as we have now been by visions preternatural and awful, it is a thing of certainty rather than of faith.

Ost. That such things are, it makes the brain confused and giddy.—These are tremendous thoughts!

(*Leans his back against the wall, and gazes fixedly on the ground.*)

Prior. Let us leave him to the bitterness of his thoughts. We now must deliberate with the brethren on what is to be done. There must be no delay; the night advances fast. Conduct him to another apartment. I must assemble a council of the whole order.

Jer. (*to* Osterloo.) We must lead you to another apartment, Count, while we consider what is to be done.

Ost. (*roused.*) Aye, the expiation, you mean: let it be severe, if atonement in this world may be made.

(*Turning to* Prior *as* Jerome *leads him off.*)

Let your expiation be severe, holy Father; a slight penance matches not with such a crime as mine.

Prior. Be well assured it shall be what it ought.

Ost. (*turning again, and catching hold of the* Prior's *robe.*) I regard not bodily pain. In battle once, with the head of a broken arrow in my thigh, I led on the charge, and sustained all the exertions of a well-fought field, till night closed upon our victory. Let your penance be severe, my reverend Father; I have been long acquainted with pain.

[EXEUNT Osterloo *and* Jerome.

Ben. You seem greatly moved, Father; but it is not with pity for the wretched. You would not destroy such a man as this, though his crime is the crime of blood?

Prior. He shall die: ere another sun dawn on these walls, he shall die.

Ben. Oh, say not so! Think of some other expiation.

Prior. I would think of another, were there any other more dreadful to him than death.

Ben. He is your penitent.

Prior. He is the murderer of my brother.

Ben. Then Heaven have mercy on him, if he must find none here! —————— Montero was your brother?

Prior. My only brother. It were tedious to tell thee now, how I was separated from him after the happy days of our youth. —————— I saw him no more; yet he was still the dearest object of my thoughts. After escaping death in many a battle, he was slain, as it was conjectured, by banditti, in travelling across the mountains. His body was never discovered. Ah! little did I think it was lying so near me!

Ben. It is indeed piteous, and you must needs feel it as a brother: but consider the danger we run, should we lay violent hands on an Imperial General, with his enraged soldiers, within a few hours' march of our walls.

Prior. I can think of nothing but revenge. Speak to me no more. I must assemble the whole order immediately.

[EXEUNT.

SCENE III.

Another Apartment. Enter OSTERLOO, *as from a small Recess at the bottom of the Stage, pacing backwards and forwards several times in an agitated manner; then advancing slowly to the front, where he stands musing and muttering to himself for some moments, before he speaks aloud.*

Ost. That this smothered horrour should burst upon me at last! And there be really such things as the darkened fancy imageth to itself, when the busy day is stilled. An unseen world surrounds us: spirits and powers, and the invisible dead, hover near us; while we in unconscious security — Oh! I have slept upon a fearful brink! Every sword that threatened my head in battle, had power in its edge to send me to a terrible account. — I have slept upon a fearful brink. —————————— Am I truly awake? (*Rubbing his eyes, then grasping several parts of his body, first with one hand and then with the other.*) Yes, yes! it is so! — I am keenly and terribly awake.

(*Paces rapidly up and down, and then stopping short.*)

Can there be virtue in penances suffered by the body to do away offences of the soul? If there be — O if there be! let them runnel my body with stripes, and swaith me round in one continued girth of wounds! Any thing that can be endured here is mercy compared to the dreadful abiding of what may be hereafter.

Enter WOVELREID *behind, followed by* Soldiers, *who range themselves at the bottom of the stage.* Osterloo, *turning round, runs up to him eagerly.*

Ha! my dear Albert, returned to me again, with all my noble fellows at thy back.——— ——— Pardon me, I mistook you for one of my Captains.

Wov. I am the Prior's Captain.

Ost. And those men too?

Wov. They are the Prior's soldiers, who have been ordered from distant quarters to repair to the monastery immediately.

Ost. In such haste!

Wov. Aye, in truth: we received our orders after sun-set, and have marched two good leagues since.

Ost. What may this mean?

Wov. Faith, I know not. My duty is to obey the Prior, and pray to our good saint; and whether I am commanded to surprise the stronghold of an enemy, or protect an execution, it is the same thing to me.

Ost. An execution! can aught of this nature be intended?

Wov. You turn pale, Sir: wearing the garb of a soldier, you have surely seen blood ere now.

Ost. I have seen too much blood.

Enter Prior, JEROME, PAUL, *and* Monks, *walking in order; the* Prior *holding a paper in his hand.*

Prior (*with solemnity.*) Count Osterloo, Lieutenant-General of our liege Lord the Emperor, authorized by this deed, which is subscribed by all the brethren of our Holy Order here present, I pronounce to you our solemn decision, that the crime of murder, as, by the mysterious voice of Heaven, and your own confession, your crime is proved to be, can only be expiated by death: you are therefore warned to prepare yourself to die this night. Before day-break you must be with the inhabitants of another world, where may the great Maker of us all deal with you in mercy!

(Osterloo *staggers back from the spot where he stood, and remains silent.*)

Prior. It is a sentence, Count, pronounced against you from necessity, to save the lives of our whole community, which you yourself have promised to submit to; have you any thing to say in reply to it?

Ost. Nothing: my thoughts are gone from me in the darkness of astonishment.

Prior. We are compelled to be thus hasty and severe: ere day-break you must die.

Ost. Ere day-break! not even the light of another sun to one so ill prepared for the awful and tremendous state into which you would thrust him! this is inhuman! it is horrible!

Prior. He was as ill prepared for it, who, with still shorter warning, was thrust into that awful state in the narrow pass of St. Gothard.

Ost. The guilt of murder was not on his soul. ——— Nay, nay, holy Prior, consider this horrible extremity: let the pain of the executioner's stroke be twenty-fold upon me; but thrust me not forth to that state from which my soul recoils with unutterable horror! ——— ——— Never but once, to save the life of a friend, did I bend the knee to mortal man in humble supplication. I am a soldier; in many battles I have bled for the service of my country: I am a noble soldier, and I was a proud one; yet do I thus — contemn not my extremity — my knee is on the ground.

Prior. Urge me no further. It must not be; no respite can be granted.

Ost. (*starting up furiously from the ground, and drawing his sword.*)

Then subdue as you may, stern priest, the strength of a desperate man.

(Wovelreid *and* Soldiers *rush forward, getting behind him, and surrounding him on every side, and after a violent struggle disarm him.*)

Wov. What a noble fellow this would be to defend a narrow breach, though he shrinks with such abhorrence from a scaffold. It is a piteous thing to see him so beset.

Prior. (*to* Wovelreid.) What sayest thou, fool?

Wov. Nay, it is no business of mine, my Lord, I confess. Shall we conduct him to the prison chamber?

Prior. Do so; and see that he retain no concealed arms about him.

Wov. I obey, my Lord: every thing shall be made secure.

(Exit Osterloo, *guarded by* Wovelreid *and* Soldiers; *and at the same time enter* Benedict, *by the opposite side, who stands looking after him piteously.*)

Prior. (*sternly to* Benedict.) What brings thee here? Dost thou repent having refused to concur with us in an act that preserves the community?

Ben. Say rather, reverend Father, an act that revenges your brother's death, which the laws of the empire should revenge.

Prior. A supernatural visitation of heaven hath commanded us to punish it.——— What! dost thou shake thy head? Thou art of a doubting and dangerous spirit; and beware lest, sooner or later, the tempter do not lure thee into heresy. If reason cannot subdue thee, authority shall.——————— Return again to thy cell; let me hear of this no more.

Ben. I will, reverend Father. But, for the love of our holy saint, bethink you, ere it be too late, that though we may be saved from the pestilence by this bloody sacrifice, what will rescue our throats from the swords of Osterloo's soldiers when they shall return, as they have threatened, to demand from us their General?

Prior. Give thyself no concern about this. My own bands are already called in, and a messenger has been dispatched to the Abbess Matilda; her troops, in defence of the church, will face the best soldiers of the empire.—— But why lose we time in unprofitable contentions? Go, my sons, (*speaking to other* Monks.) the night advances fast, and we have much to do ere morning.

(*Knocking heard without.*)

Ha! who knocks at this untimely hour? Can the soldiers be indeed returned upon us?— Run to the gate, but open it to none.

(Exeunt *several* Monks *in haste, and presently re-enter with a* Lay-Brother.)

Lay-B. Please ye, reverend Father; the Marchioness has sent a messenger from the castle, beseeching you to send a confessor immediately to confess one of her women, who was taken ill yesterday, and is now at the point of death.

Prior. I'm glad it is only this.—What is the matter with the penitent?

Lay-B. I know not, please you: the messenger only said, she was taken ill yesterday.

Prior. (*shaking his head.*) Aye, this malady has got there also.—I cannot send one of the brothers to bring infection immediately amongst us.—————What is to be done? Leonora is a most noble Lady; and the family have been great benefactors to our order.—I must send somebody to her. But he must stop well his nostrils with spicery, and leave his upper garment behind him, when he quits the infected apartment. Jerome, wilt thou go? Thou art the favorite confessor with all the women at the castle.

Jer. Nay, Father; I must attend on our prisoner here, who has most need of ghostly assistance.

Prior. (*to another* Monk.) Go thou, Anselmo; thou hast given comfort to many a dying penitent.

Monk. I thank you, Father, for the preference; but Paul is the best of us all for administering comfort to the dying; and there is a sickness come over my heart o' the sudden, that makes me unfit for the office.

Prior. (*to* Paul.) Thou wilt go then, my good son.

Paul. I beseech you, don't send me, reverend Father; I ne'er escaped contagion in my life, where malady or fever were to be had.

Prior. Who will go then?

(*A deep silence.*)

Ben. What! has no one faith enough in the protection of St. Maurice, even purchased, as it is about to be, by the shedding of human blood, to venture upon this dangerous duty? I will go then, Father, though I am sometimes of a doubting spirit.

Prior. Go, and St. Maurice protect thee!

[Exit Ben.

Let him go; it is well that we get rid of him for the night, should they happily detain him so long at the castle. — He is a troublesome, close-searching, self-willed fellow. He hath no zeal for the order. Were a miser to bequeath his possessions to our monastery, he would assist the disappointed heir himself to find out a flaw in the deed. — But retire to your cells, my sons, and employ yourselves in prayer and devotion, till the great bell warn you to attend the execution.

[Exeunt.

SCENE III.

An Apartment in the Castle. Enter Leonora *and* Agnes, *speaking as they enter.*

Ag. But she is asleep now; and is so much and so suddenly better, that the confessor, when he comes, will be dissatisfied, I fear, that we have called him from his cell at such an unreasonable hour.

Leo. Let him come, nevertheless; don't send to prevent him.

Ag. He will be unwilling to be detained, for they are engaged in no common matters to-night at the monastery. Count Osterloo, as I told you before, is doing voluntary penance at the shrine of St. Maurice to stop the progress of this terrible malady.

Leo. I remember thou did'st.

Ag. Ah, Marchioness! you would not say so thus faintly, had you seen him march through the pass with his soldiers. He is the bravest and most graceful man, though somewhat advanced in years, that I ever beheld. — Ah, had you but seen him!

Leo. I have seen him, Agnes.

Ag. And I spoke of him all the while, yet you did not tell me this before! Ah, my noble Mistress and Friend! the complexion of your cheek is altered; you have indeed seen him, and you have not seen him with indifference.

Leo. Think as thou wilt about this. He was the friend and fellow-soldier of my Lord, when we first married; though before my marriage I had never seen him.

Ag. Friend! Your Lord was then in the decline of life; there must have been great disparity in their friendship.

Leo. They were friends, however; for the Marquis liked society younger than himself; and I, who had been hurried into an unequal marriage, before I could judge for myself, was sometimes foolish enough to compare them together.

Ag. Aye, that was natural enough. (*Eagerly.*) And what happened then?

Leo. (*offended.*) What happened then! (*drawing herself up proudly.*) Nothing happened then, but subduing the foolish fancy of a girl, which was afterwards amply repaid by the self-approbation and dignity of a woman.

Ag. Pardon me, Madam; I ought to have supposed all this. But you have been long a widow, and Osterloo is still unmarried; what prevented you when free?

Leo. I was ignorant what the real state of his sentiments had been in regard to me. But had this been otherwise; received, as I was, into the family of my Lord, the undowried daughter of a petty nobleman; and left as I now am, by his confiding love, the sole guardian of his children and their fortunes; I could never think of supporting a second lord on the wealth entrusted to me by the first, to the injury of his children. As nothing, therefore, has ever happened in consequence of this weakness of my youth, nothing ever shall.

Ag. This is noble.

Leo. It is right. ——— But here comes the father Confessor.

Enter BENEDICT.

You are welcome, good Father! yet I am almost ashamed to see you; for our sick person has become suddenly well again, and is now in a deep sleep. I fear I shall appear to you capricious and inconsiderate in calling you up at so late an hour.

Ben. Be not uneasy, Lady, upon this account: I am glad to have an occasion for being absent from the monastery for some hours, if you will permit me to remain here so long.

Leo. What mean you, Father Benedict? Your countenance is solemn and sorrowful: what is going on at the monastery? (*He shakes his head.*) Ha! will they be severe with him in a voluntary penance, submitted to for the good of the order?—What is the nature of the penance? It is to continue, I am told, but one night.

Ben. It will, indeed, soon be over.

Leo. And will he be gone on the morrow?

Ben. His spirit will, but his body remains with us for ever.

Leo. (*uttering a shriek.*) Death, dost thou mean?—O horror! horror! Is this the expiation? Oh most horrible, most unjust!

Ben. Indeed I consider it as such. Though guilty, by his own confession, of murder, committed, many years since, under the frenzy of passion; it belongs not to us to inflict the punishment of death upon a guilty soul, taken so suddenly and unprepared for its doom.

Leo. Murder! didst thou say murder? Oh Osterloo, Osterloo! hast thou been so barbarous? and art thou in this terrible state?—Must thou thus end thy days, and so near me too!

Ben. You seem greatly moved, noble Leonora: would you could do something more for him than lament.

Leo. (*catching hold of him eagerly.*) Can I do any thing? Speak, Father: O tell me how! I will do any thing and every thing.—— Alas, alas! my vassals are but few, and cannot be assembled immediately.

Ben. Force were useless. Your vassals, if they were assembled, would not be persuaded to attack the sacred walls of a monastery.

Leo. I did indeed rave foolishly: but what else can be done?—Take these jewels and every thing of value in the castle, if they will bribe those who guard him, to let him escape.—Think of it.—O think well of it, good Benedict!

Ag. I have heard that there is a secret passage, leading from the prison-chamber of the monastery under its walls, and opening to the free country at the bottom of the rocks.

Ben. By every holy saint, so there is! and the most sordid of our brothers is entrusted with the key of it. But who will be his conductor? None but a Monk of the Order may pass the soldiers who guard him; and the Monk who should do it, must fly from his country for ever, and break his sacred vows. I can oppose the weak fears and injustice of my brethren, for misfortunes and disgust of the world, not superstitious veneration for monastic sanctity, has covered my head with a cowl; but this I cannot do.

Ag. There is the dress of a Monk of your Order in the old wardrobe of the castle, if some person were disguised in it.

Leo. Thanks to thee! thanks to thee, my happy Agnes! I will be that person. — I will put on the disguise. ——————— Good Father! your face gives consent to this.

Ben. If there be time; but I left them preparing for the execution.

Leo. There is, there is! — Come with me to the wardrobe, and we'll set out for the monastery forthwith. — Come, come! a few moments will carry us there.

[EXIT *hastily, followed by* Ag. *and* Ben.

SCENE IV.

A Wood near the Castle; the Stage quite dark: Enter Two Servants *with Torches.*

1*st Ser.* This must surely be the entry to the path, where my Lady ordered us to wait for those same Monks.

2*d Ser.* Yes; I know it well, for yonder is the postern. It is the nearest path to the monastery, but narrow and difficult. The night is cold: I hope they will not keep us long waiting.

1*st Ser.* I heard the sound of travellers coming up the eastern avenue, and they may linger belike; for Monks are marvellously fond of great people and of strangers; at least the good Fathers of our monastery are.

2d Ser. Aye, in their late Prior's time they lived like lords themselves; and they are not very humble at present. — But there's light from the postern: here they come.

Enter BENEDICT, LEONORA *disguised like a* Monk, *and* AGNES *with a Peasant's cloak thrown over her.*

Leo. (*speaking as she enters.*) It is well thought of, good Benedict. Go thou before me to gain brother Baldwin, in the first place; and I'll wait without on the spot we have agreed upon, until I hear the signal.

Ben. Thou comprehendest me completely, Brother; so God speed us both!

(*To 1st* Ser.)

Torch-man, go thou with me. This is the right path, I trust?

1st Ser. Fear not, Father; I know it well.

[EXIT Ben. *and 1st* Ser.

Leo. (*to* Agnes, *while she waves her hand to 2d* Servant *to retire to a greater distance.*) After I am admitted to the monastery, fail not to wait for me at the mouth of the secret passage.

Ag. Fear not: Benedict has described it so minutely, I cannot fail to discover it.

Leo. What steps are those behind us? Some body following us from the castle?

Enter 3d Servant *in haste.*

3d Ser. There are travellers arrived at the gate, and desire to be admitted for the night.

Leo. In an evil hour they come. Return, dear Agnes, and receive them. Benighted strangers, no doubt. Excuse my absence any how: go quickly.

Ag. And leave you to proceed alone?

Leo. Care not for me: there is an energy within me now, that bids defiance to fear.

(*Beckons to 2d* Servant, *who goes out before her with the torch, and* EXIT.)

Ag. (*muttering to herself, as she turns to the castle.*) The evil spirit hath brought travellers to us at this moment: but I'll send them to their chambers right quickly, and join her at the secret passage, notwithstanding.

[EXEUNT.

ACT III.

SCENE I. — *The Prison-chamber of the Monastery:* OSTERLOO *is discovered, sitting in a bending Posture, with his clenched Hands pressed upon his Knees and his Eyes fixed on the Ground,* JEROME *standing by him.*

Jer. Nay, sink not thus, my Son; the mercy of Heaven is infinite. Let other thoughts enter thy soul: let penitence and devotion subdue it.

Ost. Nothing but one short moment of division between this state of humanity and that which is to follow! The executioner lets fall his axe, and the dark veil is rent; the gulf is uncovered; the regions of anguish are before me.

Jer. My Son, my Son! this must not be; thine imagination overpowers thy devotion.

Ost. The dead are there; and what welcome shall the murderer receive from that assembled host? Oh, the terrible form that stalks forth to meet me! the stretching out of that hand! the greeting of that horrible smile! And it is thou, who must lead me before the tremendous majesty of my offended Maker! Incomprehensible and dreadful! What thoughts can give an image of that which overpowers all thought!

(*Clasping his hands tightly over his head, and bending himself almost to the ground.*)

4

Jer. (*after a pause.*) Art thou entranced? art thou asleep? art thou still in those inward agonies of imagination? (*Touching him softly.*) Speak to me.

Ost. (*starting up.*) Are they come for me? They shall not yet: I'll strangle the first man that lays hold of me. (*Grasping* Jerome *by the throat.*)

Jer. Let go your hold, my Lord; I did but touch you gently to rouse you from your stupor.

(Osterloo *lets go his hold, and* Jerome *shrinks to a distance.*)

Ost. I have grasped thee, then, too roughly. But shrink not from me thus. Strong men have fallen by my arm, but a child might contend with me now.

(*Throwing himself back again into his chair, and bursting into tears.*)

Jer. Forgive me, my Son, there was a wildness in your eyes that made me afraid.

Ost. Thou need'st not be afraid: thou art a good man, and hast days of life still before thee; thou need'st not be afraid.——————

But, as thou art a good man, speak to me, I conjure thee, as a man, not as a monk: answer me as the true sense and reason of a man doth convince thee.

Jer. I will, my Son.

Ost. Dost thou in truth believe, that the very instant after life has left the body, we are forthwith awake and conscious in the world of Spirits? No intermediate state of slumbering insensibility between?

Jer. It is indeed my belief. Death is but a short though awful pass; as it were a winking of the eyes for a moment. We shut them in this world and open them in the next: and there we open them with such increased vividness of existence, that this life, in comparison, will appear but as a state of slumber and of dreams. ——— But wherefore dost thou cross thine arms so closely on thy breast, and coil thyself together so wretchedly? What is the matter, my Son? Art thou in bodily anguish?

Ost. The chilly night shoots icy coldness through me.

Jer. O regard not the poor feelings of a fleshly frame, which thou so soon must part withal: a little time will now put an end to every thing that nature can endure.

Ost. (*raising his head quickly.*)
Ha! how soon? Has the bell struck again since I listened to it last?

Jer. No; but it will soon strike, and day-break is at hand. Rouse ye then, and occupy the few minutes that remain in acts of devotion becoming thine unhappy state. O, my Son, pour out thy soul in penitent prayers to an offended but merciful God. We, too, will pray for thee. Months, nay years after thy death, masses shall be said for the repose of thy soul, that it may at last be received into bliss. O my unhappy Son! pour forth thy spirit to God; and let thy prayers also ascend to our blessed Saint and Martyr, who will intercede for thee.

Ost. I cannot: I have not thoughts for prayer, —the gulph yawns before me—the unknown, the unbounded, the unfathomable!—Prayers! prayers! what prayers hath despair?

Jer. Hold, hold, refractory Sprit! This obstinacy is destruction. ———— I must call in brother Bernard to assist me: I cannot be answerable alone, in a service of such infinite moment.

(Exit; *and after a pause, in which* Osterloo *seems absorbed in the stupor of despair, enter* Leonora *disguised.*)

Leo. (*coming eagerly forward, and then stopping short to look at him.*)

There is some mistake in this: it is not Osterloo. ———————— It is, it is! but Oh, how changed! Thy hand, great God! has been upon him.

(*Going closer to him.*)

Osterloo! Osterloo!

Ost. I hear thee, Father.

Leo. (*throwing aside her disguise.*)

Oh no! it is no Father. Lift up thine eyes and see an old friend before thee, with deliverance in her hand. (*Holding out a key.*)

Ost. (*looking up wildly.*) Is it a sound in my ears, or did any one say deliverance?

(*Gazing on her.*)

What thing art thou? A form of magic or delusion?

Leo. Neither, Count Osterloo; but an old friend, bringing this key in her hand for thy deliverance. Yet much I fear thou hast not strength enough to rise and follow me.

Ost. (*bounding from his seat.*) I have strength for any thing if there be deliverance in it. — Where go we? They will be upon us immediately.

Leo. (*lifting a small lamp from a table, and holding it to examine the opposite wall.*)

The door, as he described it, is to the right of a small projection of the wall. — Here — here it is! (*Opens a small door, and beckons* Osterloo *to follow her.*)

Ost. Yes, blessed being! I will follow thee. — Ha! they are coming!

(*Strides hastily to the door, while* Leonora *holds up the lamp to light him into it, and then going in herself, shuts the door softly behind her.*)

SCENE II.

An old ruinous Vault, with a strong grated Door on one side, through which the Moon-beams are gleaming: on the other Side, an old winding staircase, leading from the upper Regions of the Monastery, from which a feeble Light is seen, increasing by degrees; and presently Leonora *appears, descending the Stairs with a Lamp in her Hand, followed by* Osterloo.

As she enters, something on the Wall catches her Robe, and she turns round to disentangle it, bending her Face close to the Light.

Ost. (*stopping to assist her, and then gazing on her.*)

Thou art something I have known and loved somewhere, though it has passed away from my mind with all my better thoughts. ———— Great power of Heaven! art thou Leonora?

Leo. (*smiling.*) Dost thou know me now?

Ost. I do, I do! My heart knew thee before, but my memory did not.

(*Kneeling and kissing both her hands.*)

And so it is to thee—thou whom I first loved—Pardon me, pardon me!—thou whom I loved, and dared not love; thou from whom I fled to be virtuous—thou art my deliverer. Oh! had I never loved another after thee, it had been well. ———————— Knowest thou it is a murderer thou art saving?

Leo. Say no more of this: I know thy story, and I came ——

Ost. O! thou camest like a blessed Spirit to deliver me from many horrors. I was terribly beset: thou hast snatched me from a tremendous brink.

Leo. I hope so, if this key prove to be the right one.

Ost. (*alarmed.*) Dost thou doubt it?

Leo. It seems to me smaller than it ought to be, when I consider that massive door.

Ost. Give it me.

(*Snatches the key from her, and runs to the door; then turns the key in the lock, and finding it too small, stamps with his feet, throws it from him, and holds up his clenched hands in despair.*)

Leo. Oh, cross fate! But I'll return again for the right one. Baldwin cannot be so wicked as to deceive me, and Benedict is still on the watch, near the door of the prison-chamber. Stay here till I return.

(*She ascends the stairs, whilst* Osterloo *leans his back to the wall, frequently moving his body up and down with impatient agitation: a bell tolls;* Osterloo *starts from his place, and* Leonora *descends again, re-entering in great alarm.*)

Leo. Oh! I cannot go now: that bell tolls to warn them to the great hall: I shall meet them on their way. What is to be done? The strength of three men could not force that heavy door, and thou art feeble and spent.

Ost. (*running furiously to the door.*)
Despair has strength for any thing.

(*Seizes hold of the door, and, making two or three terrible efforts, bursts it open with a loud jar.*)

Leo. Supernatural strength has assisted thee: now thou art free.

(*As* Osterloo *and* Leonora *are about to pass on through the door,* Wovelreid *and three armed* Soldiers *appear in the porch beyond it, and oppose their passage.)*

Wov. Hold! we are the Prior's Soldiers, and will suffer no prisoner to escape.

Ost. Those who dare prevent me!

(Wrests a sword from one of the Soldiers, *and, fighting furiously, forces his way past them all, they not daring to pursue him; when* Wovelreid *seizing on* Leonora *to prevent her from following him, she calls out.)*

Leo. O let me pass! and I'll reward you nobly.

Ost. (returning to rescue Leonora.*)*
Let go thine unhallowed grasp.

Leo. For Heaven's sake care not for me! Save thyself— save thyself! I am in no danger. Turn not again to fight, when such terrible odds are against thee.

Ost. I have arms in my hand now, and my foes are before me! *(Fights fiercely again, till* Morand, *with a strong band of* Soldiers, *entering the porch behind him, he is overpowered and secured;* Leonora *sinks down by the wall in a swoon.)*

Wov. Give me a rope. We must bind him securely; for the Devil has put the strength of ten men into him, though, but half an hour ago, his face was as pale as a moon-light icicle, and he could scarcely walk without being supported.

Mor. Alas, alas! his face has returned to its former colour; his head sinks on his breast, and his limbs are again feeble and listless. I would rather see him fighting like a fiend than see him thus.

Wov. Let us move him hence; would'st thou stop to lament over him?

Mor. It was base work in Baldwin to betray their plot to the Prior, for he took their money first, I'll be sworn.

Wov. He had betrayed the Prior then, and all the community besides.

Mor. Well, let us move him hence: this is no business of ours.

[EXEUNT Morand, Wovelreid *and* Soldiers, *leading out* Osterloo.

Enter AGNES *by the grated door, and discovers* LEONORA *on the ground.*

Ag. O holy Virgin! On the ground, fainting and ill! Have the barbarians left her thus?

(*Chafing her temples and hand.*)

She begins to revive. It is me, my dearest Lady: look up and see me: those men are all gone.

Leo. And Osterloo with them?

Ag. Alas, he is.

Leo. It is fated so. Let me lie where I am: I cannot move yet, my good Agnes.

Ag. Nay, do not yet despair of saving the Count.

Leo. (*starting up and catching hold of her eagerly.*)

How so? is it possible?

Ag. The travellers, arrived at the castle, are the Imperial Ambassador and his train. Night overtook them on the mountains, and they are now making merry in the hall.

Leo. Thank Heaven for this! Providence has sent him hither. I'll go to him instantly, and conjure him to interpose his authority to save the life of Osterloo. Representing his liege Lord, the Emperor, the Prior dare not disobey his commands, and the gates of the monastery will be opened at his call. Who comes here? Let us go.

Re-enter MORAND.

Mor. (*to* Leonora.) You are revived again: I am glad to see it. Pardon me, Lady, that I forgot you in your extremity, and let me conduct you safely to the castle.

Leo. I thank you, but my servants are without. Let me go. Don't follow me, I pray you.

Mor. Let me support you through the porch, and I'll leave you to their care, since you desire it. [EXEUNT, Leonora *supported by* Morand *and* Agnes.

SCENE. III.

A grand Hall, prepared for the Execution; Soldiers *are discovered drawn up on each side of the Scaffold, with* BENEDICT *and several of the* Monks *on the front of the Stage. A bell tolls at measured Intervals, with a deep pause between; after which enter* MORAND, *hanging his Head sorrowfully.*)

Ben. (*to* Mor.) Is he come forth?

1*st Monk.* Hast thou seen him?

Mor. They are leading him hither, but they move slowly.

1*st Monk.* Thou hast seen him then; how does he look now?

Mor. I cannot tell thee. These few hours have done on him the work of many years: he seems broken and haggarded with age, and his quenched eyes are fixed in their sockets, like one who walks in sleep.

Ben. Alas, alas! how changed in little time the bold and gallant Osterloo!

1*st Monk.* Have I not told thee, Morand, that fear will sometimes couch under the brazen helmet as well as the woollen cowl?

Mor. Fear, dost thou call it! Set him this moment in the field of battle, with death threatening him from a hundred points at once, and he would brave it most valiantly.

Ben. (*preventing* 1*st* Monk *from answering.*) Hush, Brother! Be not so warm, good Lieutenant; we believe what thou sayest most perfectly. The bravest mind is capable of fear, though it fears no mortal man. A brave man fears not man; and an innocent and brave man united, fears nothing.

Mor. Aye, now you speak reason: call it fear then if you will. — But the Prior comes; let us go to our places.

(*They arrange themselves; and then enter the* Prior, *with a train of* Monks, *who likewise arrange themselves: a pause, in which the bell tolls as before, and enter* OSTERLOO, *supported by* JEROME *and* PAUL, WOVELREID, *and* Soldiers *following.*)

Prior. (*meeting him with solemnity.*) Count Osterloo; in obedience to the will of Heaven, for our own preservation, and the just punishment of guilt, I am compelled with the Monks of this monastery over whom I preside, to see duly executed within the time prescribed, this dismal act of retribution. — You have I trust, with the help of these holy men, as well as a few short moments would allow, closed your mortal account with Heaven: if there be aught that rests upon your mind, regarding worldly concerns which you leave behind you unsettled, let me know your last will, and it shall be obeyed.

(*To* Jerome, *after pausing for an answer.*) Dost thou think he understands me?

Jer. (*to* Osterloo.) Did you hear, my Son, what the Prior has been saying to you?

Ost. I heard words through a multitude of sounds.

Jer. It was the Prior, desiring to know if you have any wishes to fulfil, regarding worldly affairs left behind you unsettled.—Perhaps to your soldiers you may.

Ost. (*interrupting him eagerly and looking wildly round.*) My soldiers! are they here?

Jer. Ah, no! they are not here; they are housed for the night in their distant quarters: they will not be here till the setting of to-morrow's sun.

Ost. (*groaning deeply.*) To-morrow's sun!

Jer. Is there any wish you would have conveyed to them? Are there any of your officers to whom you would send a message or token of remembrance?

Ost. Ye speak again imperfectly, through many ringing sounds.

(Jer. *repeats the question in a slow distinct voice.*)

Ost. Aye there is: these, these ——

(*Endeavouring to tear off his cincture and some military ornaments from his dress.*)

I cannot hit upon these fastenings.

Jer. We'll assist you, my Son.

(*Undoing his cincture or girdle, &c.*)

Ost. (*still endeavouring to do it himself.*)

My sword too, and my daggers.—My last remembrance to them both.

Jer. To whom, my Lord?

Ost. Both — all of them.

Ben. (*who has kept sorrowfully at some distance, now approaching eagerly.*)
Urge him no more: his officers will themselves know what names he would have uttered.

(*Turning to* Ost. *with an altered voice.*)
Yes, noble Count; they shall be given as you desire with your farewell affection to all your brave followers.

Ost. I thank ye.

Jer. And this is all?

Ost. Nay, nay!

Ben. What is there besides?

Prior. (*angrily.*) There is too much of this: and some sudden rescue may prevent us.

Ben. Nay, reverend Father, there is no fear of this: you would not cut short the last words of a dying man?

Prior. And must I be guided by thy admonitions? beware; though Baldwin has not named thee, I know it is thou who art the traitor.

Ben. There is but one object at present to be thought of, and with your leave, reverend Father, I will not be detered from it. (*To* Ost. *again in a voice of tenderness.*) What is there besides, noble Osterloo, that you would wish us to do?

Ost. There is something.

Ben. What is it, my Lord?

Ost. I wot not.

Ben. Then let it rest.

Ost. Nay, nay! This—this——

(*Pulling a ring from his finger, which falls on the ground.*)

My hands will hold nothing.

Ben. I have found it; and what shall I do with it?

Ost. (*in a faint hurried voice.*) Leonora—Leonora.

Ben. I understand you, my Lord.

Prior. I am under the necessity, Count Osterloo, of saying, your time is run to its utmost limit: let us call upon you now for your last exertion of nature. These good brothers must conduct you to the scaffold. (Jer. *and* Paul *support him towards the scaffold, while* Benedict *retires to a distance, and turns his back to it.*)

Jer. Rest upon me, my Son, you have but few paces to go.

Ost. The ground sinks under me; my feet tread upon nothing.

Jer. We are now at the foot of the scaffold, and there are two steps to mount: lean upon us more firmly.

Ost. (*stumbling*) It is dark; I cannot see.

Jer. Alas, my Son! there is a blaze of torches round you.

(*After they are on the scaffold.*)

Now, in token of thy faith in heaven, and forgiveness of all men, raise up thy clasped hands.

(*Seeing* Ost. *make a feeble effort, he raises them for him in a posture of devotion.*)

And now to heaven's mercy we commit thee.

(Jerome *and* Paul *retire, and two* Executioners *prepare him for the block, and assist him to kneel. He then lays down his head, and they hold his hands, while a third* Executioner *stands with the raised axe.*)

1*st Ex.* (*speaking close into his ear.*)
Press my hand when you are ready for the stroke. (*A long pause.*)
He gives no sign.

2*d Ex.* Stop, he will immediately.
(*A second pause.*)
Does he not?

1*st Ex.* No.

Prior. Then give the stroke without it.

(3d *Ex. prepares to give the stroke, when the* Imperial Ambassador *rushes into the hall, followed by* Leonora *and* Agnes, *and a numerous train.*)

Am. Stop the execution! In the name of your liege Lord the Emperor, I command you to stop upon your peril. My Lord Prior, this is a treacherous and clandestine use of your seignorial power. This noble servant of our Imperial Master (*pointing* to Osterloo) I take under my protection; and you must first deprive an Imperial Ambassador of life, ere one hair of his head fall to the ground.

Ben. (*running to the scaffold.*) Up, noble Osterloo! Raise up thy head: thou art rescued: thou art free.

Leo. Rise, noble Osterloo! dost thou not know the voice that calls thee?

Ben. He moves not; he is in a swoon.

(*Raises* Osterloo *from the block, whilst* Leonora *bends over him with anxious tenderness.*)

Leo. He is ghastly pale: yet it surely can be but a swoon. Chafe his hands, good Benedict, while I bathe his temples.

(*After trying to restore him.*)

Oh, no, no! no change takes place. What thinkest thou of it? Is there any life here?

Ben. In truth I know not: this seems to me the fixed ghastly visage of compleat death.

Leo. Oh, no, no! he will be restored. No stroke has fallen upon him: it cannot be death. Ha! is not that something? did not his lips move?

Ben. No, Lady; you but deceive yourself; they moved not: they are closed for ever.

Leo. (*wringing her hands.*) Oh it is so! it is so!—after all thy struggles and exertions of despair, this is thy miserable end!—Alas, alas! thou who didst bear thy crest so proudly in many a well fought field; this is thy miserable end!

(*Turning away, and hiding her face in the bosom of* Agnes.)

Ambass. (*examining the body more closely.*) I think in very truth he is dead.

1*st Gentleman of his Train.* Yes; the face

never looks thus, till every spark of life is extinguished.

Ambass. (*turning fiercely to the* Prior.) How is this, Prior? What sorcery has been here, that your block alone should destroy its victim, when the stroke of the axe has been wanting? What account shall I carry to my master of the death of his gallant General?

Prior. No sorcery hath been practised on the deceased: his own mind has dealt with him alone, and produced the effects you behold. And, when you return to Lewis of Bavaria your Master; tell him that his noble General, free from personal injury of any kind, died, within the walls of this monastery, of fear.

Ambass. Nay, nay, my good Prior; put the fool's cap on thine own head, and tell him this tale thyself. ———— Fear! Osterloo and fear coupled together! when the lion and the fawn are found couching in the same lair, we will believe this.

Prior. All the Brothers of the order will attest it.

Ambass. Away with the testimony of your cowled witnesses!

(*Beckoning* Morand *to come near.*)

Morand, thou art a brave fellow; I have known thee of old, thou art the Prior's officer indeed; but thou art now under my protection, and shalt be received into the Emperor's service with encreased rank: speak the truth then, boldly; how died Count Osterloo?

Mor. In very truth then, my Lord, according to my simple thoughts, he died even as the Prior has told you.

Ambass. Out upon thy hireling's tongue! art thou not ashamed, thyself wearing a soldier's garb, to blast a soldier's fame? There is no earthly thing the brave Osterloo was ever known to fear.

Mor. You say true, my Lord; and on my sword's point I'll maintain it against any man as stoutly as yourself. But here is a pious Monk (*pointing to* Jerome) who will explain to you what I should speak of but lamely.

Jer. With the Prior's permission, my Lord, if you will retire with me a little while, I'll inform you of this mysterious event, even simply as it happened. And perhaps you will then confess, that, called upon suddenly, under circumstances impressing powerfully the imagination, to put off this mortal frame and stand forth in that tremendous presence, before which this globe, with all its mighty empires, hangs but as a crisped rain-drop, shivering on the threaded gossamer; the bravest mind may, if a guilty one, feel that within which is too powerful for human nature to sustain.

Ambass. Explain it as thou wilt; I shall listen to thee: but think not to cheat our Imperial Master of his revenge for the loss of his gallant General. I shall not fail, my Lord Prior, to report to him the meek spirit of your Christian authority, which has made the general weal of the community subservient to your private revenge; and another month, I trust, shall not pass over our heads, till a worthier man (*pointing to* Benedict) shall possess this power which you have so greatly abused. ——————

———— Let the body be removed, and laid in solemn state, till it be delivered into the hands of those brave troops, who shall inter it with the honours of a Soldier.

THE END OF THE DREAM.

THE SIEGE:

A COMEDY,

IN FIVE ACTS.

PERSONS OF THE DRAMA.

MEN:

Count VALDEMERE.
Baron BAURCHEL.
WALTER BAURCHEL, *his Brother.*
ANTONIO, *Baron de Bertrand.*
DARTZ, *his Friend.*
Page *to* Count Valdemere.
LORIMORE, *his Valet.*
HOVELBERG, *a Jewel or Diamond Merchant.*
Soldiers, Servants, &c.

WOMEN:

Countess VALDEMERE, *Mother to the Count.*
LIVIA.
JEANETTA, *Woman to the Countess.*
NINA,
Ladies, &c.

Scene, *a Castle on the French confines of Germany.*

THE SIEGE.

ACT I.

SCENE I. — *A Grove near the Castle, with Part of the embattled Walls seen through the Trees: Enter* Baron BAURCHEL *and* WALTER BAURCHEL, *speaking as they enter.*

Bar. HAVE done, Brother? I can bear it no longer. Hadst thou been bred in a cave of Kamschatka, instead of a mansion of civilized Europe, this savage plainness had been endurrable: but ——

Walt. I call a turnip a turnip, indeed, when other people say it is a peach or a nectarine; I call a pig a pig too, though they swear it is a fawn or an antelope; and they look at me, I confess somewhat suspiciously, as if they expected to see a tail peeping from under my jerkin, or fur upon my hands like a bear.— You would have me civilized, would you? It is too late in the day now, good sooth!

Bar. Yes, the time is indeed gone by. This bachelor's life has brutified thee past all redemption. Why did you not marry, Brother?

Walt. Nay, you who have met with so many goddesses and creatures of perfection in the world, why did not you marry, Brother? I who could light upon nothing better than women — mere women; every one of them too with some fault or failing belonging to her, as obvious as those white hairs that now look from under your peruke, was it any marvel that I did not marry?

Bar. Had your wife possessed as many faults as you do wrinkles on your forehead, you would have been the better for her; she would have saved thee, as I said before, from brutification.

Walt. And yours would have saved you from dupification, dotification, and as many 'fications besides, as an old sentimental, hypocritical, greedy Dulcinea, can fasten on a rhyme-writing beau, who is stepping most unwillingly, with his lace-cloaked hose, over that ungracious line of division, that marks out his grand climacteric.

Bar. Hypocritical! greedy! you don't know the delicacy of her mind: nothing can be more tender, more refined, more disinterested than her attachment to me. You don't understand her.

Walt. Perhaps I don't understand the attachments of the fair sex now-a-days. An old rich neighbour of mine informed me the other night that he is going to marry his poor friend Spendall's youngest daughter, who has actually fallen in love with him; and nothing, as he tells me, almost in your own words, can be more tender, more disinterested than her attachment. Not understanding these matters, brother, I'll freely confess to you I did not give much credit to his story; but I may be wrong nevertheless. I dare say you believe it entirely.

Bar. Ridiculous! What proofs can the fool possibly receive of her attachment?

Walt. The very same which the Countess so condescendingly vouchsafes to yourself; she accepts of his presents.

Bar. The very same! No, no, Walter Baurchel; very different. Does not every smile of her countenance, every look of her eyes, involuntarily express her partiality for me?

Walt. Say, rather, every word of her tongue.

Bar. With what generous enthusiasm did she not praise my sonnet to Sensibility.

Walt. Aye, she is generous in what costs her little; for what are two or three lies, more or less, in the week's confession between her and Father Benedict? She'll scarcely eat a mouthful of partridge the less for it.

Bar. O heartless infidel! thou would'st mistrust the fond smiles of a mother caressing her rosy-faced infant.

Walt. By my faith, so I would, Baron, if that same infant brought a diamond necklace or a gold snuff-box in his hand for every kiss she bestowed upon him. Every sonnet you write costs you, one with another, a hundred louis d'ors. If all the money vanity filches from rich poets could be transferred to the pockets of poor ones, versemaking would be as good a business as shoe-making, or any other handicraft in the country.

Bar. Hold thy unhallowed tongue! These subjects are not for thy rude handling. What is all this grumbling intended for? Tell me what you want, and have done with it; you who pique yourself so much on your plain speaking.

Walt. Well, then, I want you to let the next six sonnets you write go unpraised, and give the money that should have paid for the praising of them, six hundred louis d'ors, as I reckon, to Antonio. Is it not a shame that your own ward and heir, in love with the Lady of this castle, as you very well know, cannot urge his suit with advantage, for want of the equipage and appendages becoming his rank; while this conceited Count, by means of his disinterested mother, drains your purse so freely; and is thereby enabled to ruin the pretensions of him whom you ought to support?

Bar. His pretensions are absurd, and cannot be supported.

Walt. Why absurd? Is he not as brave, as well born, as handsome, too, as his rival?

Bar. What signify all his good qualities? In the presence of his mistress he is an idiot.

Walt. It is true, he loses all possession of himself in that situation, and therefore she despises him, while the gay confidence of the other delights her; but he should be supported and encouraged.

Bar. How encouraged? Silly fellow!

Walt. He feels too sensibly his disadvantages, and they depress him. He feels that he is not entitled to pretend to Livia, but as the probable heir of your estates; while your fantastical fondness for this woman and her son makes it a doubtful matter whether you may not be tempted. —— But hush! here she comes with her new-ruddled face, bearing her morning's potation of flattery with her, for a stomach of most wonderful digestion.

Enter Countess VALDEMERE, *who, after slightly noticing* WALTER, *runs up caressingly to the* Baron.

Countess. How do you do, my dear Baron? I hope you have passed the night in sweet repose. — Yet, why do I hope it? You scarcely deserve that I should.

Bar. And why so, Belinda?

Walt. (*aside, making a lip at them.*) Belinda, too! Sweet innocents!

Bar. Why should you not hope that I have passed the night in repose?

Countess. Because I am vindictive, and would be revenged upon you for making me pass a very sleepless one.

Walt. (*aside.*) Will she make love to him before one's very face!

Bar. Then I am a culprit indeed, but an innocent one. What kept you awake?

Countess. O, those verses of yours! those dear

provoking verses! they haunted me the whole night. (Baron *bows.*) But don't think I am going to talk to you of their beauties — those tender easy graces which they possess, in common with every thing that comes from your pen: I am going to tell you of their defects. You know well my friendship for you, my dear Baron, makes me sometimes severe.

Bar. (*aside to* Walt.) There now, you churl, do you call this flattery? (*Aloud.*) My dear Countess, your severity is kindness.

Countess. Receive it then as such; for indeed I must be very severe on the two last lines of the second stanza, which have disturbed me exceedingly. In the verses of an ordinary poet I should not find fault with them; but in a work where every thing besides is easy, harmonious, and correct, the slightest defect is conspicuous; and I must positively insist on your altering them, though you should hate me for being so fastidious.

Bar. (*aside to* Walt.) There now, ungracious canker-tongue, do you call this hypocrisy? (*Aloud.*) Madam, I kiss the rod in so fair and so friendly a hand. Nay, it is a sceptre, to which I bow with devotion.

Countess. (*to* Walt.) You see, good Sir, I take great liberties with the Baron, as, I doubt not, with the privilege of a brother, you yourself sometimes do.

Walt. Yes, Madam, but my way of finding

fault with him is somewhat different from yours.

Countess. Yet you still find his generous spirit, I am sure, submissive to the rod.

Walt. I can't say I do, Madam.

Countess. You are unfortunate enough, perhaps, to use it unskilfully.

Walt. I am fortunate at present, however, in receiving so good a lesson from you, Madam.

Countess. O no! there is no skill with me. There are persons to whom one cannot say one-half of what one really thinks, without being deemed a flatterer.

Walt. In this, however, I have been more fortunate than you, Madam; for I have said to him what I have really thought for these forty years past, and have entirely escaped that imputation.

Bar. Aye, flattery is a sin thou wilt never do penance for. Thou can'st rub the side of a galled jade with any tender-hearted innocent in Christendom, and be mighty surprised withal that the poor devil should be so unreasonable as to winch at it.

Countess. Nay, nay, Baron! say not this of so good a brother, the shrewdness and penetration of whose mind are tempered, I am sure, with many amiable qualities.

Walt. Nay, pray, Madam, spare me, and deal with but one of us at a time. Such words will intoxicate a poor younger brother like myself, who is scarcely able to get a fowl for his pot, or new facings for his doublet, and cannot therefore be supposed to be accustomed to them.

Countess. Sir, I understand not your insinuation.

Bar. Regard him not, Madam: how should a mind, noble and delicate as your own, comprehend the unworthy thoughts of contemptible meanness? — Let me conduct you to company more deserving of you. Our fair hostess, I suppose, is already in her grotto.

Countess. No, she and my son are to follow me. But you must not go to the grotto with me now: nobody is to see it till the evening.

Bar. (*offering to lead her out.*) A step or two only.

Countess. O, not a step for the world.

[EXIT, Baron *kissing her hand as she goes off.*

Bar. (*turning fiercely upon* Walt.) Thy unmannerly meanness is intolerable. Still hinting at the presents she receives. Greedy as thou call'st her, she never asked a gift from me in her life, excepting my picture in miniature, which could only be valuable to her as she prized the original.

Walt. Say rather, as her jeweller shall prize the goodly brilliants that surround it.

Bar. What do you mean?

Walt. What I should have told you before, if she had not interrupted us; that her trinket-broker is this very morning coming secretly, by appointment, to the castle, to treat with her for certain things of great value which she wishes to dispose of; and if your picture be not amongst them, I'll forfeit my head upon it.

Bar. It is false.

Walt. Here comes one who will confirm what I say.

Enter DARTZ.

Walt. I'm glad to see you, Chevalier, for you can bear evidence to a story of mine that will not be believed else.

Dart. This is a better reason for being so than most of my friends have to give.

Walt. Is not Hovelberg, the jeweller, coming secretly to the castle to-day to confer with the Countess?

Dart. Yes, he told me so himself; and added, with a significant smile, that she had some of her old ware to dispose of.

Walt. Do you hear that, brother? It was as much as so say, she had often had such truckings with him before. Aye, you are not the only man who has thought his own dear resemblance lapped warmly behind the stomacher of his mistress, while, stripped of its jewels, it has been tossed into the drawer of some picture-monger, to be changed into a General of the last century, or one of the Grand-dukes of Austria. As for you, brother, they'll put a black velvet cap on your head, and make you a good sombre doctor of theology.

Bar. You shall not, however, make me the credulous man you think of, Walter Baurchel, with all your contrivances.

Walt. And you don't believe us then?

Bar. Are you fool enough to imagine I do?

Walt. That were foolish enough, I grant you; for though an old lover has generally a strong vein of credulity about him, the current of his belief always sets one way, carrying withered nosegays, tattered billet-doux, broken posies, and all kinds of trumpery along with it at fifteen knots by the hour.

Bar. Walter Baurchel! Walter Baurchel! flesh and blood cannot endure the offensive virulence of thy tongue.

Dart. He is indeed too severe with you, Baron; but what he tells you of Hovelberg is, nevertheless, very true.

Bar. I'll believe neither of you: you are both hatching a story to deceive me.

[EXIT *in anger.*

Walt. (*shrugging his shoulders and casting up his eyes.*) What strong delusion we poor mortals may be blinded withal! That poor brother of mine believes, that the woman who refused to marry him when he was young and poor, yet smiles upon him, praises him, accepts presents from him when he is old and rich, must certainly entertain for him a most delicate, disinterested attachment; and you might as well overturn the walls of that castle with one stroke of your foot, as beat this absurdity out of him.

Dart. But you are too violent: it will not be beat out; it must be got out as it got in, with craft and discretion.

Walt. Then devil take me for attempting it! for craft I have none, and discretion is a thing ——

Dart. You will never have any thing to do with, I believe.

Walt. What then is to be done? If it were not that I cannot brook to see the conceited overbearing son of this Jezebel, carrying off the mistress of Antonio, I would even let the old fool sit under the tickling of her thievish fingers, and make as great a noodle of himself as he pleases. — But it must not be. — Fie upon it, Dartz! thou hast a good head for invention, while I, heaven help me! have only a good tongue for railing; do thou contrive some plot or other to prevent the disgrace of thy friend.

Dart. Plots are not easily contrived.

Walt. I know this, else I should have tried it myself.

Dart. Are you well acquainted with the Count?

Walt. I am but just come to the castle, where I have thrust myself in, though an unwelcome guest, to look after the interest of De Bertrand; and should be glad to know something more of the man who has so much intoxicated the gay Livia. What kind of a being is he?

Dart. It would puzzle me as much as the contriving of your plot to answer that question. There is nothing real in him. He is a mere package of pretences, poorly held together with sense and capacity enough, were it not for one defect in his nature, to make him all that he affects to be. He is a thing made up of seemings.

Walt. Made up of seemings!

Dart. Even so; for what in other men is reckoned the sincerest part of their character, his very self-conceit, is assumed.

Walt. And what is the defect you hinted at?

Dart. It has been whispered to me by an old school-fellow of his, that he is deplorably deficient in personal courage; which accounts for his mother's having placed him in the regiment of a superannuated General, and also, for the many complaints he makes of the inactivity of his commander. It is a whisper I am inclined to credit; and, if we must have a plot, it shall hinge upon this.

Walt. My dear fellow! nothing can be better. Give it a turn or two in thy brains, and I'll warrant thou drawest it out again, shaped into an admirable plot. Direct all thyself, and I'll work under thee as a journeyman conspirator; for, as I said before, I have a ready tongue, but a head of no invention.

Dart. We must speak of this another time. See who approaches.

Walt. Ha! the man we are speaking of, and

the deluded Livia. By my faith he has a specious appearance! and the young fool looks at him too, as she would not look at a worthier man, whose merit might be tarnished with a few grains of modesty.

Enter VALDEMERE *and* LIVIA, *followed by* JEANETTE *carrying a basket filled with flowers, &c.*

Dart. (*to* Liv.) Permit me, Madam, to pay you my profound homage.

Liv. You are welcome here, Chevalier: what accident procures me this pleasure? (*aside to* Count.) He'll make one more at our midnight revel in the grotto.

Vald. (*aside with some chagrin.*) Are there not enow of us?

Dart. Being in this part of the country on military duty, I could not resist the pleasure of paying my respects at the castle: and I honestly confess I had a secondary motive for my visit, expecting to find amongst your guests, my old friend and school-fellow Antonio.

Liv. Baron de Bertrand, you mean. He was here yesterday, but I really forget whether he went away or remained in the evening. (*Affecting to yawn.*) Is he with us, or not, Count?

Walt. (*aside to* Dart.) Meet me by-and-by in my chamber. My tongue is unruly, and I had better go while I can keep it between my teeth.

[EXIT.

Liv. Does not his amiable relation there, who steals from us so quietly, know where he is?

Vald. If you are in quest of your friend, Chevalier, had you not better enquire at some of the peasants' houses in the neighbourhood? There may be some beauty in the village, perhaps, whose august presence a timid man may venture to approach, particularly if her charms should be somewhat concealed behind the friendly flax of her distaff.

Dart. Pardon me, Count; I thought my friend had aspired to a beauty, whose charms would have pleased him, indeed, behind the flax of a distaff, but will not, I trust, entirely intimidate him from the more brilliant situation in which fortune has placed them. Aye; that glance in your eye, and that colour in your cheek, charming Livia, tell me, I am right.

Liv. They speak at random then; for it would puzzle a much wiser head than I wear on my shoulders to say what are his pretensions. He visits me, it is true, but suddenly takes his leave again, and the very next day, perhaps, as suddenly returns.

Vald. Like poor puss with roasted chesnuts before her, who draws back her burnt paw every time she attempts them, but will not give up the attack. He may, however, after some more of those hasty visits, find courage for it at last.

Dart. There is one attack, however, for

which he never lacks courage, when the enemies of his country are before him.

Vald. True, he is brave in the field, but he is fortunate also. He serves under an active commander, while I waste my ardour in listless inactivity.

Dart. Cheer up then, noble Count, I have good news to tell you upon this score.

Vald. On this score! Is any change to take place? (*In a feeble voice.*)

Dart. (*after a pause.*) You are too well bred to be impatient for an answer.

Vald. O no; you mistake me; I am very impatient; I am on fire to hear it.

Dart. Expand then your doughty breast at thoughts of the glorious fields that are before you: your old General is set aside, and the most enterprising man in the service, Count ——— himself is now your Commander. (*After a momentary pause, and eyeing him keenly.*) Silent joy, they say, is most sincere; you are, I perceive, considerately and profoundly glad.

Vald. (*assuming suddenly great animation.*) O, immeasurably so. Great news indeed!— Strange — I mean very admirable news, if one could be sure it were true.

Dart. True! Who doubts what delights him?

Vald. I thought the regiment was promised to another person; I was not prepared to hear it.

Dart. So it appeared.

Vald. But I am delighted — I can't express it: — I am glad to a folly. Tol de rol — tol de rol —

(*Singing and skipping about affectedly.*)

Liv. Cruel creature! to sing at what, perhaps, will make others weep.

Vald. Weep! — No, I don't weep. I am happy to a folly, but I don't weep. (*Skipping about again.*) Tol lol de rol! — Plague take these stones! this ground is abominably rough.

Dart. Fie upon it! any ground is smooth enough for a happy man to skip upon.

Liv. You smile, Dartz; your news is of your own invention.

Dart. Not absolutely, Madam; there was such a rumonr.

Vald. (*eagerly.*) A rumour! only a rumour! Why did you say it was true?

Dart. To give you a moment's pleasure, Valdemere. If you have enjoyed it, you are a gainer; and the disappointment, I hope, will not break your heart.

Vald. It is cruel indeed.. But who can feel disappointment in this fair presence? (*Bowing to* Liv.) Let us go to the grotto, charming Livia; we waste our time here with folly. — Give me thy basket, child, (*to* Jean.) I'll dispose of every chaplet it contains to admiration. I'll hang them all up with mine own hand.

Liv. Don't be so very active: you positively shan't follow me to the grotto; I told you so before.

Vald. Positive is a word of no positive meaning when it enforces what we dislike. However, since you forbid it, I will not *follow* you; I'll go by your side, which is far better, and support your fair hand on my arm. (*Putting* Livia's *arm in his with conceited confidence.*)

Liv. What a sophistical explanation of my words! a heretical theologian is a joke to you.

Vald. (*casting a triumphant look behind him to* Dartz, *as he leads her off.*) Good morning, Chevalier, you go in quest of your friend, I suppose. Pray tell him to take courage, and be less diffident of his own good parts, and he may at last be promoted, perhaps, to the good graces of his Quarter-master's daughter.

Dart. Nobody at least, who sees Count Valdemere in his present situation, will think of recommending modesty to him.

[EXEUNT Vald. *and* Liv. *followed by* Jean.

Dart. Impudent puppy! his triumph shall be short. Blind woman! are flattery and impudence so necessary in gaining your favour, that all other qualities, without them, are annihilated? He shall this very night pay dearly for his presumption. [EXIT.

ACT II.

SCENE I.—*A Room in the Castle.* *Enter* WALTER BAURCHEL *and* DARTZ, *by opposite sides.*

Walt. Ha! my good friend, punctual to a wish. You have got your head stored, I hope, with a good plot.

Dart. I am at least more in the humour for it than I was. I have found his conceit and arrogance more intolerable than I imagined. I have touched him in the weak part too, and find him vulnerable.

Walt. Well, but the plot.

Dart. I have discovered also a trait of villainy in him, that would prick me on to the charge, were I sluggish as a tortoise.

Walt. So much the better. Now for the plot.

Dart. As I passed just now through the little green copse near the postern, a beautiful girl crossed my way, and in tears.

Walt. Tut! she has crossed thy wits too.

Dart. Have patience! she'll be useful.—I questioned her gently.

Walt. Aye, gently enough I doubt not.

Dart. And find she is sister to that shrewd little fellow, the Count's page: that her affections have been gained and betrayed by Valdemere; and she is now hovering about the castle, for an opportunity of upbraiding him, or in the vain hope, perhaps, of moving his pity.

Walt. She has moved thy pity at least; what has all this to do with our plot?

Dart. A great deal: I am telling you before hand what we shall have to work upon: a plot cannot, any more than a coat, be made without materials.

Walt. Well, but shew me thy pattern first, and talk of the buttons and buckram afterwards.

Dart. Be it so then, since you are so impatient. There is a friend of mine stationed about a league hence with his regiment; where he is to wait till he is joined by another detachment of the army, as the enemy, it is feared, may penetrate to these parts, and overrun the country. I mean to go to him immediately; make him privy to our design, and engage him to send a party of his soldiers to make a sham attack upon the castle at midnight, when we shall all be assembled at this fanciful banquet in the grotto.

Walt. (*nodding his head.*) Good.

Dart. Valdemere then, as the gallant soldier he affects to be, and the favoured admirer too of the lady, must of course take upon himself the defence of her castle.

Walt. (*nodding again.*) Very good.

Dart. This will quell his presumption, I trust; and expose him to Livia for the very paltry being that he is.

Walt. Aye, so far good; you'll make some furtherance to the plot out of this.

Dart. Some furtherance to the plot! Why this is the plot itself.

Walt. The plot itself! Any simple man in the country might have devised as much as this comes to.

Dart. It does not please you then because it is not intricate. But don't despise it entirely; though the outline is simple, tricks and contrivances to work up the mind of our victim to the state that is suited to our purpose, will enrich it as we proceed; and the Page I have mentioned, provoked by the wrongs of his sister, will be our subtle and diligent agent. Nay, should we draw Valdemere into great disgrace, we may bribe him, by concealing his dishonour, to marry the poor girl he has wronged.

Walt. Ha! this indeed is something like a plot.—And Antonio's marriage with Livia, how is that to be fastened to the end of it?

Dart. Nay, I have no certain hook, I confess, to hang that upon. It must depend on the Baron; for unless he declare Antonio his heir, he will never venture to propose himself as a match for the well-dowried Livia. But we shall manage matters ill, if we cannot draw the Baron into our scheme.

Walt. Then a fig for your plot! It is as bare of invention as the palm of my hand.

Dart. This is always the case with those who lack invention themselves: they are never pleased with that of any other person, if it be not bristled over with contrivances like a hedgehog. And I must be allowed to say, Mr. Walter Baurchel, that he who racks his brains for your service, works for a thankless master.

Walt. He works for an honest one, then.

Dart. Away with the honesty that cannot afford a few civil words to a friend, who is doing his best to oblige you! As much duplicity as this amounts to, would not much contaminate your virtue.

Walt. Well, well, I am wrong, perhaps, but thou art as testy as myself.

Dart. Because I won't bear your untoward humour. Some people find every body testy who approaches them, and marvel at their own bad luck.—But no more of this: let us think of our friend. Does the Baron believe what you told him of Hovelberg's appointment with the Countess?

Walt. He makes a show of not believing it, but I think he has his own suspicions at bottom; for his valet tells me, he has sent to desire Hovelberg to speak with him as soon as he arrives.

Dart. Here comes De Bertrand; I hear his steps.

Walt. Is he returned to the castle?

Dart. Yes; I forgot to tell you so, you were in such a hurry for your plot,

Walt. Silly fellow! he cannot stay away from his capricious mistress, though the first glance of her eye sinks him to a poltron at once.

Enter ANTONIO.

Ant. (*to* Walt.) Good morning, gentle Kinsman;—but methinks you are not very glad to see me; these are not looks of welcome.

Walt. Thou art one of those that trouble me.

Ant. I am of a pretty numerous class of beings then, from the kitten that gnaws at your shoe-string, to the Baron, who spoils your best pen in writing love-verses to his mistress.

Walt. Well; and they would torment any man. Love-verses! with such an old painted hypocrite for the object of them!

Ant. His first love, you know; his Delia.

Walt. His Delia! His delusion. Is there such a thing as witchcraft in the world? I believe in good earnest there is. Her dominion over him is a mystery: a more than Egyptian blindness.

Ant. Nay, you have yourself in a good degree to blame for it, my good Sir. Had you encouraged his humour, harmless as it is; bestowing some praise on his verses, and less abuse on the too youthful cut of his peruke, she could never have taken possession of him as she has done.

Walt. Praise his verses, and not abuse his peruke! it had been beyond the self-denial of a saint.

Dart. And had you—

Walt. (*to* Dart.) One assailant at a time, if you please.

Dart. Excuse me, Sir; I must needs say, had you even paid a little attention to the Countess herself, when she first renewed her intimacy with the Baron, she would have been less anxious, perhaps, to estrange him from his old friends.

Walt. Attention to her! I could not have done it to gain myself, like Mahomet, the entrance to the seventh heaven. I must tell people plainly what I think of them, though I should hang for it.

Dart. Had you said starve for it, you had named the fate that more commonly attends plain speaking.

Ant. And in telling people disagreeable truths to gratify your own humour too, are you surprised, my good Sir, that they should not be edified thereby?

Walt. (*to* Ant.) What, young Soldier, you are become a plain speaker too.

Ant. Just to shew you, Sir, how agreeable it is.

Walt. Ha, ha, ha! Well; thou hast the better of me now. Would thou could'st prate as briskly to thy mistress! that would do more for thee in one hour than all thy bashful tenderness in a year.

Ant. I might — I should indeed — I defend not my weakness. — You promised on this point to spare me.

Walt. Aye, the very sound of her name quells

thy spirit, and makes thee hesitate and stammer like a culprit. It is provoking.

Dart. You profess a violent detestation of conceit, my shrewd Sir; where, then, is your indulgence for modesty?

Walt. You mistake the matter, Dartz. Your friend there, has as good a conceit of himself as any man: he is not modest, but bashful; a weakness too that only besets him in the presence of his mistress. By this good fist of mine! it provokes me almost to the cudgelling of such an unaccountable ninny. But I would cudgel thee, and serve thee too, De Bertrand. Take courage; we have a plot in our heads to make a man of thee at last.

Dart. (*aside, pulling* Walt. *by the sleeve.*) Say not a word of the plot: his sense of honour is so delicate, he would recoil at it.

Ant. A plot did you say?

Walt. Aye, a kind of a plot; — that is to say — What kind of a plot is it, Dartz?

Dart. Have you forgot your own scheme for cheating the virtuoso, when your cabinet of antiquities comes to the hammer?

Walt. By my fay! this memory of mine is not worth a pinch of tobacco. (*Seeing* Ant. *look at his watch.*) Art thou going any where?

Ant. No; — I did think — I believe I shall take a turn on the terrace.

Dart. (*to* Ant.) I understand you: take a turn in the cabinet of paintings rather; that will suit your purpose better.

Ant. May I presume to go there?

Walt. Presume, simpleton! That impudent puppy of a Count lords it in her dressing-room. Go thy ways! (*pushing him off the stage with slight anger.* Exit Antonio.) That fellow provokes me; yet there is something in him that goes so near my heart: he is more akin to me than his blood entitles him to be: he is like a part of myself.

Dart. Not the least like it. Now that you have taught us to speak plainly, I must needs say, were he at all like yourself, you would disinherit him in the course of a month.

Walt. You are right, perhaps. But, alas! he would not be much the poorer for being disinherited by me. O that old fool of a brother! I could flog him for his poetry.

Dart. Have patience, and we may find a better way of dealing with him. If we could persuade him to disguise himself like a diamond merchant, and accompany Hovelberg when he visits the Countess, he would be convinced of the true nature of her regard for him.

Walt. An excellent thought! This is just what was wanting to make our plot really like a plot.

Dart. I'm glad it pleases you at last. Before I leave the castle to negociate with my friend for his myrmidons, I'll find out the Baron, and endeavour to persuade him.

Walt. Heaven prosper thee! but return, ere thou goest, and let me know the result.

Dart. Depend upon it.

[EXEUNT *severally.*

SCENE II.

A Room hung with Paintings, and enriched with Carving and Ornaments, &c. Enter VALDEMERE *and* ANTONIO.

Vald. Here are some good paintings, De Bertrand; if you have any taste for the art, they will please you. This Guido on the left is a divine thing. The Magdalen in Count Orrinberg's collection was considered as superior to it; but I always maintained this to be the best painting of the two, and the world have at last adopted my opinion. I have always decidedly thought — but you are not looking at it. Is there any thing in that door to arrest your attention? The carving on it is but indifferent.

Ant. I thought I heard footsteps. She's coming.

Vald. Pooh! she won't be here this half hour; so you need not yet take alarm, as if an enemy were advancing upon you.

Ant. You connect the idea of alarm with an enemy; would I had firmness to face what I love! You are a happy man, Valdemere, and a bold one too, most assuredly: what would not I give for a little of your happy self-possession.

Vald. Aye, it is an article of some value: he who can't possess himself, must not expect to possess his mistress.

Ant. A very specious maxim this from a young fellow's mouth, with the manliness of well-curled whiskers to support it: yet I have seen the embarrassment of a diffident character plead its own cause more effectually than the eloquence of a brazen-browed barrister. At least I have always felt it have more power over me.

Val. That is natural enough: it is a common selfish sympathy: one thief pities another when the rope is round his neck. Feeling for others is the consequence of our own imperfections; this is a known truth.

Ant. Establish it if you can, Valdemere, for it will go well nigh to prove you immaculate.

Vald. How far soever I may be from that degree of perfection, jealousy at least is not one of my faults, since I have introduced a rival into the apartments of my mistress, where he had not the courage to venture alone, and am also pointing out to him what he has not discovered for himself, that her picture is now before his eyes.

(*Pointing to a picture.*)

Ant. (*looking up to it eagerly.*) It is somewhat like.

Vald. She sat for it at my request: no one else could prevail on her. The painter knew my taste in these matters, and has taken wonderful pains with it.

Ant. (*sighing.*) You have indeed been honoured.

Vald. He has made the eyes to look upon you with such expression.

Ant. Think you so? To me he appears to have failed in this respect; or perhaps it is because any semblance of eyes which I can thus stedfastly look upon, are not to me the eyes of Livia.

Vald. I did not suspect you of being so fastidious.

Ant. Not so neither: but had they been turned on some other object instead of the spectator, one should then have seen them as one is accustomed to see them.

Vald. Yes, speaking for your single self, this may be true. I beg leave to dissent.

Ant. Yet surely you will agree, that the direct thrilling glance, from eyes of such vivid expression, cannot possibly be imitated, and ought not by a skilful painter to be attempted.

Enter LIVIA *behind them.*

Vald. Perhaps you are right: you talk like a connoisseur on the subject.

Liv. I come in good time then; for connoisseur or not, to hear De Bertrand talk at all is a very lucky adventure. You have wronged us much, Baron, to keep us so long ignorant of your taste for the fine arts.

Ant. (*embarrassed.*) Madam, I am much honoured. I am very little — (*mumbling words in a confused way that are not heard.*) I am very much obliged to you.

Liv. You are grateful for slight obligations. But you are looking at my picture I see, which was painted two years ago at the request of a good old uncle of mine; pray give me your opinion of it.

Ant. It appears — it is very charming. It is — that is, I suppose, it is very finely painted.

Liv. It is reckoned so: and it certainly does more than justice to the original. (Ant. *hesitates as if he would speak, but remains silent.*) You are of my opinion, I perceive, or at least too well bred to contradict me. Confess it freely; you are of my opinion.

Ant. O entirely, Madam.

Liv. You flatter me exceedingly.

Ant. I meant it in simple sincerity.

Liv. O, sincere enough I doubt not.

Vald. And surely you will not question its simplicity.

Liv. (*to* Vald., *turning from* Ant. *with pity and contempt*) Don't let us be too hard upon him. Pray look at that picture of my great aunt, who was a celebrated beauty.

Vald. (*gazing with affected admiration at* Livia's *picture.*) I have no eyes for any other beauty than what I now gaze upon.

Liv. And do you indeed admire this picture so much?

Vald. The faintest resemblance of its fair original is fascinating. Yet, methinks, the painter should have represented it as looking on some other object than the spectator.

Liv. Why so?

Vald. The direct thrilling glance, from eyes of such vivid expression, cannot possibly be imitated, and ought not to have been attempted.

Ant. (*aside.*) My own words in the coxcomb's mouth!

Liv. This is an objection proceeding from genuine sensibility: yet you never mentioned it before.

Vald. Perhaps I am too fastidious; but any eyes that I can thus stedfastly look upon, are not to me the eyes of Livia.

Liv. Ah! these are in truth the words of a too partial friend.

Vald. Words from the heart, divine Livia, will tell from whence they came. (*They both walk to the bottom of the stage, speaking in dumb-shew, while* Ant. *remains in the front.*)

Ant. (*aside.*) With my own words he woos her, and before my face too: matchless impudence! — And such a man as this pleases Livia! — He whispers in her ear, and she smiles. — My heart sickens at it: I'll look no more, lest I become envious and revengeful, and hateful to myself. — O Nature! hast thou made me of such poor stuff as this?

Vald. (*turning round from the bottom of the stage.*) Ha! De Bertrand, are you declaiming? Some speech of a tragedy, I suppose, from the vehemence of your gesture. Pray let Livia hear you: she is partial, you know, to every thing you do, and finds every exhibition you make before her particularly amusing.

Ant. (*sternly.*) Come nearer to me, Sir; the first part of my speech is for your private ear.— Come nearer.

Liv. Pray go to him: by the tone of his voice he personates some tyrant, and must be obeyed.

Ant. Yes, Sir, I must be obeyed. (Vald. *shuffles up to him unwillingly, and* Ant. *speaks in his ear.*) Take no more impertinent liberties with me in this Lady's presence, or be prepared to justify them elsewhere. [EXIT, *looking at* Vald. *sternly, who remains silent.*

Liv. (*advancing to the front.*) What is the matter, Count?

Vald. Nothing — nothing at all.

Liv. Nay, something unpleasant has passed between you.

Vald. I believe I did wrong: I should have treated him more gently. But the strangeness of his behaviour obliged me to use threatening words, upon which he withdrew, and chose not to understand them.

Liv. How ill one judges then by dumb-shew of what passes at a distance.

Vald. I am always calm on these occasions, while he assumes the fierceness of a boaster.

Liv. But you will not call him out for such a trifle?

Vald. Not for the world, divine creature, if it give you uneasiness.

Liv. How gentle you are! The brave are always so.

Vald. How can I be otherwise with such an angel to prompt me? No, the braggard may live in safety for me; I will not harm one hair of his head.

Liv. I thank you, dear Valdemere! and now, to recompense your goodness, I'll shew the beautiful gem I promised you: follow me.

Vald. Yes, bewitching maid! to the world's end, to the bottom of the ocean, to the cannon's brazen mouth, I would follow thee. [EXEUNT.

SCENE III.

The Countess's *Dressing-room. She enters from an inner Chamber, with a small Shagreen Case in her hand, followed by* JEANETTA, *carrying a Casket, which she sets upon a Table.*

Countess. Jeanetta, let me take a last look of those dear things before I part with them for ever.

Jean. I'm sure, my Lady, they are so handsome, and you look so handsome when you wear them, it would go to my heart to part with them.

Countess. But my dear boy must have money, Jeanetta, and I have been expensive myself. (*Opens the casket, and looks at the jewels.*) My diamonds, my pearls, my rubies, my darlings! for the sake of a still greater darling I must part with you all.

Jean. But if I might presume to speak, my Lady, don't you indulge the young Count too much in extravagance?

Countess. O no, Jeanetta; I doat upon him: it is this amiable weakness of character which all the world remarks and admires in me. And he loves me entirely too; he would sacrifice his life for my sake.

Jean. He'll sacrifice nothing else, however; for he never gives up the smallest convenience of his own to oblige you.

Countess. Small things are of no consequence: he would give up for me, I am confident, the thing most dear to his heart: and for him — to see him lord of this castle and its domains, and occupying in society the brilliant place that becomes him, I would — what would I not sacrifice!

Jean. Were he to live on the fortune he has, and marry where he is attached, he might perhaps be happier.

Countess. Happier! Were he mean enough to be happy so — contemptible thought! — I would see him in his grave rather. But no more of this: have you seen Hovelberg? You say he is waiting below.

Jean. Yes, Madam, and a friend with him; an Armenian Jew-merchant, who will, he says, go halves in his purchases, and enable him to give you a better price for the jewels, as he is himself rather low in cash at present.

Countess. Well, I'll object to neither Jew nor Infidel that puts money into my pocket. (*Holding up a ruby necklace.*) This should fetch something considerable.

Jean. O la, Madam! you won't part with that surely; your neck is like alabaster under it. Did you but know how they admired you at Prince Dormach's the last time you wore it. — I would sell the very gown from my back ere I parted with it.

Countess. So they admired me at Prince Dormach's then?

Jean. O dear, my Lady! the Prince's valet told me, though two young beauties from

Brussels were there, nobody spoke of any one but you.

Countess. Well, to please thee then, I'll keep it.

Jean. La! here is a little emerald ring, my Lady; those brokers will despise such a trifle, and give you a mere nothing for it. — La! who would think it? it fits my finger to a hair. It must be a mort too large for your delicate hand.

Countess. Keep it for thyself, then, since it fits thee. He was a great fool who gave it me, and had it made of that awkward size.

Jean. I thank you, my Lady: I wish you would give me every thing in this precious casket that has not been the gift of a sage.

Countess. Thou art right, child. It would put many a hundred louis-d'ors into thy pocket, and leave scarcely a marvedi for myself. A rich Knight of Malta gave me these (*holding up a string of pearls,*) whose bandy legs were tricked out most delicately in fine-clocked hose of the nicest and richest embroidery. Rest his soul! I made as much of those legs as the hosier did.

Jean. I doubt it not, Madam, and deserved what you earned full as well.

Countess. (*looking again at her pearls.*) There is not a flaw in any one of them.

Jean. Aye, commend me to such legs! had they been straighter, the pearls had been worse.

Countess. This amber box with brilliants I had from an old croaking Marquis, who pestered every music room in the principality to the day of his death, with notes that would have frightened a peacock. As long as he sang, poor man! I considered myself as having a salary on the musical establishment at the rate of two hundred ducats per month.

Jean. Aye; God send that all the old Marquises in these parts would croak for us at this rate.

Countess. I have no reason to complain: my present friend bleeds as freely as any of his predecessors.

Jean. So he should, my lady. Such nonsense as he writes ought not to be praised for a trifle. I would not do it, I'm sure.

Countess. Dost thou ever praise then for profit?

Jean. To be honest with you, Madam, I have done it, as who has not? But never since I entered your Ladyship's service; for why should you reward me for praising you, when all the world does it for nothing? — No, no, my Lady; you are too wise for that.

Countess. There is somebody at the door.

Jean. It is Hovelberg.

Countess. Open then, but let nobody else in.

(Jean. *opens the door, and* Hovelberg *enters, followed by Baron* Baurchel, *disguised as an Armenian Jew.*)

Countess. I am happy to see you, dear Hovelberg; and this gentleman also, (*curtesying to the* Bar.) I know it is only a friend. whom we may trust, that you would introduce to me on the present occasion.

Hov. To be sure, Madam: a friend we may depend on. (*Drawing* Countess *aside, and speaking in her ear.*) A man of few words: better to do in this quarter than this. (*Pointing first to his pocket, and then to his head.*) And that is a good man, you know, to be well with.

Countess. O the best stuff in the world for making a friend of. (*Returning to the* Bar.) Sir, I have the highest regard and esteem for you.

Bar. (*in a feigned voice.*) On vatch account, Madam?

Countess. O good Sir! on every account.

Bar. You lov'sh not my religion?

Countess. I respect and reverence it profoundly.

Bar. You lov'sh not my pershon?

Countess. It is interesting and engaging, most assuredly.

Bar. No body telsh me sho before!

Countess. Because the world is full of envious people, who will not tell you truths that are agreeable.

Bar. (*nodding assent.*) Now I understant.

Countess. Yes, dear Sir; you must do so; your understanding is unquestionable. (*Looking archly to* Hovel.) And now, gentlemen, do me the honour to be seated, and examine these jewels attentively.

Hov. We would rather stand if you'll permit us.

Countess. (*aside to* Hovel., *while the* Baron *examines the jewels.*) My dear Hovelberg, be liberal: for the sum I want is a large one, and those jewels would procure it for me any where; only, regarding you as my friend, I give you the first offer. — But your friend, methinks, examines every thing with great curiosity.

Hov. Yes, poor man! he likes to appear as knowing as he can: this is but natural, you know, when one is deficient in the upper department. — But he'll pay like a prince, if you flatter and amuse him.

Bar. Vasht fine stones! Vasht pretty ornaments! (*To* Countess.) You dishposhe of all deshe?

Countess. Yes, every thing.

Bar. Dere be gifsh here, no doubt, from de dear friensh.

Hov. Or some favoured lover, perhaps.

Countess. (*sighing affectedly.*) Perhaps so; but I must part with them all.

Bar. (*aside to* Hov.) Nay, she has some tenderness for me: put her not to too severe a trial.

Hov. (*aside.*) We shall see.

Bar. (*returning to* Countess.) You be woman; and all womansh have de affections for some one lover or frient. . .

Countess. O how good and amiable and considerate you are! I have indeed a heart formed for tenderness.

Bar. (*drawing* Hovel. *aside again.*) She does love me, Hovelberg; tempt her not with an extravagant price for the picture.

Hov. (*aside.*) I'll take a better way of managing it. (*Returning to the* Countess.) My friend desires me to say, Madam, that, if there is any thing here you particularly value, he'll advance you money upon it, which you may repay at your leisure, and you shall preserve it.

Countess. (*to* Baron.) How generous you are, my dear Sir! Yes; there is one thing I would keep.

Bar. (*eagerly.*) One ting — dere be one ting: tish picture, perhaps.

Countess. This ruby necklace.

Bar. You sell tish picture, den?

Countess. To be sure, if you'll purchase it.

Hov. The diamonds are valuable, indeed; but you will not sell the painting?

Countess. That will depend on the price you offer for it.

Hov. Being a portrait, it is of no value at all, but to those who have a regard for the original.

Jean. And what part of the world do they live in, Mr. Hovelberg? Can you find them out any where?

Countess. Nay, peace, Jeanetta. — As a portrait, indeed, it is of no value to any body, but, as a characteristic old head, it should fetch a good price. (*Shewing it to* Baron.) Observe, my dear Sir, that air of conceit and absurdity over the whole figure: to those who have a taste for the whimsical and ridiculous, it would be invaluable. Don't you perceive it?

Bar. Not very sure.

Countess. Not sure! Look at it again. See how the eyes are turned languishingly aside, as if he were repeating, "Dear gentle idol of a heart too fond." (*Mimicking the* Baron's *natural voice.*)

Hov. Ha, ha, ha! Your mimickry is excellent, Countess. Is it not, Friend Johnadab?

Bar. O, vasht comical.

Hov. (*aside to him.*) She has a good talent.

Bar. (*aside.*) Shrewd witch! The words of my last sonnet, indeed; but I did not repeat them so.

Hov. (*aloud.*) Though you are an admirable mimick, Madam, my Friend Johnadab does not think your imitation of the Baron entirely correct.

Countess. (*alarmed.*) He knows the Baron then; I have been very imprudent. — But pray don't suppose I meant any disrespect to the worthy Baron, whom I esteem very much.

Bar. O vasht much!

Hov. Be not uneasy, Madam; my friend will be secret, and loves a joke mightily.

Countess. I'll trust, then, to his honour: and since he does not like my imitation of the Baron, he shall have it from one who does it better than I. Jeanetta, amuse this worthy gentleman by repeating the Baron's last sonnet.

Jean. Nay, my Lady, you make me do it so often, I'm tired of taking him off.

Countess. Do as you are bid, child.

Jean. " Dear gentle idol of a heart too fond,
" Why doth that eye of sweetest sympathy ——"

Hov. Ha, ha, ha! Excellent!

Bar. (*off his guard.*) By Heaven, this is too bad! Your servants taught to turn me into ridicule!

Countess. (*starting.*) How's this? Mercy on me!

Hov. Be not alarmed, Countess; I thought he would surprise you. My friend is the best mimick in Europe.

Countess. I can scarcely recover my surprise. (*To* Baron) My dear Sir, I cannot praise you enough. You have a wonderful talent. The Baron's own mouth could not utter his voice more perfectly than yours.

Bar. (*pulling off his cap and beard.*) No, Madam, not easily. (Jean. *shrieks out, and the* Countess *stands in stupid amazement.*) This disguise, Madam, has procured for me a specimen of the amiable dispositions of a heart formed for tenderness, with a sample of your talents for mimickry into the bargain; and so I wish you good day, with thanks for my morning's amusement.

Countess. (*recovering herself.*) Ha, ha, ha! You understand mumming very well, Baron, but I still better. I acted my part well.

Bar. Better than well, Madam: it was the counter-part of my enacting the Baron.

Jean. Indeed, dear Baron, the Countess knew it was you, and so did I too. Indeed, indeed, we did. I'm sure it is a very good joke: I wonder we don't laugh more at it than we do.

Bar. Be quiet, subordinate imp of this arch tempter! My thraldom is at an end; and all the jewels in that shameful heap were not too great a price for such emancipation. (*Bowing very low to* Countess.) Adieu! most amiable, most sentimental, most disinterested of women! [Exit.

Countess. Hovelberg, you have betrayed me.

Hov. How so, Madam? You told me yourself you were the most sincere woman in the world; the Baron doubted your regard for him; how could I then dissuade him from putting it to the proof, unless I had doubted your word, Madam? an insult you could never have pardoned.

Countess. What, you laugh at me, too, you villian! (Exit Hovel.) Oh! I am ruined, derided, and betrayed! (*Throws herself into a chair, covering her face with her hand, while* Jeanetta *endeavours to comfort her.*)

Jean. Be not so cast down, my Lady, there are more than one rich fool in the world, and you have a good knack at finding them out.

Countess. O, that I should have been so unguarded! That I should never have suspected!

Jean. Aye, with his vasht this, and his vasht that: it was, as he said, vasht comical that we did not.

Countess. Bring not his detested words again to my ears; I can't endure the sound of them.

Enter VALDEMERE.

Vald. Well, Madam, you can answer my demands now, I hope: Hovelberg has been with you. Money, money, my dear mother! (*Holding out his hand.*) There is a fair broad palm to receive it; and here (*kissing her hand coaxingly.*) is a sweet little hand to bestow it.

Countess. (*pushing him away sternly.*) Thy inconsiderate prodigality has been most disastrous. Had'st thou been less thoughtless, less profuse — a small portion of prudence and economy would have made us independent of every dotard's humour.

Vald. Notable virtues indeed, Madam; but where was I to learn them, pray? Did you ever before recommend them to me, by either precept or example? Prudence! Economy! What has befallen you? I'm sure there is something wrong when such words come from your lips. — Ha! in tears, too! Hovelberg has brought no money then?

Countess. No, no, barbarian! He has ruined me.

Vald. How so?

Countess. I cannot tell thee: it would suffocate me.

Jean. La, Count! My Lady may well call him barbarian. He brought the old Baron with him to purchase the jewels, disguised like an Armenian Jew; and when bargaining with her for his own picture, my Lady said something of the original not much to his liking, and so the old fool tore off his disguise, and bounced out of the room in a great passion.

Vald. By my faith, this is unlucky! I depended on touching 500 louis d'ors immediately.

Countess. Thinking only of yourself still, when you may well guess how I am distressed.—I shall never again find such a liberal old cully as he.

Vald. Yes, you will, mother: more readily than I shall find the 500 louis.—I owe half that sum to Count Pugstoff, for losses at the billiard table; all the velvet and embroidery, the defunct suits of two passing years, haunt me wherever I go, in the form of unmannerly taylors: and, besides all this, there is a sweet pretty Arabian in the stables of Huckston, my jockey, that I am dying to be master of.—By my faith, it is very hard! Had you no suspicion? How came you to be so much off your guard?

Countess. I believe it was fated to be so, and therefore I was blinded for the moment. I dreamt last night that I had but one tooth in my head, and it dropped on the ground at my feet. This, it is said, betokens the loss of a friend by death, and I trembled for thee, my child; but now, too surely, my dream is explained and accomplished.

Vald. And, methinks, you would have preferred the first interpretation.

Countess. Ah! ungrateful boy! You know too well how I have doated on you.

Vald. I do know too well: it has done me little good, I fear.

Countess. It has done me little good, I'm sure, since this is all the gratitude thou hast. I should never, but for thee, have become the flatterer of those I despise, to amass those odious jewels.

Vald. Ha! the jewels are still here then! I shall have my louis' still. Thank you, dear mother, that you did not part with them, at least. (*Kissing her hand hastily, and running to the table.*) I'll soon dispose of them all.

Countess. (*running after him.*) No, no! not so fast, Valdemere: thou wilt not take them all. Haste thee, Jeanetta, and save some of them.

(*They all scramble round the table for the jewels, and the scene closes.*)

ACT III.

Scene before the Gate of the Castle. Enter NINA, *who crosses the Stage timidly, stopping once or twice, and then with hesitation giving a gentle knock at the Gate. Enter* Porter *from the Gate, which he opens.*

Porter. (*after waiting to hear her speak.*)

WHAT do you want, young woman? Did you only knock for amusement?

Nin. No, Sir; Is Count Valdemere in the castle? I would speak with him, if he is at leisure.

Port. He is in the castle; but as to speaking with him, no man of less consequence than his valet can answer that question.

Enter LORIMORE, *by the opposite side.*

Here he is. You come opportunely, Mr. Lorimore; this young person would speak with your master.

Lor. (*aside.*) O, Nina, I see. (*aloud.*) How do you do, my pretty Nina? You can't speak with my master, indeed; but you may speak with the next most agreeable personage in these parts, my master's man, as long as you please; and that, be assured, is a far better thing for your purpose, my princess.

Nin. Dare you insult me? You durst not once have done it.—I do not ask then to see him; but give him this letter.

Lor. (*taking the letter.*) Do you wish this precious piece to be read, child, or to be burnt?

Nin. Why ask that? to be read, certainly.

Lor. I must not give it to the Count, then, but keep it to myself: and if you'll just allow me to make the slight alteration of putting Lorimore the valet for Valdemere the master, as I read, it will be a very pretty, reasonable letter, and one that may advance your honour withal.

Nin. Audacious coxcomb! Give it me again. (*Snatches the letter from him, and turns away.*)

Lor. She is as proud as that little devil of a page, her brother.

Enter Page *behind from the gate.*

Page. The more devil he be, the fitter company for you. Whom spoke you to? (*seeing* Nina) Oh, oh! Is Nina here?—— Nina, Nina, (*Running after her.*)

Nin. (*returning.*) My dear Theodore, is it thee? I did not ask for thee, lest thou should'st chide me for coming to the castle.

Page. I won't chide, but I'm sorry to see thee here. Fie, woman! thou art the daughter of as brave an officer, though a poor one, as any in the service; art thou not ashamed to come, thus meanly, after a lover who despises thee?

Nin. He promised to marry me.

Page. He promised a fiddle-stick! Poor deluded simpleton!

Nin. Ah! dost thou chide me, boy as thou art?

Page. Who is there to chide thee now, when both our parents are dead? But as they would have done, so do I, sister; I chide thee, and love thee too.—Go now; return to the good woman from whose house thou hast stolen away, and I'll buy thee a new gown as soon as my quarter's salary is paid me.

Nin. Silly child, what care I for a new gown? But if thou hast any pity for me, give this letter to thy master.

Page. I will, I will: but go thy ways now; there is a gentleman coming. And do, dear Nina, return no more to the castle till I send thee word. Good be with thee, poor simpleton!

[EXIT Nina, *and enter* Dartz *by the opposite side.*]

Dart. Is it thy sister thou hast parted from? I met her in the wood this morning! she need not avoid me now.

Page. Let her go, Sir; the farther she is from the castle the better.

Dart. Thou hast a letter in thy hand.

Page. Yes, Sir.

Dart. Which thou art to give to the Count.

Page. No, Sir; I'll see him choked first.

(*Tearing the letter.*)

Dart. Nay, see what it contains ere thou destroyest it.

Page. (*putting it together again and reading it.*) Only upbraiding his unkindness, and stuff of that sort, with some nonsense about a dream she has had, which makes her afraid she shall never see him again.

Dart. Let me look. (*After reading it.*) This letter may be useful. Come with me, my little friend; and we'll devise a way of revenging thy sister on her cruel seducer.

Page. Will you? I'll worship you like a saint of the calendar, if you do this.

Dart. (*considering.*) Is not your master somewhat superstitious?

Page. Marry is he! but mightily afraid to be thought so. He laughed at me, — when the bad fever prevailed, — for wearing a charm on my breast against infection! but the very next night when he went to bed, what should drop out, think you, as he opened his vest, but the very same charm, which he had procured immediately, and worn with such secrecy, that even valet Lorimore knew nothing of the matter.

Dart. This is good; come with me, and I'll instruct thee what to do with thy letter.

[Exeunt.

SCENE II.

VALDEMERE'S *Dressing-Room: Enter* Page *treading softly on tiptoe, and looking about the Room.*

Page. Aye; the coast is clear, and the door of his chamber is a-jar; now is my time. (*Pulling the torn letter from his pocket, and stamping on the floor as he raises his voice.*) There, cursed letter, I'll make an end of thee! Give thee to my master, indeed! I'll give thee to the devil first. (*pretending to tear the letter, and strew the pieces about, while* Valdemere, *looking from the door of his chamber, steals behind him, and seizes his hands with the remainder of the letter in them.*) Mercy on me! is it you, my Lord?

Vald. What art thou doing? What scares thee so? What letter is this? Let me see it.

Page. O no, my Lord! I beseech you, for your own sake, don't read it.

Vald. Why should not I read it, boy?

Page. Lud, I don't know! you may not mind it, perhaps; but were any body to send such a letter to me, I should be mainly terrified. To be sure, death comes, as they say, at his own time, and we can't keep him away, though we should hang ourselves; but one don't like to be told before-hand the very year or day we are to die, neither.

Vald. The year and day! give me the letter: give it me immediately. (*Snatching the frag-*

ments of the letter from him, and picking up a piece or two from the floor, which he puts together hastily on a table near the front of the stage.) I can't make it piece any way.

Page. So much the better, my Lord: don't try to do it.

Vald. It is Nina's hand, I see, but I can make no sense of it.—Aye, now it will do, (*reading*) "I have been terrified with a dream, and fear I shall see you no more." But where is the dream; it is torn off; give it me.

Page. I have it not.

Vald. Thou liest! give it me, I say.

Page. Lud have mercy! as I tore it off just now, your black spaniel ran away it.

Vald. No, varlet! that is a sham; go find it; thou knowest where it is well enough.

Page. Indeed, my Lord, if it is not in the black spaniel's custody, it is no where else that I know of.

Vald. (*reading again.*) I fear I shall see you no more! But it may be her own death as well as mine, that her dream has foretold; and therefore she may see me no more.

Page. Very true, you had better think so; though it does not often happen that a woman is killed at a siege.

Vald. At a siege!

Page. Pest take this hasty tongue of mine; I could bite it off for the tricks it plays me.

Vald. At a siege!

Page. O, never mind it, Sir. It may be some

lie after all: some wicked invention to make you afraid.

Vald. (*sternly.*) What sayest thou?

Page. O no, I don't mean afraid; only uneasy as it were: — no, no! not uneasy neither; only somewhat as you feel at present, my Lord; you know best what to call it.

Vald. At a siege!

Page. Dear my Lord, those words are glued to your tongue.

Vald. (*not heeding him.*) My grandfather perished at a siege, and his grandfather also: is this fate decreed in our family for alternate generations? (*Sinks into a chair by the table, and* Page, *seeing him so much absorbed, comes close to him, staring curiously in his face.*)

Vald. Take thy varlet's face out of my sight; why art thou so near me? Leave the room, I say. [Exit Page.

(*Rising, and pacing to and fro as he speaks to himself.*)

A hundred dreams prove false for one that prefigures any real event. — It should not have been, however: my mother should have found for me some other occupation than a military life. — Quit it? No, I can't do that: the world would cry out upon me; Livia would despise me. — 'Tis a strange thing that women, who can't fight themselves, should so eagerly push us to the work. — Pooh! am I a fool that it seizes me thus? — I would this boy, however, had really destroyed the letter.

Enter DARTZ, *looking at* VALD. *some time before he speaks.*

Dart. (*aside.*) This will do; it is working with him. (*Aloud, advancing.*) My dear Count—but don't start, I bring no bad tidings; I come to beg a favour of you.

Vald. (*recovering himself.*) Say you are come to oblige me.

Dart. I thank you, Valdemere; but faith I'm ashamed to mention it; you will laugh at me for being so superstitious.

Vald. Ha! somebody has been dreaming about you too.

Dart. Should you deem me very credulous if a thing of this nature had power to disturb me?

Vald. 'Tis even so; they have been dreaming all over the house. Ha, ha, ha! And thou art really uneasy about such flummery as this: ha, ha, ha! ha, ha, ha! this is admirable! delightful!—ha, ha, ha, ha!

Dart. Be more moderate with your merriment: your tears and your laughter come so strangely together, one would take you for an hysterical girl.

Vald. I can't chuse but laugh at your dreamers; ha, ha, ha!

Dart. Don't laugh at me then; for I am neither a dreamer, nor believer in dreams.

Vald. (*becoming serious at once.*) No! what is it then?

Dart. I'm almost ashamed to tell you, yet I'll throw myself on your mercy and do it. I am in love then, and fearful of the fortunes of war; for you know we must expect sharp fighting this ensuing campaign.

Vald. (*ruefully.*) You think so?

Dart. I am certain of it. Now, though I have no faith in dreams, I must own I have some in fortune-tellers; and there is a famous one just come to the castle, whom I would gladly consult. Will you permit me to bring him to your inner apartment there, that he may tell me of my future destiny whatever his art may reveal to him? Laugh as you please, but refuse me not this favour, for there is no other room in the castle where I can meet him secure from interruption.

Vald. (*smiling affectedly.*) And thou art really in earnest with this folly?

Dart. When you have heard the wonderful things this wizard has foretold, you will not call it folly.

Vald. Can'st thou tell me any of them?

Dart. Take a turn with me on the terrace, and thou shalt hear things that will astonish thee.

Vald. Ha, ha! it is whimsical to see thee so serious. Such stories are pleasant amusement: I'll attend thee most willingly. [EXEUNT.

ACT IV.

SCENE I. — *A small Room in* Valdemere's *Apartments.* Baron BAURCHEL *is discovered in the Disguise of a Fortune-teller, with* DARTZ *standing by him, adjusting part of his Dress.*

Dart. 'Twill do well enough. Stand majestically by this great chair, with your worsted robe thrown over the arm of it; it will spread out your figure, and make it more imposing. — Bravo! you assume the astrological dignity to admiration; the rolling of your eyes under that black hood almost appals me. Be as good an astrologer as you have been an Armenian Jew, Baron, and we shall be triumphant.

Bar. As good, Dartz! if I am not a dolt, I shall be better; for there is no danger of losing my temper now; and being fairly engaged in it, methinks I could assume as many shapes as Proteus, to be revenged on this false hyena and her detestable cub.

Dart. Aye, that is your true spirit. But I must leave you now, and wait in the anti-room for the Count, who will be here presently.

[EXIT.

Bar. (*after musing some time.*) Superlative baseness and ingratitude! That sonnet, of all the sonnets I ever wrote, is the most exquisitely feeling and tender. When I read it to her, she wept. Were her tears feigned? I can't believe it. Assassins will weep at a high-wrought scene of tragedy, and cut the author's throat when it is over. — Even so: it suited her purposes better to laugh at my verses, than acknowledge their genuine effect; and so, forgetting every kindness she owed me —— O, the detestable worldling! I'll — hush, hush, hush! they are coming.

Re-enter DARTZ, *followed by* VALDEMERE, *who walks shrinkingly behind, peeping past his shoulder to the* Baron, *who slightly inclines his body, putting his hand with great solemnity three times to his forehead.*

Dart. (*aside to* Vald. *after a pause.*) Faith, Valdemere, I dare scarcely speak to him; 'tis well you are with me; will you speak to him?

Vald. No, 'tis your own affair; stand to it yourself.

Dart. (*aloud.*) Learned and gifted mortal, we come to thee —

Vald. (*aside, jogging his arm.*) Don't say *we*; 'tis your own affair entirely.

Dart. Well, I should say, gifted sage, not *we*, but *I* come to thee, to know what fortune is abiding me in this up-and-down world. I am a lover and a soldier, and liable, as both, to great vicissitudes.

Bar. Thou say'st truly, my Son; and who is

this young man, so much wiser than thyself, who does not desire to look into futurity?

Dart. It is my friend.

Bar. (*after examining the faces of both for some time.*) Say, more than friend.

Dart. How so?

Bar. (*still continuing to gaze alternately at them.*) 'Tis very wonderful! in all the years of my occult experience, I never met the like before, but once.

Vald. (*aside to* Dart.) What does he mean? Ask him, man.

Dart. You never met the like but once! What mean you, Father?

Bar. (*awswers not, but continues to look at them, while* Vald., *unable to bear it longer, shrinks again behind* Dart.) Shrink not back, young man; my eyes make not the fate they see, and cannot do you harm.—'Tis wonderful! there is not in your two faces one trait of resemblance, yet your fortunes in the self-same mould are cast: ye are in fate twin-brothers.

Dart. Indeed! then my friend need only listen to my fortune, and he'll have his own into the bargain.

Bar. Nay, nay, my Sons, be advised, and enquire not into futurity. They are the happiest men who have fewest dealings with such miserable beings as myself—beings who are compelled to know the impending evils of hapless humanity, without the power of averting them. Be advised, and suppress unprofitable curiosity.

Dart. By my fay, sage, I cannot suppress it.

Bar. Then let your friend go. He is wise enough not to wish to know his future fate, and I have already said you are in this twin-brothers.

Dart. Retire then, Valdemere.

Vald. (*agitated and irresolute.*) I had better, perhaps.—Yet there is within me a strange and perverse craving—I will retire (*going to the door, and stopping short.*)—Live in fearful ignorance, fancying evils that may never be! 'twere better to know all at once. (*Returning.*) Is it our general fortunes only, or is there some particular circumstance of our fate, now present to your mind, of which you advise us to be ignorant?

Bar. There is —

Vald. (*pulling* Dart. *by the arm.*) Come away, come away; don't hear it.

Dart. I am bound by some spell; I must stay to hear it.

Vald. I am certainly bound also; I know not how it is; I must hear it too.

Bar. Be it as you will. (*After writing characters on a table, with other mummeries.*) Propose your questions.

Dart. The name, age, and quality of her who is my love! (Bar. *writes again.*) The initials of her name, I protest; and her age to a day, nineteen years and a half! And her quality, good Father?

Bar. Only daughter and heiress of an eminent Dutch butter-dealer.

Dart. Nay, you are scarcely right there, sage; you might at least have called him Burgo-master; but let it pass. She loves me, I hope? (Bar. *nods.*) I knew it. And now let me know if she shall ever be my wife, and how many children we shall have?

Vald. (*aside to* Dart.) Deuce take wife and children too! what is all this drivelling for?

Dart. (*aside to him.*) I thought you were in love as well as myself.

Vald. So I am; but be satisfied that she loves you, and pass on to things of deeper import.

Dart. (*aside.*) Can any thing be of deeper import? (*Aloud.*) I should like very well, gifted Father, to have two or three black-haired burly knaves, and a little fair damsel, to play with.

Vald. (*aside to* Dart.) Would they were all drowned in a horse-pond! Look how ruefully the sage shakes his head at thee: wife or children thou wilt never have.

Dart. Shall I never be married, Father? what shall prevent it?

Bar. Death.

Dart. Shall I lose her? (*Turning to* Vald.) Do you not tremble for Livia?

Vald. Is it her death? did he say so? Ask him.

Bar. Death will prevent it. Let me leave you.

Vald. (*seizing the* Baron's *robe.*) Whose death? whose death? is it only the lady's?

Bar. Nay, do not detain me. There is a deep depression on my mind. Good night to you! I'll tell you the remainder when you are better prepared to hear it.

Dart. No, no! the present time is the best.

Vald. (*in a feeble voice.*) You had better let him go.

Dart. (*catching hold of the* Bar.) You must not leave us in this tremendous uncertainty. Whose death shall prevent my marriage?

Bar. Let me examine, then. Stretch out your hand. (Dartz *holds out his hand, and* Vald. *involuntarily does the same, but draws it back again as* Bar. *begins to inspect it.*) Nay, don't draw back your hand: I must examine both palms to see if the line of death be there.

Dart. The line of death must be on every man's hand.

Bar. But if it be early or impending death, the waving of the shroud will lie across it. (Vald. *shudders and turns away his head, and the* Bar., *after looking at both their hands, starts back from them, and shakes his head piteously.*)

Dart. What is the matter, Father? What is the matter?

Bar. Ask not; I will not tell what I know; nothing shall compel me. [Exit *hastily.*

Vald. (*turning round.*) Is he gone? Went he by the door?

Dart. What way he went I know not. He has vanished I believe: did you hear his steps on the floor?

Vald. I heard nothing.

Dart. (*after a short pause.*) How do you feel, Count?

Vald. Ha! do you feel it too?

Dart. Feel what?

Vald. As if a cold shroud were drawn over you.

Dart. Aye, so I think I do.—But never mind it: we may still have some good months or weeks before us; let us go to the banquet and put a merry face upon it: a cup of wine will warm us again. What, though my grandam dreamt at my birth that I should be slain in a breach, and the weird witch of Croningberg confirmed it; I'll live and be merry while I may.

Vald. Ha! and thy grandam had such a dream!

Dart. Never mind it: a cup of wine will soon cheer us again.

Vald. Would to God I had one now!

Dart. You have no time to take wine at present: I hear a bustle below: they are going to the grotto already.—Who's at the door? (*Opens the door.*) Your valet with your new suit for the banquet. I'll leave you then. (Exit Dartz, *and enter* Lorimore *with a suit of cloaths over his arm, followed by* Page.)

Lor. I have waited this half hour, my Lord, to hear your bell, and the ladies are waiting for you to go to the grotto. Look at this coat, my Lord: the fashion of it is exquisite, and it has such an air with it; there is not, besides yourself, a man in the empire that would know how to wear it.

Page. His consummate valet excepted.

Lor. Hold your peace, Sirrah. — Look here, my Lord; if I had not myself given the tailor a few hints, he could never have had genius enough to finish it in this style. I'd give a ducat that the Marquis De Florimel's valet could see it. He pretends — But you don't look at it, my Lord: what is the matter with you?

Vald. (*eagerly.*) Is any thing the matter?

Lor. Nothing, my Lord; but the ladies are waiting for you to go with them to the grotto: won't you be pleased to put on your new coat?

Vald. Put it on then. (*Stretching out his arms to put on the coat.*)

Lor. But we must first take off the old coat.

Vald. I forgot that. (*Trying to pull off his coat.*) It sticks strangely to me: doff it if thou can'st.

Lor. (*after pulling off his coat.*) Now, my Lord, thrust your arm into this beautiful sleeve; the whole *beau monde* of Paris can't shew you its fellow. — That is the wrong arm, my Lord.

Vald. It will do; it will do.

Lor. Pardon me, my Lord; your left arm won't do for the right sleeve of the coat.

Vald. (*holding out his other arm and fumbling some time.*) There is no hole at all to put my arm into.

Lor. Nay, you push your hand past it; here, here.

Vald. Where sayest thou? 'Tis mightily perplexed.

Page. (*aside to himself.*) Either the coat or the coat's master is perplexed enough. (*Aloud, offering him his hat.*) You won't go, my Lord, without your new hat and plume.

Vald. Plume?

Page. Yes, my Lord, and it will wave so handsomely too, for the company walk by torch-light in procession.

Vald. Let them move on, and I'll follow.

Page. No, they can't go without you, my Lord.

Vald. How is it? Am I one of the pall-bearers?

Page. It is not a funeral, my Lord.

Vald. I forgot; the chillness of the night has bewildered me.

Lor. You are not well, my Lord; what is the matter with you?

Vald. Nothing, leave me alone for a little.

Lor. Will you not join the company? The procession is prepared to set out.

Vald. Aye, very true; tell me when they move the body, and I'll follow it.

Page. He, he, he! a funeral again.

Lor. Unmannerly imp; what art thou snickering at? (*To* Vald. *in a loud distinct voice.*) It is not a funeral, my Lord. The Lady Livia, and the Countess your mother, are going to the grotto, and are waiting impatiently below till you join them.

Vald. (*rubbing his forehead.*) It is so: how went it out of my head? That wine after dinner must have fuddled me. I'll join them immediately.

Lor. Lean on me, my Lord; you are not well, I fear.

Vald. No, no; the fumes of that diabolical champaign have left my head now.

Lor. It must have been mixed with some black drug, I think, to produce such a sombre intoxication.

Page. It may rest in the cellar long enough for me; I'll none on't.

Lor. Peace, young Sir; and go before with one of these lights.

[EXEUNT, Page *lighting them.*

SCENE II.

An arched Grotto, the Roof and Sides of which are crusted over with Shells and Corals, &c.; a Banquet set out, ornamented with Lamps and Festoons of Flowers. Enter Countess, *led in by* DARTZ, *and* LIVIA *by* VALDEMERE, *two other Ladies by the* Baron *and* WALTER BAURCHEL, Page *and* Attendants *following.*

Liv. Welcome all to my sea-nymph's hall; and do me the honour to place yourselves at table, as best pleases your fancy, without ceremony. If you hear any sound without, 'tis but the rolling of forty fathom water over-head; and nothing can intrude on our merriment, but a whale, or a mermaid, or a dolphin.

Walt. This same sea-nymph must have an ingenious art of cultivating roses in the bottom of the ocean.

Liv. It must be a perfect contrivance indeed that escapes the correct taste of Mr. Walter Baurchel. Fruit and ices perhaps may likewise be an incongruity: shall I order them away, and feast you on salt water and limpits?

Bar. Aye, pickle him up with brine in a corner by himself, for he has a secret sympathy with every thing uncherishing and pungent.

Liv. Do me the honour to take your places. I can pretty well divine which of the ladies will be your charge, gentle Baron. — But how is this? The Countess and you exchange strange looks, methinks, as if you did not know one another.

Bar. Some people exchange strange looks, fair Livia, from the opposite cause.

Liv. I don't comprehend you: should you have preferred being in masks? That indeed would have been a less common amusement.

Bar. By no means, Madam; the Countess and I meeting one another unmasked is a very uncommon one.

Countess. You know best, Baron, as far as you

are yourself concerned: you always appeared to me a good and amiable man, and a most tender and elegant poet.

Bar. Of which, Madam, you always took great care to inform me, as a sincere and disinterested friend.

Liv. Ha! what is all this? Poo, poo, take your places together as usual: a love-quarrel never mars merry-making.

Walt. Yes, tender doves! let them smooth down their ruffled feathers by one another as sweetly as they can. Why should you, Madam, give yourself any uneasiness about it? — But the Count, methinks, is less sprightly than usual: there are no more love-quarrels, I hope, in the party.

Liv. (*looking at* Vald.) Indeed you are very silent: I have been too much occupied to observe it before. You don't like my grotto, I fear.

Vald. Pardon me; I like it very well; I like it very much.

Liv. But this is not your usual manner of expressing approbation.

Vald. Is it not? you do me honour to remember it. (*Speaking confusedly as the company sit down to table.*) My spirits are very — that is to say, not altogether, but considerably —

Dart. Low, Valdemere?

Vald. (*snatching up a glass, and filling a bumper of wine, which he swallows hastily.*) No, Dartz; light as a feather. My tongue was so confoundedly parched: this wine is excellent (*drinking another bumper.*) There is more beauty in these decorations than I was aware of: the effect, the taste is incomparable. (*Drinks again.*) It is truly exquisite.

Walt. The champaign you mean, Count? I should have guessed as much.

Vald. No, no; the decorations.—Is it champaign? Let me judge of its flavour more considerately (*drinks again*): upon honour it is fit for the table of a god. But our hostess *is* a divinity, and 'tis nectar we quaff at her board.— Wine! common earthly wine! I'll thrust any man thro' with my rapier that says it is but wine.

Bar. Keep your courage for a better cause, Count. Report says the enemy are near us, and you may soon have the honour to exert it in defence of your divinity.

Walt. Which will be a sacred war, you know, and will entitle you perhaps to the glory of martyrdom.

Vald. The enemy?

Walt. Aye, report says they are near us.

Vald. Be it so: I shall be prepared for them (*drinks again*).

Dart. (*aside to* Walt.) By my faith, he will be prepared for them, for he'll fill himself mortal drunk, and frustrate our project entirely. (*Aside to* Page.) Go, boy, and bid them make haste: thou understandest me?

Page. (*aside.*) Trust me for that: the Philistines shall be upon him immediately.

Countess. Valdemere is immeasurably fond of war and of military glory, which the tenderness of a too fearful mother has hitherto with difficulty restrained; and in your cause, charming Livia, he will be enthusiastically devoted.

Liv. I claim him then as my Knight, whene'er I stand in need of his valorous arms; though it may, perhaps, prove but a troublesome honour.

Vald. It is an honour I would purchase — aye, purchase with a thousand lives —— I say it, divine Livia, with a thousand lives. —— Life! — life! —What is it but the breath of a moment: I scorn it. (*Getting up from table, and reeling about.*) The enemy, did they say? Let an host of them come: this sword shall devour every mother's son of them. — I'm prepared for them all.

Bar. (*aside to* Dart.) He is too well prepared; we were foolish to let him drink so much.

Countess. (*aside to* Vald.) Be seated again, you disturb the company.

Vald. (*still reeling about.*) Aye, divine Livia; but the breath of a moment; I scorn it.

(*An alarm without: re-enter* Page, *as if much frightened.*)

Page. O my Lady Livia! O my master! O gentles all! a party of the enemy is coming to attack the castle, and they'll murder every soul of us.

Vald. Speak plainer, wretch; what said'st thou?

Page. (*speaking loud in his ear.*) The enemy are coming to attack the castle.

Vald. Thou liest.

Page. I wish I did; but he will confirm my words.

(*Pointing to a* Servant, *who now enters in alarm.*)

Ser. (*to* Vald.) He speaks truth, my Lord! they are approaching in great strength.

Vald. Approaching! are they near us then?

Page. Aye, marry! too near. They beat no drum, as you may guess; but the heavy sound of their march strikes from the hollow ground most fearfully.

(Valdemere *becoming perfectly sober, stands confounded.*)

Liv. (*and the* Ladies, *much alarmed.*) What shall we do? What will become of us?

Dart. Have courage, Madam; have courage, Ladies; the valiant Valdemere is your defender; you have nothing to fear.

Liv. (*and* Ladies, *crowding close to* Vald.) Aye, dear Count; our safety depends on you. Save us! Save us! We have no refuge but you. (*All clamouring at once.*)

Vald. Hush, hush, hush! They'll hear you. (*In a low choked voice.*)

Dart. Nay, don't whisper, Valdemere; they are not so near us yet.

Bar. Rouse ye, Count, and give your orders for the defence of the castle immediately.

Dart. We are ready to execute them, be they ever so daring.

Walt. There is no time to be lost; your orders, Count: do you comprehend us?

Vald. My orders!

Dart. Your orders quickly.

Vald. I am thinking —— I was thinking——

Page. (*aside.*) How to save yourself, I believe.

Bar. Well, noble Count, what are your thoughts.

Vald. I — I — I am considering ——

Walt. Thought and consideration become a good Commander, with some spice of activity into the bargain.

Dart. There is no time to deliberate; issue your orders immediately. Under such an able commander we may stand a siege of some days.

Vald. A siege! — Aye, the very thing — and so suddenly!

Page. You tremble, my Lord; shall I bring you drops?

Countess. Thou liest, Boy; get thee gone! (*Aside to* Vald.) Are you beside yourself? Tell them what to do; they wait for your orders.

Vald. I order them all to the walls. Haste, haste, (*pushing off the* Ladies *who stand next him,*) and man them as well as you can.

Bar. Woman them, you mean, Valdemere; these are Ladies you push.

Countess. Nay; you crowd upon him too much — you confuse him: he is as brave as his sword, if you would leave off confounding him so.

Liv. Dear Valdemere! What is the matter? Rouse yourself, rouse yourself! (*A great alarm without.*) Hear that sound: they are at hand; what shall we do? There is a vault by the side of this grotto, where we poor miserable women may be concealed, but ——

Vald. (*eagerly.*) Where is it? My duty is to take care of you, dear Livia: come, come with me, and I'll place you in security. (*Catches hold of the* Page *in his hurry, and runs off with him.*)

Countess. Stop, stop! That is the Page you have got. Will you leave me behind you?

(*As* Vald. *is about to drag the* Page *into a recess at the side of the stage, the* Boy *laughs outright, and he discovers his mistake.*)

Vald. Off, Wretch! Where is Livia; come, come, my Life! where are you? (*Stretching out one hand to her, while his body bends eagerly the other way.*)

Liv. No, Count; I will not go. Alarm overcame me for the moment; but now I will enter the castle; and if the enemy should take it, they shall find me there in a situation becoming its mistress.

Omnes. Bravely said, Lady! Let us all to the castle.

Dart. With or without a commander, we'll defend it to the last extremity.

Countess. (*going to* Vald. *and speaking in his ear, while she pulls him along with her.*) Come with the rest, or be disgraced for ever. Did I put a sword by your side, a cockade in your hat, for this?

(*A still louder alarm without, and* EXEUNT *in great hurry and confusion.*)

SCENE III.

A Grove by the Castle; the Scene darkened, and moving Lights seen through the Trees from the Castle, sometimes gleaming from the Battlements, and sometimes from the Windows: Enter NINA, *with a Peasant's Surtout over her Dress.*

Nin. O, if in this disguise I could but enter the castle! Alas! the company are gone in, and the gate is now shut. I'll wait here till day-break.—Woe is me! He past by me quickly, and heard me not when I spoke to him.——O mercy! Soldiers coming here! (*Hides herself amongst some bushes.*)

Enter BOUNCE, *followed by* Soldiers.

Bounce. Come, let us hector it here awhile: I'll warrant ye we make a noise that might do for the siege of Troy.

1*st Soldier.* Aye, you're a book-learned man, Corporal: you're always talking of that there siege. Could they throw a bomb in those days, or fire off an eighteen-pounder any better than ourselves? (*Firing heard without.*)

Bounce. Hark! our comrades are at it on the other side: let us to it here at the same time. I'll warrant ye we'll make the fair Lady within, and my Lady's fair gentlewomen, and the village Cure himself, should he be of the party, cast up their eyes like boiled fish, and say ten pater-nosters in a breath.

(*Voices without.*)

Hallo! hallo! comrades!

Who goes there?

Enter 2d Soldier *and others.*

2d Sold. What makes you so quiet, an' be hanged to you! An old woman with her spinning-wheel might be stationed here to as much purpose. I could not tell where to find you.

Bounce. By my faith, 'tis the first time Corporal Bounce was ever accused of not making noise enough. Come; we'll give you a round shall make the whole principality tremble.

(*They prepare to fire, when 3d* Soldier *enters in haste.*)

3d Sold. Hold, there! Spare your powder for better purpose: an advanced corps of the enemy is coming in good earnest, and marching in haste to the castle.

Bounce. So, we're to have real fighting then! Faith, comrade, valiant as I am, a little sham thunder, and a good supper after it, would have pleased my humour full as well at this present time. Pest take it! They must open the gates and let us in. What gentlemen are in the castle? We have no officer to command us.

3d Sold. The Chevalier Dartz is there, and Count Valdemere.

Bounce. Ah! he's but a craven-bird, that same Count: a kind of Free-mason-soldier, for parades and processions, and the like. If the young Baron de Bertrand were there, we should be nobly commanded.

3d Sold. Don't stand prating here; let us give the alarm to the rest of our comrades, and get into the castle ere the enemy come up with us.

Bounce. Come, then! But what moves amongst the bushes? (*Pulling out* Nina.) A girl, i'faith, disguised in a countryman's surtout.

Nin. O dear — O mercy! Don't be angry with me: I'm a poor harmless creature.

Bounce. Blessings on thee, pretty one! thou'rt harmless enough: don't think we're afraid of thee. Come away with us: we'll lodge thee safely in the castle.

[Exeunt.

ACT V.

SCENE I. — *A Hall in the Castle: Enter* LIVIA *and the* Baron, *talking as they enter.*

Liv. Yes, Baron; you and your friends have, by this plot of yours, taught me a severe lesson; and I thank you for it, though my own understanding ought to have made it unnecessary.

Bar. Dear Livia; why should a young woman like you be so much affronted at finding her understanding—for you are mighty fond of that word *understanding*—not quite infallible? At the age of 63, an age I shall henceforth honestly own I have attained, one is not surprised at some small deficiencies even in one's own understanding. One can then, as I shall henceforth do, give up the vanity of being a wise man.

Liv. And a poet, too, Baron? That were too much to give up in one day.

Bar. Posterity will settle that point, Madam, and I shall give myself very little concern about the matter.

Liv. Which one can easily perceive is perfectly indifferent to you. (*Noise without.*) What encreased noise is that? Since your poor victim is already sacrificed, (for they tell me he is gone, on pretence of violent illness, to the vaults under the castle,) why continue this mock-war any longer?

Enter Servant.

Bar. By this man's looks one might suppose that our mockery had turned to earnest.

Liv. (*to* Serv.) What is the matter?

Serv. A party of the real enemy, Madam, *has* come to attack the castle, and is now fighting with the Chevalier's men at the gate.

Liv. Why did you not open the gate to receive the Chevalier's men?

Serv. They called to us to get in; but we could not distinguish them from the enemy, who were close on their heels; so we let down the portcullis, an't please you, and they must fight it out under the walls as they can.

Bar. Is the Chevalier in the castle?

Serv. O lud, no, Sir! he sallied out by the postern with Mr. Walter Baurchel and some of the domestics, and is fighting with them like a devil. But his numbers are so small, we fear he must be beaten; and ——

Liv. And how can we hold out with neither men, ammunition, nor provisions. Merciful Heaven deliver us!

Enter Maid-Servants, *wringing their hands.*

Maids. O lud, lud! What will become of us? What will become of us? What shall we do?

Bar. Any thing you please but stun us with such frantic clamour. Get off to your laundries and your store-rooms, and your dressing closets, and don't encrease the confusion here.

(EXEUNT Maids, *clamouring and wringing their hands.*)

Liv. You are rough with those poor creatures; they are very much frightened.

Bar. Not half so frightened as those who make less noise. They think it necessary to raise an out-cry, because they are women, and it is expected from them. I have been long enough duped in this way; I have no patience with it now. — But I must go to the walls and try to be of use. (*going.*)

(*Voice without.*) Succour! succour!

Liv. Ha! there is a welcome cry.

Enter JEANETTA.

Succour did they say?

Jean. Yes, my lady: a band of men come to relieve us; and their leader is charging the enemy so furiously sword in hand! — the Chevalier, they said, fought like a devil; but he fights like forty devils. We have been looking down upon them by torch-light from the walls; and their swords flash, and their plumes nod, and their eyes glare in the light so gallantly, I could almost sally out myself and take a bout with them.

Bar. (*to* Jean.) Aye, Minx; thou'rt forward enough to do any thing.

Liv. Nay, chide her not when she brings us good news.— Heaven be praised for this timely aid! What brave man has brought it to us? Dost thou know him, Jeanetta?

Jean. No, Madam: for, thank God! his back is to us and his face to the foe; but there is a smack in his air of the Baron de Bertrand.

Bar. Ha! my brave Antonio! I'll be sworn it is he. Come; let us to the ramparts, and look down on the combatants.

Liv. Heaven grant there be not much bloodshed! [EXEUNT.

SCENE II.

A dark Vault: Enter VALDEMERE, *followed by* Page, *carrying a torch in one hand, and his plumed Cap in the other.*

Vald. (*after hurrying some paces onward, stops short, and looks wildly round him.*) Is there no passage this way?

Page. No, my Lord; but you run marvellously fast for one so ill as you are; I could scarcely keep up with you: pray stop here awhile and take breath.

Vald. Stop here, and that sound still behind me!

Page. What sound?

Vald. Did'st thou not hear the tread of heavy steps behind us? The trampling of a whole band?

Page. It was but the sound of my feet following you.

Vald. Only that. The castle is taken thou say'st, and the ruffians are in quest of me.

Page. Aye, marry are they! Their savage leader says, as the old tale book has it, that he'll have the heart's blood of Count Valdemere on his sword before he eat or sleep.

Vald. His sword!

Page. Aye, my Lord, a good heavy rapier, I assure you; and he swears, since you have not fought like a man on the walls, he'll kill you like a rat in your hole.

Vald. I am horribly beset!

Page. Aye, hot work, my Lord; the big drops fall from your forehead, like a thunder shower.

Vald. Thou liest; I am cold as the damp of a sepulchre.

Page. And pale too, as the thing that lies within it.

Vald. (*listening.*) Hark, hark! they are coming.

Page. I hear nothing.

Vald. Thou dost! thou dost! lying varlet, with that treacherous leer upon thy face: thou hast decoyed me here for destruction. (*Catching him by the throat.*)

Page. For mercy, my Lord, let go your hold! I hear nothing, as I hope to be saved, but our own voices sounding again from the vaulted roof over our heads.

Vald. Aye, it is vaulted; thou'rt right perhaps. — This strange ringing in my ears will not suffer me to know the sounds that really are, from those are not. — Why dost thou grin so? I have a frenzy, I believe; I know I am strangely disordered. It was not so with me yesterday. I could then —— Dost thou grin still? Stand some paces off: why art thou always so near me?

Page. (*retiring to the opposite side of the stage.*) I had best, perhaps: his hand has the gripe of a madman.

Vald. (*leans his back against the side-scene, pressing his temples tightly with both hands, and speaking low to himself.*) This horrible tumult of nature! it knows within itself the moments that precede its destruction.

Page. I must let him rest for a time. (*Pause.*) — It is cold here doing nothing. (*Puts on his cap.*) — He moves not: his eyes have a fixed ghastly stare; truly he is ill. (*Going up to him.*) You are very ill, my Lord.

Vald. (*starting.*) Have mercy upon me!

Page. Don't start, my Lord; it was I who spoke to you.

Vald. Who art thou?

Page. Your Page, my Lord.

Vald. Ha! only thou! thy stature seemed gigantic.

Page. This half-yard of plume in my cap, and your good fancy, have made it so.

Vald. Aye; thou wert unbonnetted before. Keep by me then, but don't speak to me. (*Putting his hand again to his temples.*)

Page. Nay, I must ask what is the matter. You are very ill: what is the matter with you?

Vald. There is a beating within me like the pendulum of a great clock.

Page. Is it in your heart or your head, my Lord?

Vald. Don't speak to me: it is every where.

Page. Rest here a while; they will not discover you. You are indeed very ill.—Are you worse?

Vald. Speak not; my mouth is parched like a cinder; I can't answer thee.

Page. I'll fetch you some water. (*Going.*)

Vald. (*springing across the stage after him.*) Not for the universe.

Page. (*aside.*) He's strong enough still I see. (*Turning his ear to the entry of the vault.*)

Vald. Thou'rt listening; thou hear'st something.

Page. By my faith, they are coming now.

Vald. Merciful heaven! where shall I run?

Page. Where you please, my Lord.

Vald. (*hurrying two or three steps on, in a kind of groping way.*) The light fails me: I don't see where I am going.

Page. Nay, it burns very clearly; I fear it will discover where we are.

Vald. Put it out! put it out, for God's sake!

— Where is it? (*Seizes on the torch, puts it out, stamping on it with his feet, then laying himself on the floor.*) I am gone — I am dead; tell them so, for God's sake!

Page. I shall tell but half a lie when I do.

Enter Baron *and* WALTER BAURCHEL, *with Soldier's Cloaks thrown over them, and* LIVIA *in the same Disguise with a military Cap drawn over her Eyes, a* Servant *preceding them with Torches.*

Liv. (*shrinking back as she enters.*) Is he dead?

(Page *nods, and winks to her significantly.*)

Bar. (*in a rough voice.*) Has the caitiff escaped my sword? Have I thirsted for his blood in vain?

Walt. (*in a rough voice also.*) Is he really dead? I'll lay my hand on his breast, and feel if his heart beats.

Page. O don't do that, gracious, merciful Sir! You'll but defile your worshipful fingers in touching of a dead corse, which brings bad luck with it.

Walt. Well then, Boy, I will not; but there are a couple of brawny knaves without, who are burying the dead for us; they shall come forthwith, and cast him into the pit with the rest.

Page. O lud, no, Sir! don't do that, please your worshipful goodness! What if he should come alive again?

Walt. Never fear that: I'll draw this rapier cross his laced cravat, and make it secure.

Vald. (*starting up upon his knees.*) Mercy,

mercy! slay not a dying man; let me breathe my last breath without violence.

Liv. (*covering her eyes, and turning away her head.*) Torment him no more, I beseech you!

Enter Antonio, *and* Dartz *with his arm bound up.*

Ant. Nay, Gentlemen, this is unfeeling, ungenerous, unmanly. Stand upon your feet, Count Valdermere, (*raising him up,*) there are none but friends near you, if friends they may be called, who have played you such an abominable trick.

Vald. How is this? Art thou Antonio? Where are those who would have butcher'd me?

Omnes, Liv. and *Ant. excepted.* Ha, ha, ha! (*laughing some time.*)

Bar. No where, Valdemere, but in your own imagination. We have put this deceit upon you to cure you of arrogance and boasting.

Walt. Running the usual risk, gentle Count, of not having our services very thankfully acknowledged.

Vald. You have laid a diabolical snare for me, and I have fallen into it most wretchedly.—I have been strangely overcome. I have been moved as with magic.—I have been ——I— I know not—What shall I call it?

Walt. Give yourself no trouble about that, Count; we can find a name for it.

Ant. Nay, good Sir; you shall not call it by any name a man would be asham—— (*correct-*

ing himself.) unwilling to hear. The Count, as Dartz has informed me, while I bound up his wound above stairs, has been tampered with, by dreams and fortune-telling and other devices, in a way that might have overcome many a man, who, differently circumstanced, would not have shrunk from his duty in the field. And shall we sport wantonly with a weakness of our nature in some degree common to all? We admire a brave man for overcoming it, and should pity the less brave when it overcomes him.

Liv. (*catching his hand eagerly.*) Noble Antonio!

Ant. Young man, I thank you: this squeeze of the hand tells me I have you upon my side.

Vald. And let me also say, "Noble Antonio!"—And what more can I say! I have not deserved this generous treatment from you.

Ant. Say nothing more: the transactions of this night shall be as if they had never been: they will never be mentioned by any of us.

Walt. Speak for yourself, Antonio de Bertrand; my tongue is a free agent, and will not be bridled by another person's feelings. But there is one condition on which I consent to be silent as the grave; and the Baron and Chevalier concur with me.

Bar. and *Dartz.* We do so.

[Exit Bar.

Dart. We but require of Valdemere to do what, as a man of honour he is bound to do; and satisfied on this point, our silence is secured for ever.

Re-enter BARON *leading in* NINA.

Bar. (*to* Vald.) Look on this fair gentlewoman: her father was a respectable officer, though misfortunes prevented his promotion. You have taken advantage of her situation, being under the protection of the Countess your mother, as a god-daughter and distant relation, to use her most unworthily. Make her your wife, and receive, as her dowry, your reputation in the world untarnished.

Walt. Now, good, heroic, sentimental Antonio; is this too much to require of the noble personage you plead for?

Ant. On this I am compelled to be silent.

Bar. Will Count Valdemere vouchsafe us an answer? Will you marry her or not, Count?

Vald. I have indeed—I ought in strict justice——She will not accept of one who has used her so unworthily.

Page. (*eagerly.*) I hope not: I would rather than a thousand crowns she would refuse him.

Dart. Will you have him or not, pretty Nina? Don't be afraid to refuse him: we shan't think the worse of you if you do. (Nina *stands silent and weeping.*)

Page. (*aside to* Nina.) Don't have him, woman; he's a coward and a coxcomb, and a—— don't have him.

Nina. (*aside.*) Ah, you have never loved him as I have done, Brother.

Page. (*aloud.*) Murrain take thee and thy love too! thou hast no more spirit in thee than a worm.

Bar. Bravo, Boy! thou hast enough of it, I see; and I'll put a stand of colours into thy hand as soon as thou art strong enough to carry them. Thou art my boy now; I will protect thee.

Page. I thank you, Baron. — And my sister; will you protect her too?

Bar. Yes, Child; both of you.

Page. Refuse him then, Nina: hast thou no more pride about thee?

Nina. Alas! I should have more pride: I know I should; but I have been sadly humbled.

Page. Thou'lt be still more so if thou art his wife, trust me! for he'll despise thee, and cow thee, and make thee a poor slave to his will. Thou'lt tremble at every glance of his eye, and every turn of his humoursome fancy. — He'll treat thee like a very ——

Vald. Stop, spiteful wretch! I'll cherish and protect her, and turn every word thou hast uttered to a manifest and abominable falsehood. — Give me thy hand, Nina; thou really lovest me; no one will do it but thee; and I shall have need of somebody to love me.

Omnes. Well said, Count! this is done like a man!

Ant. (*to* Page.) Faith, Boy! those sharp words of thine were worth a store of gentle persuasion. Thou hast woo'd for thy sister in a spell-like fashion as witches say their prayers backwards.

I wish somebody would court my mistress for me in the same manner: 'tis the only chance I have of winning her.

Liv. (*in a feigned voice.*) I'll do that for thee, gallant De Bertand; for I know faults enough of yours to acquaint her with, besides the greatest of all faults, concealing good talents *under a bushel;* every tittle of which I will tell her forthwith, and she'll marry you, no doubt, out of spite.

Ant. Thanks, pleasant stripling! May thy success be equal to thy zeal! (*taking her hand.*) Thy name, youth? thou hast a pretty gait in that warlike cloak of thine, but thy cap overshadows thee perversely.—Ha! this is not a boy's hand!—That ring—O Heavens!

(*Retires some paces back in confusion, while* Livia, *taking off her cap and cloak, makes him a profound curtesy; and pauses, expecting him to speak. Finding him silent, she begins to rub her hand, and look at it affectedly.*)

Liv. It is not a boy's hand, Baron de Bertrand: 'tis the hand of a weak foolish woman, which shall be given to a lover of hers who is not much wiser than herself, whenever he has courage to ask it.

Walt. (*aside, jogging* Ant.) That is thyself: dost thou not apprehend her, man?

Liv. (*still looking at her hand.*) Even so; whenever he has courage to ask it. That, I suppose, may happen in about five or six years from this present time.

Ant. (*running up to her, catching her hand, and putting his knee to the ground.*) Now, now, dear Livia! O that I could utter what I feel! — I am a fool still; — I cannot.

Liv. Nothing you can possibly say will make me more sensible of your generous worth, or more ashamed of my former injustice to it.

(*All crowd round* Ant. *and* Liv. *to congratulate them, when the* Countess *is heard speaking angrily without.*)

Dart. We must pay our compliments another time; I fear there is a storm ready to burst upon us.

Enter Countess.

Countess. Yes, Gentlemen; I have heard of your plot, as you call it; a diabolical conspiracy for debasing the merit you envy. I despise you all: you are beneath my anger.

Walt. Let us escape it then.

Countess. (*to* Walt.) Aye, snarling Cynic! who hast always a prick of thy adder's tongue to bestow upon every one whom the world admires or caresses; thou are the wicked mover of all these contrivances. (*To the* Bar.) As for you, poor antiquated *rhime-maker!* had I but continued to praise your verses, you would have suffered me to ruin your whole kindred very quietly; nor had one single grain of compunction disturbed the sweet calm of your gratified vanity.

Bar. Nay, Madam; I cannot charge my memory with any interruption of your goodness, in this repect, to my face: had you been as perseveringly obliging behind my back, we might indeed have remained longer friends than would have been entirely for the interest of my heir.

Countess. Well, well; may every urchin of the principality learn by rote some scrap of your poetry, and mouth it at you as often as you stir abroad! (*To* Liv.) And you, Madam; you are here, too, amongst this worshipful divan! This is your hospitality — your delicacy — your —— O! may you wed a tyrant for your pains, and these walls prove your odious prison! — But I spend my words vainly: where is the unhappy victim of your envious malevolence? They told me he was here. (*Discovering* Vald. *and* Nina *retired to the bottom of the stage.*) Ha! you *are* here, patiently enduring their triumph, degenerate boy! Is this the fruit of all my cares? Did I procure for you a military appointment, did I tease every creature connected with me for your promotion, did I ruin myself for your extravagant martial equipments — and has it all come to this?

Vald. You put me into the army, Madam, to please your own vanity; and they who thrust their sons into it for that purpose, are not always gratified.

Countess. And you answer me thus! I have spoilt you, indeed; and an indulged child, I find, does not always prove a dutiful one. Who is that you hold by the hand?

Vald. My wife, Madam.

Countess. Your wife! You do not say so: you dare not say so. Have they imposed a wife upon you also? Let go her unworthy hand.

Vald. No, Madam; never. It is my hand that is unworthy to hold so much innocent affection.

Countess. You are distracted: let go her hand, or I renounce you for ever.—What, will you not?

Vald. I will not.

Countess. Thou can'st be sturdy, I find, only for thine own ruin. They have confounded and bewildered thee: thou hast joined the conspiracy against thyself, and thy poor mother.—O, I could hate thee more than them all!—Heaven grant me patience!

Walt. I like to hear people pray for what they really want.

Countess. Insolent! Heaven grant you what you need not pray for, the detestation of every one annoyed with your pestiferous society.

[Exit *in rage.*

Dart. Let us be thankful this tornado is over, and the hurry of an eventful day and night so happily concluded.—I hope, charming Livia, you forgive our deceit, and regret not its consequences.

Liv. The only thing to be regretted, Chevalier, is the wound you have received.

Dart. Thank God! this, though but slight, is the only harm that has been done to-night, a broken pate or two excepted; and our feigned attack upon the castle has been providentially the means of defending it from a real one. Had not Antonio, however, who was not in our plot, come so opportunely to our aid, we had been beaten. — But now that I have time to enquire, how did'st thou come so opportunely?

Ant. I have been in the habit of wandering after dark round the walls. Livia knows not how many nights I have watched the light gleaming from the window of her chamber. Wandering then, as usual, I discovered a corps of the enemy on their march to the castle, and went immediately for succour, which I fortunately found. We have both fought stoutly, my friend, with our little force; but the blows have fallen to your share, and the blessing to mine.

Dart. Not so; friends keep not their shares so distinctly.

Liv. True, Chevalier; and you claim, besides, whatever satisfaction you may have from the gratitude of this good company, for contriving a plot that has ended so fortunately.

Dart. Nay, there is, I fear, one person in this good company, from whom my claims, of this kind, are but small. — Count Valdemere, can you forgive me?

Vald. Ask me not at present, Dartz. I know that my conduct to Antonio did deserve correction; but you have taken a revenge for him with merciless severity, which he would himself have been too generous, too noble, to have taken.

Dart. Well, Count, I confess I stand somewhat reproved and conscience-stricken before you.

Walt. (*to* Dart.) Why, truly, if he forgive thee, or any of us, by this day twelve-month, it will be as much as we can reasonably expect.

Dart. Be it so! And now we have all pardon to ask, where, I hope, it will be granted immediately. (*Bowing to the audience.*)

THE END OF THE SIEGE.

THE BEACON:

A SERIOUS MUSICAL DRAMA,

IN TWO ACTS.

PERSONS OF THE DRAMA.

MEN.

ULRICK, *Lord of the Island.*
ERMINGARD.
BASTIANI, *Friend of* Ulrick.
GARCIO, *Friend of* Ermingard.
Page.
Pope's Legate.
Knights of St. John of Jerusalem.
Fishermen, Singers, Attendants of the Legate, &c.

WOMEN.

AURORA.
TERENTIA, *a noble Lady, and Governante to* Aurora.
VIOLA, EDDA, } *Ladies attending on* Aurora.

Scene, *a small Island of the Mediterranean.*

Time, *towards the middle of the* 14*th Century.*

THE BEACON.

ACT I.

SCENE I. — *A Grove adjoining to a castellated Building, part of which only is seen. Several People are discovered near the Window of one of its Towers, who begin to sing as the Curtain draws up.*

Song of several voices.

Up! quit thy bower, late wears the hour;
Long have the rooks caw'd round thy tower;
On flower and tree, loud hums the bee;
The wilding kid sports merrily:
A day so bright, so fresh, so clear,
Shineth when good fortune 's near.

Up! Lady fair, and braid thy hair,
And rouze thee in the breezy air;
The lulling stream, that sooth'd thy dream,
Is dancing in the sunny beam;
And hours so sweet, so bright, so gay,
Will waft good fortune on its way.

Up! time will tell; the friar's bell
Its service-sound hath chimed well;

The aged crone keeps house alone,
And reapers to the fields are gone;
The active day so boon and bright,
May bring good fortune ere the night.

Enter Page.

Page. Leave off your morning songs, they come too late;
My Lady hath been up these two good hours,
And hath no heart to listen to your lays!
You should have cheer'd her sooner.

1*st. Sing.* Her nightly vigils make the ev'ning morn.
And thus we reckon'd time.

Page. Well, go ye now;
Another day she'll hear your carols out.

(Exeunt Page *and* Singers *severally, by the bottom of the stage, while* Ulrick *and* Terentia *enter by the front, speaking as they enter.*)

Ul. Thou pleadest in vain: this night shall be the last.

Ter. Have patience, noble Ulrick; be assur'd,
Hope, lacking nourishment, if left alone,
Comes to a natural end. Then let Aurora,
Night after night, upon the lofty cliff,
Her beacon watch: despondency, ere long,
Will steal upon the sad unvaried task.

Ul. Sad and unvaried! Aye; to sober minds
So doth it seem indeed. I've seen a child,
Day after day, to his dead hedgeling bring
The wonted mess, prepared against its waking,

'Till from its putrid breast each feather dropt :
Or on the edge of a clear stream hold out
His rod and baitless line from morn till noon,
Eyeing the spotted trout, that past his snare
A thousand times hath glided, till by force
His angry Dame hath dragg'd him from his station.
Hope is of such a tough continuous nature,
That, waiting thus its natural end, my life
Shall to an end wear sadly. Patience, say'st thou!
I have too long been patient.

Ter. Then, be it known to thee, despondency
Already steals upon her ; for she sits not
So oft' as she was wont upon the beach,
But in her chamber keeps in sombre silence ;
And when the night is come, less eagerly
She now enquires if yet the beacon's light
Peer down the woody pass, that to the cliff
Nightly conducts her toilsome steps. I guess,
Soon of her own accord she'll watch no more.

Ul. No, thou unwisely guessest. By that flame
I do believe some spirit of the night
Comes to her mystic call, and soothes her ear
With whisper'd prophecies of good to come.

Ter. In truth my Lord, you do yourself talk strangely ;
These are wild thoughts.

Ul. Nay, be thou well assur'd,
Spell-bound she is : night hath become her day :

On all wild songs, and sounds, and ominous things,
(Shunning the sober intercourse of friends
Such as affliction courts,) her ear and fancy
Do solely dwell. This visionary state
Is foster'd by these nightly watchings; therefore,
I say again, I will no more endure it;
This night shall be the last.

Ter. That Ermingard upon the plains of Palestine
Fell on that fatal day, what sober mind
Can truly doubt; altho' his corpse, defaced,
Or hid by other slain, was ne'er discover'd.
For, well I am assured, had he survived it,
Knowing thou wer't his rival, and Aurora
Left in this isle, where thou bear'st sov'reign sway,
He, with a lover's speed, had hasten'd back.
All, whom the havoc of the battle spared,
Have to their homes return'd. —— Thou shak'st thy head,
Thou dost not doubt?

Ul. We'll speak of this no more.
I'm sick and weary of these calculations.
We must and will consider him as dead;
And let Aurora know ——

Enter BASTIANI.

(*To* Bast. *angrily.*) Why, Bastiani,
Intrud'st thou thus, regardless of my state:

These petty cares are grown most irksome to me;
I cannot hear thee now.
Bast. Indeed, my Lord, it is no petty care
Compels me to intrude. Within your port
A vessel from the holy land has moor'd.
Ul. (*starting.*) Warriors from Palestine?
Bast. No, good my Lord!
The holy legate on his way to Rome;
Who, by late tempests driven on our coasts,
Means here his shatter'd pinnace to refit,
And give refreshment to his weary train.
Ul. In evil hour he comes to lord it here.
Bast. He doth appear a meek and peaceful man.
Ul. 'Tis seeming all. I would with mailed foes
Far rather in th' embattled plain contend
Than strive with such my peaceful town within.
Already landed say'st thou?
Bast. Yes, from the beach their grave procession comes.
Between our gazing sight and the bright deep,
That glows behind them in the western sun,
Crosses and spears and croziers shew aloft
Their darken'd spikes, in most distinct confusion;
While grey-cowl'd monks, and purple-stoled priests,
And crested chiefs a closing group below,
Motley and garish, yet right solemn too,
Move slowly on.—
Ul. Then must I haste to meet them.

Bast. Or be most strangely wanting in respect.
For every street and alley of your city
Its eager swarm pours forth to gaze upon them:
The very sick and dying, whose wan cheeks
No more did think to meet the breath of heaven,
Creep to their doors, and stretch their wither'd arms
To catch a benediction. Blushing maids,
Made bold by inward sense of sanctity,
Come forth with threaded rosaries in their hands
To have them by the holy prelate bless'd;
And mothers hold their wond'ring infants up,
That touch of passing cowl or sacred robe
May bring them good. And in fair truth, my Lord,
Amongst the crowd the rev'rend legate seems
Like a right noble and right gentle parent
Cheering a helpless race.

Ul. Aye, 'tis right plain thou art besotted too.
Were he less gentle I should fear him less.

[Exit.

Bast. He's in a blessed mood: what so disturbs him?

Ter. What has disturb'd him long, as well thou knowest:
Aurora's persevering fond belief
That her beloved Ermingard still lives,
And will return again. To guide his bark
Upon our dang'rous coast, she nightly kindles
Her watch-fire, sitting by the lonely flame;

For so she promis'd, when he parted from her,
To watch for his return.

Bast. Ulrick in wisdom should have married them
Before he went, for then the chance had been
She had not watch'd so long.
Your widow is a thing of more docility
Than your lorn maiden.—Pardon, fair Terentia.

Ter. Thy tongue wags freely. Yet, I must confess,
Had Ulrick done what thou call'st wisely, he
The very thing had done which as her kinsman
He was in duty bound to. But, alas!
A wayward passion warp'd him from the right,
And made him use his power ungen'rously
Their union to prevent.

Bast. But tho' the death of Ermingard were prov'd,
Think'st thou Aurora would bestow her hand
On one who has so long her wishes cross'd,
A lover cloth'd in stern authority?

Ter. I know not; Ulrick fondly so believes;
And I, altho' allied to him by blood,
The playmate also of his early days,
Dare not an opposite opinion utter.

Bast. Hark there! I hear without th' approaching crowd.
My duty on this public ceremony
I must attend for honour of the state.
In petty courts like this, on such occasions,
One spangled doublet more or less bears count.

[EXEUNT *severally.*

SCENE II.

An Arbour, supported by rustic wooden Pillars, twined round with Flowers and green Plants, and a Flower Garden seen in the back Ground between the Pillars. Enter Page, *followed by* Edda, *speaking as she enters.*

Ed. Yes, do so, boy; Aurora is at hand.—
But take with thee, besides, this little basket,
And gather roses in the farther thicket,
Close to the garden gate.—

Page. (*taking the basket.*)
Give it me then. She chid me yesterday
For gath'ring full-spread roses, whose loose leaves
Fell on her lap: to-day I'll fill my basket
With buds, and budlings, and half-open'd flowers,
Such as nice dames do in their kerchiefs place.

Ed. Prate less and move thee quicker. Get thee hence.
See there thy mistress comes: haste to thy task.
[Exit Page.

Enter Aurora *and* Terentia.

Ter. Here you will find a more refreshing air;
The western sun beats fiercely.

Aur. Western sun!
Is time so far advanced? I left my couch
Scarcely an hour ago.

Ter. You are deceived.
Three hours have past, but past by you unheeded;

Who have the while in silent stillness sat,
Like one forlorn, that has no need of time.

Aur. In truth I now but little have to do
With time or any thing besides. It passes;
Hour follows hour; day follows day; and year,
If I so long shall last, will follow year:
Like drops that thro' the cavern'd hermit's roof
Some cold spring filters; glancing on his eye
At measured intervals, but moving not
His fix'd unvaried notice.

Ed. Nay, dearest Lady, be not so depress'd.
You have not ask'd me for my song to-day —
The song you prais'd so much. Shall I not sing it?
I do but wait your bidding.

Aur. I thank thy kindness; sing it if thou wilt.

(*Sits down on a low seat, her head supported between both her hands, with her elbows resting on her knees.*)

SONG.

Where distant billows meet the sky,
A pale, dull light the seamen spy,
As spent they stand and tempest-tost,
Their vessel struck, their rudder lost;
While distant homes where kinsmen weep,
And graves full many a fathom deep,
By turns their fitful, gloomy thoughts pourtray:
" 'Tis some delusion of the sight,
Some northern streamer's paly light."
" Fools!" saith rous'd Hope with gen'rous scorn,
" It is the blessed peep of morn,
And aid and safety come when comes the day."

And so it is ; the gradual shine
Spreads o'er heaven's verge its lengthen'd line:
Cloud after cloud begins to glow
And tint the changeful deep below;
Now sombre red, now amber bright,
Till upward breaks the blazing light;
Like floating fire the gleamy billows burn:
Far distant on the ruddy tide,
A black'ning sail is seen to glide ;
Loud bursts their eager joyful cry,
Their hoisted signal waves on high,
And life and strength and happy thoughts return.

Ter. Is not her voice improved in power and sweetness?

Ed. It is a cheering song.

Aur. It cheers those who are cheer'd.

(*After a pause.*)

Twelve years are past;
Their daughters matrons grown, their infants youths,
And they themselves with aged furrows mark'd;
But none of all their kin are yet return'd;
No, nor shall ever.

Ter. Still run thy thoughts upon those hapless women
Of that small hamlet, whose advent'rous peasants
To Palestine with noble Baldwin went,
And ne'er were heard of more?

Aur. They perish'd there; and of their dismal fate
No trace remain'd — none of them all return'd.

Did'st thou not say so?—Husbands, lovers, friends,
Not one return'd again.
Ter. So I believe.
Aur. Thou but believest then?
Ter. As I was told———
Ed. Thou hast the story wrong.
Four years gone by, one did return again;
But marr'd, and maim'd, and chang'd—a woeful man.
Aur. And what tho' every limb were hack'd and maim'd,
And roughen'd o'er with scars?—he did return.
(*Rising lightly from her seat.*)
I would a pilgrimage to Iceland go,
To the Antipodes or burning zone,
To see that man who did return again,
And her who did receive him.—Did receive him!
O what a moving thought lurks here!—How was't?
Tell it me all: and oh, another time,
Give me your tale ungarbled.—

Enter VIOLA.

Ha, Viola! 'tis my first sight of thee
Since our long vigil. Thou hast had, I hope,
A sound and kindly sleep.
Viol. Kindly enough, but somewhat cross'd with dreams.
Aur. How cross'd? what was thy dream? O tell it me!
I have an ear that craves for every thing

That hath the smallest sign or omen in it.
It was not sad?

Viol. Nay, rather strange; Methought
A christ'ning feast within your bower was held;
But when the infant to the font was brought,
It prov'd a full-grown man in armour clad.

Aur. A full-grown man! (*considering for a moment, and then holding up her hands.*)
O blessing on thy dream!
From death to life restor'd is joyful birth.
It is, it is! Come to my heart, sweet maid,
(*Embracing* Viola.)
A blessing on thyself and on thy sleep!
I feel a kindling life within me stir,
That doth assure me it has shadow'd forth
A joy that soon shall be.

Ter. So may it prove!
But trust not such vain fancies, nor appear
Too much elated; for unhappy Ulrick
Swears that your Beacon, after this night's watch,
Shall burn no more.

Aur. He does! then will we have
A noble fire. This night our lofty blaze
Shall through the darkness shoot full many a league
Its streamy rays, like to a bearded star
Preceding changeful — aye, and better times.
It may in very truth. O if his bark
(For many a bark within its widen'd reach
The dark seas traverse) should our light descry!
Should this be so — it may; perhaps it will.

O that it might! — We'll have a rousing blaze!
Give me your hands. (*Taking* Viola *and* Terentia *gaily by the hands.*)
So lightly bounds my heart,
I could like midnight goblins round the flame
Unruly orgies hold. — Ha! think ye not,
When to the font our mail-clad infant comes,
Ulrick will a right gracious gossip prove?

Viol. Assuredly, so will his honour prompt.

Aur. Nay, rather say his pride. Methinks I see him;
His darken'd figure striding cross the hall,
While his high plume, that noddles to and fro,
Shews his perturb'd and restless courtesy.
Good, noble, happy wight! Yet woe betide
The luckless hound that fawns on him that day!
His dismal yell disturbs the ceremony.
Ha, ha! I needs must laugh.

Ter. Indeed you let your fancy wildly run,
And disappointment will but prove the sharper.

Aur. Talk not of disappointment; be assur'd
Some late intelligence hath Ulrick prompted
To these stern orders. On our sea there sails,
Or soon will sail, some vessel, which right gladly
He would permit to founder on the coast,
Or miss its course. But no, it will not be:
In spite of all his hatred, to the shore,
Thro' seas as dark as subterraneous night,
It will arrive in safety.

Ter. Nay, sweet Aurora, feed not thus thy wishes
With wild unlikely thoughts; for Ulrick surely
No such intelligence hath had, and thou

But mak'st thy after-sorrow more acute
When these vain fancies fail.

Aur. And let them fail: tho' duller thoughts succeed,
The bliss e'en of a moment still is bliss.

Viol. (*to* Ter.) Thou would'st not of her dew-drops spoil the thorn,
Because her glory will not last till noon;
Nor still the lightsome gambols of the colt,
Whose neck to-morrow's yoke will gall. Fye on't!
If this be wise, 'tis cruel.

Aur. Thanks, gentle Viola; thou art ever kind.
We'll think to-morrow still hath good in store,
And make of this a blessing for to-day,
Tho' good Terentia there may chide us for it.

Ter. And thus a profitable life you'll lead,
Which hath no present time, but is made up
Entirely of to-morrows.

Aur. Well, taunt me as thou wilt, I'll worship still
The blessed morrow, storehouse of all good
For wretched folks. They who lament to-day,
May then rejoice: they who in misery bend
E'en to the earth, be then in honour robed.
O! who shall reckon what its brighten'd hours
May of returning joy contain? To-morrow!
The blest to-morrow! cheering, kind to-morrow!
I were a heathen not to worship thee.
(*To* Ter.) Frown not again; we must not wrangle now.

Ter. Thou dost such vain and foolish fancies cherish,
Thou forcest me to seem unkind and stern.

Aur. Ah! be not stern. Edda will sing the song
That makes feet beat and heads nod to its tune;
And even grave Terentia will be moved
To think of pleasant things.

SONG.

Wish'd-for gales, the light vane veering,
Better dreams the dull night cheering,
Lighter heart the morning greeting,
Things of better omen meeting;
Eyes each passing stranger watching,
Ears each feeble rumour catching,
Say he existeth still on earthly ground,
The absent will return, the long, long lost be found.

In the tower the ward-bell ringing,
In the court the carols singing,
Busy hands the gay board dressing,
Eager steps the threshold pressing,
Open'd arms in haste advancing,
Joyful looks thro' blind tears glancing,
The gladsome bounding of his aged hound,
Say he in truth is here, our long, long lost is found.

Hymned thanks and beadsmen praying,
With sheath'd sword the urchin playing,
Blazon'd hall with torches burning,
Cheerful morn in peace returning,
Converse sweet that strangely borrows
Present bliss from former sorrows;
O who can tell each blessed sight and sound
That says, he with us bides, our long, long lost is found.

Aur. (*who at first nods her head lightly to the measure, now bursts into tears, taking* Edda's *hands between hers, and pressing them gratefully.*)
I thank thee: this shall be our daily song:
It cheers my heart, altho' these foolish tears
Seem to disgrace its sweetness.

Enter Page.

Viol. (*to* Aur.) Here comes your page with lightly-bounding steps,
As if he brought good tidings.

Ed. Grant he may!

Aur. (*eagerly.*) What brings thee hither, boy?

Page. (*to* Aur.) A noble stranger of the Legate's train,
Come from the Holy Land, doth wait without,
Near to the garden gate, where I have left him;
He begs to be admitted to your presence;
Pleading for such indulgence as the friend
Of Ermingard, for so he bade me say.

Aur. The friend of Ermingard! the Holy Land!
(*Pausing for a moment, and then tossing up her arms in ecstasy.*)
O God! it is himself!
(*Runs eagerly some steps towards the garden, then catching hold of* Terentia, *who follows her.*)
My head is dizzy grown; I cannot go.
Haste, lead him hither, boy.
(*Waving her hand impatiently.*)
Fly; hear'st thou not? [Exit Page.

Ter. Be not so greatly mov'd. It is not likely
This should be Ermingard. The boy has seen him,
And would have known him. 'Tis belike some friend.

Aur. No; every thrilling fibre of my frame
Cries out " It is himself." (*Looking out.*)
He comes not yet: how strange! how dull! how tardy!

Ter. Your page hath scarce had time to reach the gate,
Tho' he hath run right quickly.

Aur. (*pausing and looking out.*)
He comes not yet. Ah! if it be not he;
My sinking heart misgives me.
O now he comes! the size and air are his.

Ter. Not to my fancy; there is no resemblance.

Aur. Nay, but there is: and see, he wears his cloak
As he was wont to do; and o'er his cap
The shading plume so hangs. — It is! it is!

(*Enter* Garcio; *and she, breaking from* Terentia, *runs towards him.*)

My lost, my found, my blest! conceal thee not.

(*Going to catch him in her arms, when* Garcio *takes off his plumed cap, and bows profoundly. She utters a faint cry, and shrinks back.*)

Gar. Lady, I see this doff'd cap hath discover'd

A face less welcome than the one you look'd for.
Pardon a stranger's presence; I've presumed
Thus to intrude, as friend of Ermingard,
Who bade me—

Aur. Bade thee! is he then at hand?

Gar. Ah, would he were!
'Twas in a hostile and a distant land
He did commit to me these precious tokens,
Desiring me to give them to Aurora,
And with them too his sad and last farewel.

Aur. And he is dead!

Gar. Nay, wring not thus your hands:
He was alive and well when he entrusted me
With what I now return.

(*Offering her a small casket.*)

Aur. Alive and well, and sends me back my tokens!

Gar. He sent them back to thee as Ulrick's wife;
For such, forc'd by intelligence from hence
Of strong authority, he did believe thee;
And in that fatal fight, which shortly follow'd,
He fought for death as shrewdly as for fame.
Fame he indeed hath earn'd.

Aur. But not the other?
Ah, do not say he has! Amongst the slain
His body was not found.

Gar. As we have learnt, the Knights of blest St. John
Did from the field of dying and of wounded
Many convey, who in their house of charity
All care and solace had; but with the names,

Recorded as within their walls receiv'd,
His is not found; therefore we must account him
With those who, shrouded in an unknown fate,
Are as the dead lamented, as the dead
For ever from our worldly care dismiss'd.

Aur. Lamented he shall be; but from my care
Dismiss'd as are the dead — that is impossible.

Ter. Nay, listen to advice so wise and needful:
It is the friend of Ermingard who says,
Let him within thy mind be as the dead.

Aur. My heart repels the thought; it cannot be.
No, till his corse, bereft of life, is found,
Till this is sworn, and prov'd, and witness'd to me,
Within my breast he shall be living still.

Ter. Wilt thou yet vainly watch night after night,
To guide his bark who never will return?

Aur. Who never will return! And thinkest thou
To bear me down with such presumptuous words?
Heaven makes me strong against thee:
There is a Power above that calms the storm,
Restrains the mighty, gives the dead to life:
I will in humble faith my watch still keep;
Force only shall restrain me.

Gar. Force never shall, thou noble, ardent spirit!
Thy gen'rous confidence would almost tempt me
To think it will be justified.

Aur. Ha! say'st thou so? A blessing rest upon thee

For these most cheering words! Some guardian power
Whispers within thee. — No, we'll not despair.

Enter ULRICK.

Ul. (*to* Gar.) Your dismal mission is, I trust, fulfill'd;
Then, gentle Garcio, deem it not unkind
That I entreat you to retire; for they
Who sorrow for the dead, love to be left
To grieve without constraint.

Aur. Thanks for your kind concern, most noble Sir;
And when we needs must sorrow for the dead,
We'll freely grieve without constraint. But know,
Until our corse is found, we ring no knell.
If then your ear for funeral dirges long,
Go to some other bower; hope still is here.

Ul. Ha! still perversely bent! what can convince thee?
This is distraction.

Aur. Be it what it may,
It owns not thy authority. Brave youth, (*to* Gar.)
I owe thy gentleness some kind acknowledgment,
I'll find another time to give thee thanks.

[EXIT, *followed by* Viol. *and* Ed.

Ul. Such hope is madness! yield we to her humour?
No, she must be to sober reason brought,
By steady, firm controul.

Gar. Mean you by this, my Lord, a forc'd controul?

Ul. Who shall enquire my meaning?

Gar. The holy Legate, patron of th' oppress'd,
Will venture to enquire.

Ul. Aye, as his nephew, thou presumest, I see.
But know, bold youth, I am unused to threats.

Gar. Yet brook them as you may. I take my leave. [Exit.

Manent Ulrick *and* Terentia.

Ul. Did I not say these cursed meddling priests —
These men of meekness, wheresoe'er they come,
Would rule and power usurp? Woe worth the hour
That brought them here! — And for this head-strong maniac
As such, I will ——

Ter. Hush, hush! these precincts quit.
It is not well, here to expose to view
Thy weak ungovern'd passions. Thou'rt observ'd;
Retire with me, where skreen'd from every eye,
With more possession of thy ruffled mind,
Thou may'st consider of thy wayward state.

[Exeunt.

ACT II.

SCENE I.—*A flat Spot of Ground on the top of a Cliff, with broken craggy Rocks on each Side, and a large mass of Rock in the middle, on which a great Fire of Wood is burning; a dark Sea in the back Ground: the Scene to receive no Light but from the Fire. Two Fishermen are discovered watching the Fire, and supplying it with Wood.*

SONG.

First Fisherman.

" *HIGH is the tower, and the watch-dogs bay,*
And the flitting owlets shriek;
I see thee wave thy mantle grey,
But I cannot hear thee speak.

" *O, are they from the east or west*
The tidings he bears to me?
Or from the land that I love best,
From the knight of the north countree?"

Swift down the winding stair she rush'd,
Like a gust of the summer wind;
Her steps were light, her breath was hush'd,
And she dared not look behind.

She pass'd by stealth the narrow door,
The postern way also,
And thought each bush her robe that tore,
The grasp of a warding foe.

And she has climb'd the moat so steep,
With chilly dread and fear,
While th' evening fly humm'd dull and deep,
Like a wardman whisp'ring near.

" *Now, who art thou, thou Palmer tall,*
Who beckonest so to me?
Art thou from that dear and distant hall?
Art thou from the north countree?"

He rais'd his hood with wary wile,
That cover'd his raven hair,
And a manlier face and a sweeter smile
Ne'er greeted lady fair.

" *My coal-black steed feeds in the brake,*
Of gen'rous blood and true;
He'll soon the nearest frontier make,
Let they who list pursue.

" *Thy pale cheek shows an alter'd mind,*
Thine eye the blinding tear;
Come not with me if aught behind
Is to thy heart more dear.

" *Thy sire and dame are in that hall,*
Thy friend, thy mother's son;
Come not with me, if one o' them all
E'er lov'd thee as I have done."

The lady mounted the coal-black steed,
Behind her knight I ween,
And they have pass'd thro' brake and mead,
And plain, and woodland green.

But hark, behind! the warders shout,
And the hasty larums ring;
And the mingled sound of a gath'ring rout
The passing air doth bring.

"*O noble steed! now 'quit thee well,*
And prove thy gen'rous kind!
That fearful sound doth louder swell,
It is not far behind.

"*The frontier's near — a span the plain,*
Press on and do not fail!
Ah! on our steps fell horsemen gain,
I hear their ringing mail."

2d Fish. Tush, man! give o'er; thy ballads have no end,
When thou art in the mood. I hear below
A sound of many voices on the shore:
Some boat, belike, forced by the drifting current
Upon the rocks, may be in jeopardy.

1st Fish. 'Tis all a mock to cut my ditty short.
Thou hast no mind to hear how it befel
That those two lovers were by kinsmen stern
O'erta'en; and how the knight, by armed foes
Beset, a bloody combat bravely held,
And was the while robb'd of his lady fair.
And how in Paynim land they met again.
How, as a Page disguised, she sought her knight,
Left on the field as lifeless. How she cheer'd him;
And how they married were, and home in state ———

2d Fish. Ha' done, ha' done! a hundred times I've heard it.
My Grandam lull'd me with it on her lap
Full many a night; and as my father sat,
Mending his nets upon the beach, he sung it.
I would I knew my prayers as well.—But hark!
I hear a noise again.——

(Goes to the bottom of the stage, as if he were looking down to the sea.)

Along the shore
I see lights moving swiftly.

1st Fish. Some fishermen, who, later than the rest,
Their crazy boat bring in; while, to the beach,
With flaming brands, their wives and children run.
Rare sight, indeed, to take thy fancy so!

(Sings again.)

No fish stir in our heaving net,
And the sky is dark, and the night is wet;
And we must ply the lusty oar,
For the tide is ebbing from the shore;
And sad are they whose faggots burn,
So kindly stored for our return.

Our boat is small and the tempest raves,
And nought is heard but the lashing waves,
And the sullen roar of the angry sea,
And the wild winds piping drearily;
Yet sea and tempest rise in vain,
We'll bless our blazing hearths again.

Push bravely, Mates! Our guiding star
Now from its towerlet streameth far;
And now along the nearing strand,
See, swiftly moves yon flaming brand:
Before the midnight watch is past,
We'll quaff our bowl and mock the blast.

Bast. (*without.*)
Holla, good Mate! Thou who so bravely sing'st!
Come down, I pray thee.

1*st Fish.* Who art thou who call'st?

2*d Fish.* I know the voice; 'tis Sign'or Bastiani.

1*st Fish.* What! he, at such an hour, upon the cliff!
(*Calling down.*) I cannot come. If, from my station here,
This fire untended, I were found; good sooth!
I had as lief the luckless friar be,
Who spilt the Abbot's wine.

2*d Fish.* I'll go to him. [Exit.

1*st Fish.* (*muttering to himself.*)
Aye; leave my watch, indeed! a rare entreaty!

Enter Bastiani.

Bast. Wilt thou not go? A boat near to the shore,
In a most perilous state, calls for assistance:
Who is like thee, good Stephen, bold and skilful?
Haste to its aid, if there be pity in thee,
Or any Christian grace. I will, meantime,

Thy beacon watch; and, should the lady come,
Excuse thy absence. Haste; make no reply.

1st Fish. I will; God help us all! [EXIT.

Bast. Here is, indeed, a splendid noble fire
Left me in ward. It makes the darkness round,
To its fierce light oppos'd, seem thick and palpable,
And clos'd o'er head, like to the pitchy cope
Of some vast cavern. ——Near at hand, methinks,
Soft female voices speak: I'll to my station.

(*Retires from the front of the stage behind the fire.*)

Enter AURORA, TERENTIA *and* VIOLA.

Viol. A rousing light! Good Stephen hath full well
Obey'd your earnest bidding.—Fays and witches
Might round its blaze their midnight revelry
Right fitly keep.

Ter. Aye; thou lov'st wilds and darkness,
And fire and storms, and things unsooth and strange:
This suits thee well. Methinks, in gazing on it,
Thy face a witch-like eagerness assumes.

Viol. I'll be a goblin then, and round it dance.
Did not Aurora say we thus should hold
This nightly vigil. Yea, such were her words.

Aur. They were light bubbles of some mantling thought,
That now is flat and spiritless; and yet,
If thou art so inclin'd, ask not my leave,
Dance if thou wilt.

Viol. Nay, not alone, sweet sooth!
Witches, themselves, some fiend-like partners find.

Ter. And so may'st thou. Look yonder; near the flame
A crested figure stands. That is not Stephen.

Aur. (*eagerly*,) A crested figure! Where? O call to it!

(Bast. *comes forward.*)

Ter. 'Tis Bastiani.

Aur. Aye; 'tis Bastiani:
'Tis he, or any one; 'tis ever thus;
So is my fancy mock'd.

Bast. If I offend you, Madam, 'tis unwillingly.
Stephen has for a while gone to the beach,
To help some fishermen, who, as I guess,
Against the tide would force their boat to land.
He'll soon return; meantime, I did entreat him
To let me watch his Beacon. Pardon me;
I had not else intruded; tho' full oft
I've clamber'd o'er these cliffs, ev'n at this hour,
To see the ocean from its sabled breast
The flickering gleam of these bright flames return.

Aur. Make no excuse, I pray thee. I am told
By good Terentia thou dost wish me well,
Tho' Ulrick long has been thy friend. I know
A wanderer on the seas in early youth
Thou wast, and still can'st feel for all storm-toss'd
On that rude element.

Bast. 'Tis true, fair Lady : I have been, ere now,
Where such a warning light, sent from the shore,
Had saved some precious lives; which makes the task,
I now fulfil, more grateful.

Aur. How many leagues from shore may such a light
By the benighted mariner be seen?

Bast. Some six or so, he will descry it faintly,
Like a small star, or hermit's taper, peering
From some cav'd rock that brows the dreary waste;
Or like the lamp of some lone lazar-house,
Which through the silent night the traveller spies
Upon his doubtful way.

Viol. Fie on such images!
Thou should'st have liken'd it to things more seemly.
Thou might'st have said the peasant's evening fire
That from his upland cot, thro' winter's gloom,
What time his wife their evening meal prepares,

Blinks on the traveller's eye, and cheers his
heart;
Or signal-torch, that from my Lady's bower
Tells wand'ring knights the revels are begun;
Or blazing brand, that from the vintage-house
O' long October nights, thro' the still air
Looks rouzingly. —— To have our gallant
Beacon
Ta'en for a lazar-house!

Bast. Well, Maiden, as thou wilt: thy gentle
Mistress
Of all these things may chuse what likes her best,
To paint more clearly how her noble fire
The distant seaman cheers, who bless the while
The hand that kindled it.

Aur. Shall I be bless'd——
By wand'ring men returning to their homes?
By those from shipwreck sav'd, again to cheer
Their wives, their friends, their kindred? Bless'd
by those!
And shall it not a blessing call from heaven?
It will; my heart leaps at the very thought:
The seamen's blessing rests upon my head
To charm my wand'rer home.——
Heap on more wood:
Let it more brightly blaze. —Good Bastiani,
Hie to thy task, and we'll assist thee gladly.

(*As they begin to occupy themselves with the fire, the sound of distant voices, singing in harmony, is heard under the stage as if ascending the cliff.*)

Aur. What may it be?

Viol. The songs of Paradise,
But that our savage rocks and gloomy night
So ill agree with peaceful soothing bliss.

Ter. No blessed spirits in these evil days
Hymn, thro' the stilly darkness, strains of grace.

Aur. Nay list; it comes again.

(*Voices heard nearer.*)

Ter. The mingled sound comes nearer, and betrays
Voices of mortal men.

Viol. In such sweet harmony!
I never heard the like.

Aur. They must be good and holy who can utter
Such heavenly sounds.

Bast. I've surely heard before
This solemn chorus chaunted by the knights,
The holy brothers of Jerusalem.
It is a carrol sung by them full oft,
When saved from peril dire of flood or field.

Aur. The Knights of blest St. John from Palestine!
Alas! why feel I thus? knowing too well
They cannot bring the tidings I would hear.

(*Chorus rises again very near.*)

Viol. List, list! they've gain'd the summit of the cliff:
They are at hand; their voices are distinct;
Yea, ev'n the words they sing.

(*A solemn Song or Hymn, sung in harmony, heard without.*)

Men preserv'd from storm and tide
And fire and battle raging wide;
What shall subdue our steady faith,
Or of our heads a hair shall skathe?
Men preserv'd in gladness weeping,
Praise him, who hath alway our souls in holy keeping.

And wheresoe'er in earth or sea
Our spot of rest at last shall be;
Our swords in many a glorious field,
Surviving heroes still shall wield,
While we our faithful toils are reaping
With him, who hath alway our souls in holy keeping.

(*Enter* six Knights of St. John of Jerusalem *in procession, with their followers behind them, who don't advance upon the stage, but remain partly concealed behind the rocks.*)

Aur. Speak to them, Bastiani; thou'rt a soldier;
Thy mind is more composed. — I pray thee do.
(*Motioning* Bast. *to accost them.*)

Bast. This lady, noble Warriors, greets you all,
And offers you such hospitality
As this late hour and scanty means afford.
Wilt please ye round this blazing fire to rest?
After such perilous tossing on the waves,
You needs must be forspent.

1*st Knight.* We thank you, Sir, and this most noble dame,

Whose Beacon hath from shipwreck sav'd us.
Driven
By adverse winds too near your rocky coast,
Warn'd by its friendly light, we stood to sea:
But soon discov'ring that our crazy bark
Had sprung a dangerous leak, we took our boat
And made for shore. The nearest point of land
Beneath this cliff, with peril imminent,
By help of some good fishermen we gained;
And here, in God's good mercy, safe we are
With grateful hearts.

Aur. We praise that mercy also
Which hath preserv'd you.

1st Knight. Lady, take our thanks.
And may the vessel of that friend beloved,
For whom you watch, as we have now been told,
Soon to your shore its welcome freight convey.

Aur. Thanks for the wish; and may its prayers be heard.
Renowned men ye are; holy and brave;
In every field of honour and of arms
Some of your noble brotherhood are found:
Perhaps the valiant knights I now behold,
Did on that luckless day against the Souldain
With brave De Villeneuve for the cross contend.
If this be so, you can, perhaps, inform me
Of one who in the battle fought, whose fate
Is still unknown.

1st Knight. None of us all, fair Dame, so honour'd were
As in that field to be, save this young knight.
Sir Bertram, wherefore, in thy mantle lapt,

Stand'st thou so far behind? Speak to him, Lady:
For in that battle he right nobly fought,
And may, belike, wot of the friend you mention'd.

Aur. (*going up eagerly to the young Knight.*)
Did'st thou there fight? — then surely thou did'st know
The noble Ermingard, who from this isle
With valiant Conrad went: ——
What fate had he upon that dismal day?

Young Kt. Whate'er his fate in that fell fight might be,
He now is as the dead.

Aur. Is as the dead! ha! then he is not dead:
He's living still. O tell me — tell me this!
Say he is still alive; and tho' he breathe
In the foul pest-house; tho' a wretched wand'rer,
Wounded and maim'd; yea, tho' his noble form
With chains and stripes and slav'ry be disgraced,
Say he is living still, and I will bless thee.
Thou know'st — full well thou know'st, but wilt not speak.
What means that heavy groan? For love of God, speak to me!

(*Tears the mantle from his face, with which he had concealed it.*)

My Ermingard! My blessed Ermingard!
Thy very living self restored again!
Why turn from me?

Er. Ah! call'st thou this restored?

Aur. Do I not grasp thy real living hand?
Dear, dear! — so dear! most dear! — my lost, my found!

Thou turn'st and weep'st; art thou not so to me?

Er. Ah! would I were! alas, alas! I'm lost:
Sever'd from thee for ever.

Aur. How so? What mean such words?

Er. (*shaking his head, and pointing to the cross on his mantle.*)
Look on this emblem of a holy vow
Which binds and weds me to a heavenly love:
We are, my sweet Aurora, far divided;
Our bliss is wreck'd for ever.

Aur. No; thou art still alive, and that is bliss.
Few moments since, what would I not have sacrificed,
To know that in the lapse of many years
I should again behold thee? — I had been ——
How strongly thou art moved! — Thou heed'st me not.

Ter. (*to* Aur.) Were it not better he should leave this spot?
Let me conduct him to my quiet bower.
Rest and retirement may compose his mind.

Aur. Aye, thou art right, Terentia.

Ter. (*to the other* Knights.) Noble Knights,
And these your followers! gentle Bastiani
Will to a place of better comfort lead you,
Where ye shall find some hospitable cheer,
And couches for repose. — Have we your leave
That your companion be a little time
Ta'en from your company?

1*st Knight.* You have, good Lady;
Most readily we grant it.—Heaven be with you,

And this your lovely charge!
(*To* Bast.) Sir, to your guidance
We yield ourselves right gladly.
[Exeunt Knights, &c. *by a path between the rocks, and* Aurora *and* Ermingard, &c. *by another path.*

SCENE II.

An Anti-room in the House of Aurora: *Enter* Garcio, *beckoning the* Page, *who presently enters by the opposite side.*

Gar. Come hither, little Friend, who did'st before
Serve me so willingly. Wilt thou from me
Bear to Sir Ermingard a friendly message;
And say his old companion ——
Page. Nay, I dare not.
The holy legate and the pope besides
Might not disturb him now; for dame Terentia
Hath so decreed. He is in her apartment,
And yonder is the door.
(*Pointing off the stage.*)
Gar. From which ev'n now
I saw thee turn?
Page. I listen'd not for harm.
Gar. Do I accuse thee, Boy? Is he alone?
Or is thy Lady with him?
Page. That I know not.
Do folks groan heaviest when they are alone?
Gar. Full oft' they do; for then without restraint
They utter what they feel.

Page. Then, by my beard, I think he be alone!
For as I slipp'd on tiptoe to the door,
I heard him groan so deeply!

Gar. Thou heard'st him groan?

Page. Aye; deeply.
I thought when he return'd, we should be merry:
So starting up at the good tidings, quickly,
All darkling as I was, I don'd my cloaths:
But, by my beard! I'd go to bed again,
Did I not long most curiously to know
What will betide.

Gar. Speak softly, boy; thou, and thy beard to boot,
Will badly fare if Ulrick should o'erhear thee.
I know his angry voice: he is at hand.

Page. Where shall I go?—He will not tarry here:
He will but pass to the adjoining hall.
In this dark nook I'll hide me from his sight
Lest he should chide me.

(*Retires behind the pillar.*)

Gar. Is there room for me?
He'll greet me too with little courtesy
If I remain to front him.

(*Retires behind the pillar also.*)

Enter ULRICK *and* BASTIANI, *speaking as they enter.*

Ul. And still thou say'st, forbear!

Bast. Pass on, my Lord.

Ul. No, by the holy rood! I'll keep in sight

Of that accursed door which gave him entrance.
An hour's sand well hath run, which undisturb'd
They have in converse or endearments spent.
And yet I must forbear!

Bast. They have not told the truth who told you so;
It is not yet so long.

Ul. It is! it is!
I have within these walls, who for my service
More faithfully have watch'd than Bastiani —
Aye, or Terentia either.

Bast. Wrong us not.
Since Ermingard returns by holy vows
So bound, that as a rival to your love,
You may, with honest thoughts of her you love,
No more consider him; all jealousy
Within your noble breast should be extinct.
Then think not to disturb these few short moments
Of unavailing sorrow; that were cruel.

Ul. Thou pitiest others well; I am tormented,
And no one pities me. — That cursed Beacon!
I said in vain this night should be the last:
It was a night too much: the sea had now
Roll'd o'er his lifeless corse; I been at peace.

Bast. For mercy, good my lord! curb such fell thoughts:
They bear no kindred to your better nature.

Ul. My better nature! Mock me not with words;
Who loves like me, no nature hath but one,

And that so keen —— Would the engulphing waves
Had fifty fathom deep entombed him!

Bast. Speak not so loud: pass on; we are within
The observation of a prying household,
Pass on, and presently I'll bring you notice
Of what you would. I pray you, stop not here!

[EXEUNT Ul. *and* Bast. *while* Gar. *and* Page *come from their concealment.*

Page. He would have chid me shrewdly.

Gar. He is, indeed, an angry, ruthless man,
And Bastiani no slight task will have
To keep his wrath from mischief. To the legate
I'll hie me straight, and ask his better counsel:
So fare thee well, sweet child.

Page. Nay, take me with you; I'm afraid to stay.
I can my prayers and an Ave-Maria say,
The legate will not chide me.

Gar. Nay, stay behind; thou art secure, poor elph!
I'll soon return again. [EXEUNT.

SCENE III.

The Apartment of TERENTIA: ERMINGARD *and* AURORA *are discovered with* TERENTIA, *who is withdrawn to a distance from them.* ERMINGARD *is seated with his body thrown back, and his face covered with both his hands, while*

Aurora *stands by him in the attitude of one who is entreating or soothing him.*

Erm. O cease! Thy words, thy voice, thy hand on mine,
That touch so dearly felt, do but enhance
An agony too great. —— Untoward fate!
Thus to have lost thee!

Aur. Say not, thou hast lost me.
Heaven will subdue our minds, and we shall still,
With what is spared as from our wreck of bliss,
Be happy.

Erm. Most unblest, untoward fate!
After that hapless battle, where in vain
I courted death, I kept my name conceal'd.
Ev'n brave De Villeneune, master of our Order,
When he received my vows, did pledge his faith
Not to declare it. Thus I kept myself
From all communication with these shores,
Perversely forwarding my rival's will.
O blind and credulous fool!

Aur. Nay, do not thus upbraid thyself: Heaven will'd it.
Be not so keenly moved: there still is left
What to the soul is dear.—We'll still be happy.

Erm. The chasten'd pilgrim o'er his lady's grave
Sweet tears may shed, and may without reproach
Thoughts of his past love blend with thoughts of heaven.
He whom the treach'ry of some faithless maid
Hath robb'd of bliss, may, in the sturdy pride
Of a wrong'd man, the galling ill endure;

But sever'd thus from thee, so true, so noble,
By vows that all the soul's devotion claim,
It makes me feel — may God forgive the crime!
A very hatred of all saintly things.
Fool — rash and credulous fool! to lose thee thus!

Aur. Nay, say not so: thou still art mine. Short while
I would have given my whole of life besides
To've seen but once again thy passing form —
Thy face — thine eyes turn'd on me for a moment;
Or only to have heard thro' the still air
Thy voice distinctly call me, or the sound
Of thy known steps upon my lonely floor:
And shall I then, holding thy living hand
In love and honour, say, thou art not mine?

Erm. (*shaking his head.*) This state — this sacred badge!

Aur. O no! that holy cross upon thy breast
Throws such a charm of valorous sanctity
O'er thy lov'd form: my thoughts do forward glance
To deeds of such high fame by thee achiev'd,
That ev'n methinks the bliss of wedded love
Less dear, less noble is, than such strong bonds
As may, without reproach, unite us still.

Erm. O creature of a gen'rous constancy!
Thou but the more distractest me! Fool, fool!

(*Starting from his seat, and pacing to and fro distractedly.*)

Mean, misbelieving fool! — I thought her false,

Cred'lous alone of evil — I have lost,
And have deserv'd to lose her.

Aur. Oh! be not thus! Have I no power to soothe thee?
See, good Terentia weeps, and fain would try
To speak thee comfort.

Ter. (*coming forward.*) Aye; bethink thee well,
Most noble Ermingard, heaven grants thee still
All that is truly precious of her love, —
Her true and dear regard.

Erm. Then heaven forgive my black ingratitude,
For I am most unthankful!

Ter. Nay, consider,
Her heart is thine: you are in mind united.

Erm. United! In the farthest nook o' th' earth
I may in lonely solitude reflect,
That in some spot — some happier land she lives
And thinks of me. Is this to be united?

Aur. I cannot, in a Page's surtout clad,
Thy steps attend as other maids have done
To other Knights.

Erm. No, by the holy rood!
Thou canst not, and thou should'st not. Rather would I,
Dear as thou art, weep o'er thee in thy grave,
Than see thee so degraded.

Aur. Hear me out.
I cannot so attend thee — noon and eve
Thy near companion be; but I have heard
That near the sacred houses of your Order,

Convents of maids devout in Holy Land
Establish'd are — maids who in deeds of charity
To pilgrims and to all in warfare maim'd,
In sacred warfare for the holy cross,
Are deem'd the humble partners of your zeal.

Erm. Aye, such there are; but what availeth this?

Aur. There will I dwell, a vow'd and humble sister.
We shall not far be sever'd. The same winds
That do o' nights thro' your still cloisters sigh,
Our quiet cells visiting with mournful harmony,
Shall lull my pillow too. Our window'd towers
Shall sometimes shew me on the neighbouring plains,
Amidst thy brave companions; thy mail'd form
Crested with glory, on thy pawing steed
Returning from the wars. And when at last
Thou art in sickness laid — who will forbid
The dear sad pleasure — like a holy bride
I'll by thy death-bed stand, and look to heaven,
Where all bless'd union is. O! at the thought,
Methinks this span of life to nothing shrinks,
And we are bless'd already. Thou art silent:
Dost thou despise my words?

Erm. O no! speak to me thus: say what thou wilt:
I am subdued. And yet these bursting tears!
My heart is rent in twain: I fear — I fear
I am rebellious still.

(*Kneeling, and taking both her hands be-*

tween his, and kissing them with great devotion.)

School me or chide me now: do what thou wilt:
I am resign'd and humble.

Ter. (advancing to them with alarm.)

Hear ye that noise without? — They force the door,
And angry Ulrick comes.

Erm. (starting from his knees furiously.)

Thank heaven this hated rival front to front
Shall now oppose me! God avenge the right!

Enter ULRICK, *bursting into the room, followed by* BASTIANI.

Ul. (to Erm.*)* Vow'd, holy Knight; from all vain earthly love
Pure and divided; in a lady's chamber
Do we surprise thee? Quit it instantly:
It is a place for thee unfit: and know,
In sacred wardship will I keep that maid.

Erm. In sacred wardship! O unblushing face!
What of thy baseness, treachery, and falsehood
I could declare, my choaking voice forbids,
Which utterance hath not. — Here's a ready tongue — *(Drawing his sword.)*
Defend thee, then, and heaven defend the right!

(They both draw, and fight furiously, Bastiani *endeavouring in vain to interpose; when the* Legate *and his train, with* Garcio *and the* Knights of St. John, *enter, and separate them.)*

Leg. Put up your weapons: to the holy church

This cause belongs, and to her high award
I charge you both that you in all humility
Submit. Lord Ulrick, to the Pope perforce
You must account of this your wardship give,
Or by yourself in person, or your deputy,
To Rome forthwith dispatch'd.

(Ul. *bows sullenly.*)

As for the lady, to my guardian care,
Till we before the holy Father come,
She must commit herself. And thou, Sir Ermingard,
Shalt to the sovereign Pontiff and the patron
Of thy most valiant order, fully shew
Wherein thou'st been aggriev'd. If the bless'd cross
Thou hast assum'd, supposing other vows
That did before engage thee, were annull'd,
By false reports deceived; the holy Urban,
Our wise enlighten'd father, will, I trust,
A dispensation grant, that shall empower thee
To do'ff with honour this thy sacred mantle,
And in its stead a bridegroom's robe assume.

(Ermingard *and* Aurora *both embrace the* Legate'*s knees, who raises them up gently.*)

It is enough; forbear, forbear, my children;
I am too richly thank'd.
And now we must with sober minds confer:
For when the wind is fair, we sail for Rome.
Some days, perhaps, it may adversely blow —
Perhaps some weeks; for I have known it oft
Hold vessels bound.

Aur. (*tossing up her arms joyfully as she speaks.*)

No; it will change to-morrow.

Erm. Dear ardent soul! canst thou command the winds?

(Aur. *shrinks back ashamed.*)

Leg. Blush not, sweet maid; nor check thy ardent thoughts;
That gen'rous, buoyant spirit is a power
Which in the virtuous mind doth all things conquer.
It bears the hero on to arduous deeds:
It lifts the saint to heaven. (*Curtain drops.*)

THE END.

Printed by A. and R. Spottiswoode,
Printers-Street, London.

CPSIA information can be obtained
at www.ICGtesting.com
Printed in the USA
LVHW080121300922
729649LV00024B/409

9 780526 136698